Two week loan

Please return on or before the last
date stamped below.
Charges are made for late return.

LIMITATION OF LIABILITY FOR MARITIME CLAIMS

LIMITATION OF LIABILITY FOR MARITIME CLAIMS

By

PATRICK GRIGGS
Solicitor

AND

RICHARD WILLIAMS, LL.B., LL.M.
Solicitor

SECOND EDITION

|L|L|P|

LONDON   NEW YORK   HAMBURG   HONG KONG
LLOYD'S OF LONDON PRESS LTD.
1991

Lloyd's of London Press Ltd.
Legal Publishing and Conferences Division
One Singer Street, London EC2A 4LQ

USA AND CANADA
Lloyd's of London Press Inc.
Suite 308, 611 Broadway
New York, NY 10012 USA

GERMANY
Lloyd's of London Press
59 Ehrenbergstrasse
2000 Hamburg, Germany

SOUTH EAST ASIA
Lloyd's of London Press (Far East) Ltd.
Room 1101, Hollywood Centre
233 Hollywood Road
Hong Kong

British Library Cataloguing in Publication Data
Griggs, Patrick
Limitation of liability for maritime claims.—
2nd ed
I. Title II. Williams, Richard
340.9322

ISBN 1–85044–337–8

Text set in 11/13 Linotron 202 Times by
Promenade Graphics, Cheltenham, Glos.
Printed in Great Britain by
WBC Print Ltd., Bridgend, Mid Glamorgan

PREFACE TO THE
SECOND EDITION

Five years have passed since the first edition of this book and the 1976 Limitation Convention (The London Convention) has been in force in the United Kingdom since 1 December 1986. This Convention was drafted in the way that most Conventions are—hours of intense debate in smoke-filled rooms involving many compromises. For the majority of those engaged in this task the two official Convention languages of French and English will not have been their mother tongue. In the first edition we drew attention to some of the obvious textual problems. Some of these have already caused difficulties in practice. This second edition gives us the opportunity to review the working of the Convention and to incorporate some new material. For the sake of completeness we have added sections dealing with Hague, Hague–Visby and Hamburg Rules relating to the carriage of goods and the 1974 Convention relating to the Carriage of Passengers and their Luggage by Sea (the Athens Convention). There have been a number of recent incidents in which the interrelationship between the London and Athens Conventions has been a vital factor in determining the rights of claimants (we have in mind in particular the capsizing of the *Herald of Free Enterprise* at Zeebrugge in March 1987 and the sinking of the *Marchioness* in the Thames in August 1989).

Our thanks go to Imad Elias who had the task of sifting through the material which we had accumulated since the publication of the first edition and suggesting amendments. He also did much of the research and drafting on the section dealing with the Athens Convention.

We now know that second editions take nearly as much time to prepare as first editions.

September 1991   P.J.S.G.
R.W.W.

CONTENTS

Preface	v
Table of Cases	xvii
Table of Statutes and Statutory Instruments	xix
Table of Conventions	xxiii

1. INTRODUCTION ... 1

2. HISTORY OF LIMITATION IN THE UNITED KINGDOM ... 5

3. THE 1976 LIMITATION CONVENTION ... 7

Explanatory Note	7
CHAPTER I—THE RIGHT OF LIMITATION	7
Article 1: Persons entitled to limit liability	7
Article 1 [Text]	7
(a) Shipowners	8
(b) Salvors	10
(c) Seagoing ships and hovercraft	11
(d) Other persons	12
(e) Owner/master	13
(f) Liability insurer	14
(g) Summary	16
Excluded persons/excluded vessels	16
Article 2: Claims subject to limitation	17
Article 2 [Text]	17
Article 2(1)	18

Article 2(1)(a)   19
Article 2(1)(b)   20
Article 2(1)(c)   21
Article 2(1)(d)   21
Article 2(1)(e)   22
Article 2(1)(f)   23
Article 2(2)   24
Loss of or damage to valuables; loss or damage by fire   25

Article 3: Claims excepted from limitation   25

Article 3 [Text]   25
Article 3(a)   26
Article 3(b)   26
Article 3(c)   27
Article 3(d)   28
Article 3(e)   28
Summary   29

Article 4: Conduct barring limitation   30

Article 4 [Text]   30
  I. The effect of Article 4   30
      (a) "Personal" act or omission   35
      (b) The "person liable"   35

      (c) "Loss"   36
      (d) (i) "Such loss"   37
           (ii) "Intent to cause such loss"   38
           (iii) "Or *recklessly* and with knowledge that such
                 loss would *probably* result"   38
  II. Onus of proof under Article 4   39
 III. The overall effect of the changes   40
  IV. Vestiges of section 502 of the MSA 1894   41

Article 5: Counterclaims   42

Article 5 [Text]   42

CHAPTER II—THE LIMITS OF LIABILITY   44

Article 6: The general limits [Text]   44
Article 7: The limit for passenger claims [Text]   45
Article 8: Unit of Account [Text]   45

Article 6: The general limits 47
 Article 6(1) 47
 Article 6(2) 48
 Article 6(3) 49
 Article 6(4) 49
 Article 6(5) 50
 Calculation of limitation tonnage 50
  Transitional provisions 52

Article 7: The limit for passenger claims 53

The position in the United Kingdom 55
 Summary of Limits 56
  For loss of life/personal injury claims only 56
  Other claims 56
  Total potential exposure where there are personal
   and property claims 56
  Passenger claims 57

Article 8: Unit of account 57

Article 9: Aggregation of claims 57

Article 9 [Text] 57
 Comment 58

Introduction to Articles 10–14 59

*Article 10: Limitation of liability without constitution
of a limitation fund* 59

Article 10 [Text] 59
 Article 10(1) 59
 Article 10(2) 60
 Article 10(3) 60
 The position in the United Kingdom 60

CHAPTER III—THE LIMITATION FUND 63

Article 11: Constitution of the fund [Text] 63
Article 12: Distribution of the fund [Text] 63
Article 13: Bar to other actions [Text] 64
Article 14: Governing law [Text] 64

Article 11: Constitution of the fund 65

    Article 11(1) 65
    Article 11(2) 66
    Article 11(3) 67

Article 12: Distribution of the fund 67

    Article 12(1) 67
    Article 12(2) 68
    Article 12(3) 69
    Article 12(4) 69
    Liens or other rights in respect of any ship or property—
    effect on distribution 69

Article 13: Bar to other actions 70

    Article 13(1) 70
    Article 13(2) 72
      (a) General aims of the subsection 72
      (b) The mechanics of the subsection 73
    Article 13(3) 75

Article 14: Governing law 75

CHAPTER IV—SCOPE OF APPLICATION 76

Article 15 [Text] 76
    Article 15(1) 77
    Article 15(2) 77
      (a) Non sea-going ships 77
      (b) Ships of less than 300 tons 78
    Article 15(3) 79
    Article 15(4) 79
    Article 15(5) 79

CHAPTER V—FINAL CLAUSES 81

Article 16: Signature, Ratification and Accession [Text] 81
Article 17: Entry into force [Text] 81
Article 18: Reservations [Text] 82
Article 19: Denunciation [Text] 82
Article 20: Revision and Amendment [Text] 82
Article 21: Revision of the limitation amount and of Unit of
    Account or Monetary Unit [Text] 83

Article 22: Depositary [Text] 83
Article 23: Languages [Text] 83

Article 17: Entry into force 84

Article 17(1) 84
Article 17(4) 84

Article 18: Reservations 84

Article 18(1) 84

4. LIMITATION: PASSENGER CLAIMS 85

The Passenger Contract: General Principles 85

THE ATHENS CONVENTION 1974 86

Article 1: Definitions 86

Article 1 [Text] 86
  (a) Carrier/performing carrier 88
  (b) Contract of carriage 88
  (c) Ship 89
  (d) Passenger 90
  (e) Luggage/cabin luggage 90
  (f) Loss of or damage to luggage 91
  (g) Carriage 91
  (h) International carriage 92

Article 2: Application 92

Article 2 [Text] 92
  Comment 92

Article 3: Liability of the carrier 93

Article 3 [Text] 93

Article 4: Performing carrier 93

Article 4 [Text] 93

Article 5: Valuables 94

Article 5 [Text] 94

CONTENTS

Article 6: Contributory fault   94

Article 6 [Text]   94
Articles 3–6   94

Article 7: Limit of liability for personal injury   96

Article 7 [Text]   96

Article 8: Limit of liability for loss of or damage to luggage   96

Article 8 [Text]   96

Article 9: Monetary unit and conversion   96

Article 9 [Text]   96

Article 10: Supplementary provisions on limits of liability   96

Article 10 [Text]   96
Articles 7–10   97

Article 11: Defences and limits for carriers' servants   98

Article 11 [Text]   98

Article 12: Aggregation of claims   98

Article 12 [Text]   98
Articles 11 and 12   99

Article 13: Loss of right to limit liability   99

Article 13 [Text]   99

Article 14: Basis for claims   99

Article 14 [Text]   99
Articles 13 and 14   100

Article 15: Notice of loss or damage to luggage   101

Article 15 [Text]   101

Article 16: Time-bar for actions   102

Article 16 [Text]   102
Articles 15 and 16   102

Article 17: Competent jurisdiction   103

Article 17 [Text]   103
Article 17   103

Article 18: Invalidity of contractual provisions   103

Article 18 [Text]   103
Article 18   104

Article 19: Other conventions on limitation of liability   104

Article 19 [Text]   104
Article 19   104

Article 20: Nuclear damage   105

Article 20 [Text]   105
Article 21   105

CHAPTER 5: LIMITATION: CARRIAGE OF GOODS   107

History   107
Relationship between the Hague, Hague–Visby and
    Hamburg Rules and the 1976 Limitation Convention   108

Example   110
Package limitation   111
   (i) Hague Rules   111
     (a) "Per package or unit"   112
     (b) "£100"   114
   (ii) Hague–Visby Rules   114
     Example 1—Light cargo   116
     Example 2—Heavy cargo   116
   (iii) Hamburg Rules   119
     Article 6: Limits of liability [Text]   120
     Article 7: Application to non-contractual claims [Text]   120
     Article 8: Loss of right to limit liability [Text]   121
   (iv) Can the carrier of goods rely on lower "package"
     limits?   123
   (v) No "package" limit   124
   (vi) Loss of right to rely on package limitation   125
     (a) Hague Rules   125
     (b) Hague–Visby Rules   127
     (c) Hamburg Rules   130

(vii) Persons who can limit liability 130
 (1) Owners and charterers 130
  (a) Hague/Hague–Visby/Hamburg Rules 130
  (b) 1976 Convention 131
 (2) Other "carriers" 132
  (a) Hague/Hague–Visby/Hamburg Rules 132
  (b) 1976 Convention 132
 (3) Servants and agents of a carrier 132
  (a) Hague Rules 132
  (b) Hague–Visby Rules 133
  (c) Hamburg Rules 133
(viii) Claims which are subject to limitation 134
 (a) Hague and Hague–Visby Rules 134
 (b) Hamburg Rules 135
 (c) 1976 Convention 135

APPENDICES

 I. Section 503 of the Merchant Shipping Act 1894 as amended by (a) Merchant Shipping (Liability of Shipowners and Others) Act 1958; (b) section 12 of the Merchant Shipping Act 1984 139
 II. Sections 14, 17, 18, 19, 35 and 48 of the Merchant Shipping Act 1979 143
 III. Merchant Shipping Act 1979, Schedule 3, Parts I, II and III 147
 IV. Merchant Shipping Act 1979, Schedule 4, Parts I and II 159
 V. Merchant Shipping Act 1979, Schedule 5 169
 VI. Statutory Instruments 171
  1. Merchant Shipping Act 1979 (Commencement No. 10) Order 1986 171
  2. Merchant Shipping (Liability of Shipowners and Others) (Calculation of Tonnage) Order 1986 174
  3. Merchant Shipping Act 1979 (Commencement No. 11) Order 1987 175
  4. Merchant Shipping Act 1979 (Commencement No. 13) Order 1989 179
  5. Carriage of Passengers and their Luggage by Sea [United Kingdom Carriers] [Amendment] Order 1989 182
 VII. Carriage of Goods by Sea Act 1971 (The Hague–Visby Rules) 183

VIII. United Nations Convention on the Carriage of Goods
       By Sea 1978 (The Hamburg Rules)   195
  IX. Limitation of Liability for Maritime Claims: Summary
       of Limits   217

Index   223

TABLE OF CASES

Abadesa (No. 2), The [1968] 1 Lloyd's Rep. 493 64
Aliakmon, The [1986] 2 Lloyd's Rep. 1 119
Amalia, The (1863) B. & L. 151 62
Annie Hay, The [1968] 1 Lloyd's Rep. 141 13
Antares, The [1987] 1 Lloyd's Rep. 424 126
Att-Gen. of Ceylon v. Scindia [1962] A.C. 60 117
Beauchamp v. Turrell [1952] 2 Q.B. 207 60
Bowbelle, The [1990] 3 All E.R. 476 .... 40, 70, 71, 73
Captain Gregos, The [1990] 1 Lloyd's Rep. 315 .... 119, 133
Chanda, The [1989] 2 Lloyd's Rep. 494 125–127
Chyebassa, The [1966] 2 Lloyd's Rep. 193 122
Countess, The [1923] A.C. 345 70
European Enterprise, The [1989] 2 Lloyd's Rep. 191 .... 10, 34, 35,
                                                                100, 123, 128
Eurymedon, The [1975] 2 Lloyd's Rep. 534 132
Eurysthenes, The [1976] 2 Lloyd's Rep. 171 .... 32, 41
Fanti, The (Padre Island, The) [1990] 2 Lloyd's Rep. 191 15
Funabashi, The [1972] 1 Lloyd's Rep. 371 65
Garden City (No. 2), The [1984] 2 Lloyd's Rep. 37 .... 65, 67, 75
Giacinto Motta, The [1977] 2 Lloyd's Rep. 221 68
Goldman v. Thai Airways International Ltd. [1983] 3 All E.R.
    693 .... 37–40, 129
Grant v. Norway (1851) 10 C.B. 665 187
Gypsum Carriers Inc. v. The Queen [Can.] (1978) 78 D.L.R. 175
    Fed.Ct. and [1978] 4 Current Law, para. 706 21
Hain S.S. Co. v. Tate and Lyle (1936) 41 Com.Cas. 350 126
Harlow, The (1922) 10 Ll.L.Rep. 66 58
Himalaya, The [1954] 2 Lloyd's Rep. 267 8
Hollandia/Morviken, The [1983] 1 Lloyd's Rep. 1 123
Jones v. Flying Clipper (1954) 116 Fed.Supp. 386 127
Karo, The (1887) 13 P.D. 24 62
Kirknes, The [1956] 2 Lloyd's Rep. 651 19
Kulmerland, The [1973] 1 Lloyd's Rep. 319 113
Lady Gwendolen, The [1965] 1 Lloyd's Rep. 335 31
Lennard's Carrying Co. [1915] A.C. 705 31
Lion, The [1990] 2 Lloyd's Rep. 144 .... 34, 35, 40, 86, 100, 128–130
Lucullite, The (1929) 33 Ll.L.Rep. 186 58

Marion, The [1984] 2 Lloyd's Rep. 1 32
McDermid v. Nash Dredging and Reclamation Co. Ltd. [1986] 2 Lloyd's
  Rep. 24 12
Mormaclynx, The [1971] 2 Lloyd's Rep. 276 113
Muncaster Castle, The [1961] A.C. 807 .... 12, 128
Norman, The [1960] 1 Lloyd's Rep. 1 (H.L.) 39
Photo Production v. Securicor Transport Ltd. [1980] 1 Lloyd's Rep.
  545 126
Port Jackson v. Salmond [1980] 3 All E.R. 257 132
Pyrene Co. Ltd. v. Scindia Steam Navigation Co. Ltd. [1954] 1 Lloyd's
  Rep. 321; [1954] 2 Q.B. 402 124
R. v. Caldwell [1982] A.C. 354 39
R. v. Lawrence (Stephen) [1982] A.C. 520 39
Renton, G.H., & Co. Ltd. v. Palmyra Trading Corporation; The Cas-
  piana [1956] 2 Lloyd's Rep. 379; [1957] A.C. 149, H.L. 134, 135
Rosa, S, The [1988] 2 Lloyd's Rep. 574 .... 114, 221
Satya Kailash, The [1984] 1 Lloyd's Rep. 588 .... 134, 135
Sisters, The (1876) 2 Asp.M.L.C. 589 62
Standard Electrica S.A. v. Hamburg Sudamerikanische Dampfschif-
  fahrts-Gesellschaft [1967] 2 Lloyd's Rep. 193 113
Stonedale No. 1, The [1956] A.C. 1 .... 18, 21
Studebaker Distributors Ltd. v. Charlton Steam Shipping Company Ltd.
  (1937) 59 Ll.L.Rep. 23 112
Svenska Traktor v. Maritime Agencies [1953] 2 Lloyd's Rep. 124 127
Swiss Bank Corp. v. Brink's MAT Limited [1986] 2 All E.R. 188 68
Tojo Maru, The [1971] 1 Lloyd's Rep. 341 .... 10, 19, 43
Waltraud, The [1991] 1 Lloyd's Rep. 389 61
Whaite v. Lancs & Yorks Railway (1874) L.R. 9 Ex. 67 113
Wheeler v. London & Rochester Trading Co. Ltd. [1957] 1 Lloyd's Rep.
  69 60
White Rose, The [1969] 2 Lloyd's Rep. 52 12
Wladyslaw Lokietek, The [1978] 2 Lloyd's Rep. 520 72

TABLE OF STATUTES AND STATUTORY INSTRUMENTS

Carriage by Air Act 1961 80
Carriage of Goods by Sea Act
  1924 .... 3, 6,
      107, 111, 183,
      185, 186,
      219
  s. 6(1) 42
Carriage of Goods by Sea Act
  1971 .... 3, 6, 107,
      111, 183–194, 219
  s. 1 3
    (2), (3) and (6) 123
    6(4) 42, 110, 170
  Sched. 123
Carriage of Passengers and their
  Luggage by Sea (Domestic
  Carriage) Order 1987 (S.I.
  1987 No. 670) 92, 103
Carriage of Passengers and their
  Luggage by Sea (Interim
  Provisions) Order 1980
  (S.I. 1980 No. 1092) 6, 53,
      86, 89, 92, 174,
      175, 176, 177
Carriage of Passengers and their
  Luggage by Sea (Interim
  Provisions) (Notice) Order
  1980 (S.I. 1980 No. 1125) ... 86
Carriage of Passengers and their
  Luggage by Sea (Notice)
  Order 1987 (S.I. 1987 No.
  703) 86
Carriage of Passengers and
  their Luggage by Sea
  (United Kingdom Carriers)
  (Amendment) Order 1989
  (S.I. 1989 No. 1880) .. 182, 221

Carriage of Passengers and their
  Luggage by Sea (United
  Kingdom Carriers) Order
  1987 (S.I. 1981 No.
  855) 97, 182
Coinage Act 1870 221
Crown Proceedings Act 1947
  s. 5 170

Damages (Scotland) Act 1976 .. 167

Fatal Accidents Act 1976 167
Fatal Accidents Act (Northern
  Ireland) Order 1977 167

Hovercraft Act 1968—
  s. 1(1)(h) 146, 186
      (i) 170
      (ii) 186
Hovercraft (Civil Liability)
  Order 1986 .... 11, 80
  s. 3 80
  Sched. 1 80
  Sched. 3 80

Interpretation Act 1889—
  s. 38(1) 186

Law Reform (Contributory
  Negligence) Act 1945 . 95, 155
Law Reform (Miscellaneous)
  Provisions Act (Northern
  Ireland) 1948 155
Limitation Act 1939—
  s. 27(3), (4) 156

Marine Insurance Act 1906 15
s. 33(3) 14
   39(5) 32, 41
   55(2)(a) 41
Merchant   Shipping   Act
   1894 .... 31, 35
s. 274 167
   502 .... 25, 41, 141, 157, 186
   503 .... 5, 11,
                        28, 31, 55, 73,
                        78, 139–141,
                        145, 146, 157
      (1) 8, 18, 20, 21
      (d)(i) and (ii) 48
   504 71
   Part III 167
   Part VIII 141, 170
Merchant Shipping Act 1979—
s. 1 .... 13, 170, 172, 174, 177
ss. 2–4 .... 172, 174, 177
s. 5 .... 172, 174, 177
   (2) 175
ss. 6–8 .... 172, 174, 177
   9–11 174
s. 12 .... 172, 174, 177
   13(1) 172, 173, 174,
                        177, 178
   (2)–(5) 173, 174, 178
   14 .... 2, 6, 86, 143,
            175, 176, 179, 182, 220
   (1), (2) 175, 176, 180
   (4)–(6) 176, 180
   (7) 176
   15(1) 173, 178, 180
   (2) 173, 176, 178, 180
   16 .... 86, 173, 178,
                        180, 182, 220
   (1) 174, 175, 179
   (2) 174, 179
   (4) 176
   (5) 174, 179
   17 .... 2, 5, 7, 16, 22, 26,
         27, 47, 53, 56, 69–71, 74,
            84, 143, 144, 145,
            146, 157, 166, 169,
            170, 171, 178, 180
   (1) 11, 15, 48, 50,
         60, 67, 77, 78, 79, 80
   18 .... 41, 110,
            143, 144, 145, 157,
         169, 170, 171, 178, 180

Merchant Shipping Act 1979—cont.
s. 18(1) 25
   (3) 41
   19 .... 143, 145
   (1) 171, 178, 180
   (2), (3) 173, 178, 180
   (4) 171, 180
ss. 20–22, 23(7), 26–34 173,
                        178, 181
s. 35 .... 29, 143, 145
   (1) 173, 174, 178, 181
   (2) 29, 30, 173, 179, 181
ss. 36(1),   37(1)–(5),   (7),
      (8), 38(1)–(3), (5), (6),
      39–47 .... 173, 178, 181
s. 48 .... 17, 143, 146,
                        173, 178, 181
   49 .... 173, 178, 181
   50(1)–(3) 173, 178, 181
   (4) 172, 173, 178, 181
   51(1)–(3) 173, 179, 181
   52 .... 173, 179, 181
   (2) 171, 176, 179
Sch. 1 .... 172, 177
Sch. 2 .... 173, 174
Sch. 3 .... 86, 143, 175
   Part I 3, 86, 143,
      147–155, 174, 176, 179, 181
   II 3, 86, 143, 147,
                        155, 158
   para. 3 95
      4 220
      9 86
      12 .... 42, 110
      13 55
   III 3, 143, 147,
            156, 157–158, 176
Sch. 4 ..... 144, 170, 172, 179, 181
   Part I 2, 7, 11, 17,
      48–50, 57, 60, 77, 79,
      80, 84, 144, 145,
      159–165, 169
   II 84, 144, 159,
      165–168, 169, 174
   para. 2 .... 11, 16, 78
      3 .... 22, 23, 30
      (1) 11
      4(1), (2) 27, 30
      5 .... 78, 174
      (2), (3) 50
      6(1) 53

Merchant Shipping Act 1979—*cont.*
 Sch. 4—*cont.*
  Part II, para. 8 56
     (2) 71
    9 69
    10 74
    11 .... 65, 71
    12 .. 11, 17, 79, 81
    13 .... 65, 70, 74
  III, para. 7 47
 Sch. 5 .... 2, 145,
    169–170, 174, 179,
        181
  Part I 172
 Sch. 6 .... 173, 178, 181
 Sch. 7 .... 172, 173, 178,
        181
  Part II 41, 172, 174
Merchant Shipping Act 1979
 (Commencement No. 10)
 Order 1986 (S.I. 1986 No.
 1052) 2, 84, 171
Merchant Shipping Act 1979
 (Commencement No. 11)
 Order 1987 (S.I. 1987 No.
 635) 3, 53, 86,
      175, 176
Merchant Shipping Act 1979
 (Commencement No. 12)
 Order 1987 (S.I. 1987 No.
 719) 29
Merchant Shipping Act 1979
 (Commencement No. 13)
 Order 1989 (S.I. 1989 No.
 1881) 29, 179,
        221
Merchant Shipping Act 1981—
 s. 1 47
  2(3) 190, 191
  (5) 116
  5(3), Sch. 183
Merchant Shipping Act 1984—
 s. 12 139
Merchant Shipping Act (Liab-
 ility of Shipowners and
 Others) (Rate of Interest)
 Order 1986 (S.I. 1986 No.
 1932) 66
Merchant Shipping (Liability of
 Shipowners and Others)
 Act 1900, s. 2(1) 169

Merchant Shipping (Liability of
 Shipowners and Others)
 Act 1958 .... 2, 5, 8, 18,
     21, 43, 139,
      170, 186
 s. 2 19
  (1) 21
  (2)(a) 21
  (4) 28
  (5) 21
  (6) 166
 3 8
  (1) 8, 13
  (2) 12, 13
 5 72
 6 70
 7(1) 69
 8(2) 58
 17(2) 70
Merchant Shipping (Liability of
 Shipowners and Others)
 (Calculation of Tonnage)
 Order 1986 (S.I. 1986
 No. 1040) 174
 para. 2(1), (2) 52
Merchant Shipping (Oil Pollu-
 tion) Act 1971 30
 s. 1 .... 27, 166
 5(4)(b) 170
 7 27
  (b) 170
 15(2) 170
Merchant Shipping (Tonnage)
 Regulations 1967 50
 regs. 3, 13 51
Merchant Shipping (Tonnage)
 Regulations 1982 (S.I. 1982
 No. 841) 50
 regs. 4–6 .... 52, 174, 175
 reg. 12 51

Nuclear Installations Act
 1965—
 ss. 7–11 .... 27, 28, 30, 166
 s. 12(4) 185
 14(1) 28
 16 28

Pilotage Act 1913—
 ss. 9–11 172
Pilotage Act 1983 174

Pilotage Authorities (Limitation
of Liability) Act 1936—
ss. 1(1), 4 169

Rules of the Supreme Court—
Ord. 18, r. 22 60
22, r. 1 66
74, r. 6(1A) 71
75 .... 59, 71
r. 24 66
rr. 37–43 .... 61, 65
r. 37A 65
(1) 60
rr. 41–43 68
Rules of the Supreme Court
(Amendment) 1985 (S.I.
1985 No. 69) 65

Rules of the Supreme Court
(Amendment No. 2) 1990
(S.I. 1990 No. 1689) 71

Statute of Limitation (Northern
Ireland) 1958—
s. 72(2), (3) 156
Supreme Court Act 1981—
s. 20(1)(b) and (3)(c) 65

Third Parties (Rights Against
Insurers) Act 1930 .. 14–16, 36
s. 1(1) 14–16, 36

Unfair Contract Terms Act
1977 85

TABLE OF CONVENTIONS

Athens Convention, 1974 ...... 2, 3,
6, 34, 35, 37, 40, 53–55,
86–105, 109, 128, 143,
147–158, 175, 176, 177, 218
Art. 1 .... 86–92, 105, 147, 155
(1)–(3) 87, 147
(4) 87, 104, 105, 147
(5) 87, 147
(6), (7) 87, 148
(8)(a), (b) 87, 148
(c) 88, 148
(9) 88, 92, 148
2 .... 92–93, 148, 149
(1)(a) 92, 148
(b), (c) 92, 149
(2) 92, 93
3 .... 93–95, 149
(1) 93, 94, 149
(2) 93, 149
(3) 93, 95, 149
4 .... 88, 93, 95, 149–150
(1) 93, 95, 149
(2) 149
(3) 97, 150
(4) 150
(5) 93, 150
5 .... 94, 95–96, 150
6 .... 94, 95, 150
7 .... 96, 97, 98,
99, 100, 129, 151, 152,
156, 157, 158, 221
(1) 53, 54, 96, 97,
100, 150, 156
(2) 96, 150
8 .... 87, 91, 96, 97, 98,
99, 100, 129, 148, 151,
152, 156, 157, 158, 221

Athens Convention, 1974—
cont.
Art. 8(1) 96, 150, 151
(2) 96, 151
(3) 94, 96, 150, 151
(4) 96, 97, 104, 151, 154
9 .... 96, 97, 156,
157, 158
(1), (2) 96, 151
10 96–97
(1) 94, 96, 100,
150, 151, 152
(2) 97, 151
11 .... 98, 99, 151, 152
12 .... 98–99, 156
(1) 98, 151
(2) 98, 99, 152
(3) 99, 152
13 .... 33, 38, 54,
99, 100, 101, 129
(1), (2) 99, 152
14 ...... 55, 99, 101, 105, 152
15 .... 101, 102
(1)(a) 101, 152
(b) 101, 153
(2), (3) 101, 153
16 .... 102, 156
(1)–(4) 102, 153
17 .... 103, 104, 154, 156
(1) 103, 104, 154
(a)–(d) 103, 154
(2) 103, 154
18 .... 103–104, 154
19 ...... 55, 56, 101, 104, 154
20 .... 105, 154
(a), (b) 155
21 .... 105, 155

Brussels Convention, 1957. *See* Limitation Convention, 1957

Convention on Limitation of Liability for Maritime Claims, 1976 (London Convention). *See* Limitation Convention 1976

Convention on the Liability of Operators of Nuclear Ships 1962 28

Convention relating to the Carriage of Passengers and Their Luggage by Sea 1974. *See* Athens Convention

Hague Protocol, 1955, to the Warsaw Convention, 1929 .. 37
  Art. 13 32

Hague Rules 2, 3, 6, 42, 107–119, 121, 123, 125–127, 131, 132, 134–135, 136, 183, 186, 188, 192, 214, 219
  Art. I(a) 130, 132
    (b) 131
    (c) 126
  II 127
  III 108
    (2) 127
    (4) 187
    (8) 123, 127, 134
  IV 108, 127
    (2)(q) 122
    (5) 108, 111, 114, 124, 125, 126, 127, 130, 134, 135, 190
  VIII 110

Hague-Visby Rules 2, 3, 6, 34, 35, 37, 40, 62, 107–119, 121, 123, 127–130, 131, 132, 136, 183–194, 219
  Art. I 186
    (a) 130, 186
    (b) 131, 186
    (c) 184, 186
    (d), (e) 184
  II 118, 186
  III 108, 187

Hague-Visby Rules—*cont.*
  Art. III(1) 12, 110, 128, 187, 189
    (a)–(c) 187
    (2) 128, 187
    (3) 117, 187, 189
      (a)–(c) 187
    (4) 117, 118, 184, 187
    (5) 117, 188
    (6) 126, 188
    (6) *bis* 188
    (7) 184, 188
    (8) 123, 124, 189
  IV 187, 189
    (1) 189
    (2) 130, 189
      (a)–(f) 189
      (g)–(p) 190
      (q) 122, 190
    (3), (4) 190
    (5) 108, 114, 123, 124, 130, 190, 193
      (a) 114, 116, 118, 129, 134, 135, 190
      (b) 114, 116, 190
      (c) 115, 116, 117, 118, 191
      (d) 115, 191
      (e) 33, 37, 38, 115, 118, 127, 128, 129, 191
      (f), (g) 115, 191
      (h) 115, 124, 191
    (6) 191
  IV *bis* 192
    (1) 118, 192
    (2) 119, 122, 128, 133, 192
    (3) 119, 192
    (4) 119, 128, 192
  V 192
  VI 125, 186, 193
  VIII 42, 110, 186, 193
  IX 193
  X 193
    (a), (b) 194
    (c) 183, 194

Hamburg Rules 2, 3, 34, 35, 37, 108, 119–123, 130, 131, 132, 133–134, 135, 220, 221
  Art. 1 195

Hamburg Rules—*cont.*

Art. 1(1) 130, 132, 195
   (2) 122, 130, 131, 195
   (3)–(5) 195
   (6) 131, 195
   (7) 196, 204
   (8) 196
 2 .... 196, 214
   (1)–(2) 196
   (3) 131, 196
   (4) 196
 3 197
 4(1) 197
   (2) 197, 207
    (a), (b) 197
   (3) 197
 5 .... 120, 197, 203
   (1) 108, 197, 201
   (2)–(7) 197
 6 .... 108, 120,
      121, 130, 199, 200,
      201, 212, 214
   (1) 108, 120, 135, 199
    (a) 120, 121, 122,
       135, 199
    (b) ... 120, 123, 135, 199
    (c) 120, 199
   (2) 120, 135, 199
    (a), (b) 120, 199
   (3) 120, 121, 199
   (4) 120, 199, 204
 7 .... 108, 120–121, 199
   (1) 120, 199
    (i) 122
   (2) 120, 121, 122,
       133, 200, 201
   (3) 121, 122, 200, 201
 8 .... 108, 121, 122, 200, 201
   (1) 33, 101, 121,
       130, 200
   (2) 121, 130, 200, 201
 9(1)–(3) 200
   (4) 201
 10 .... 122, 130, 201
   (1) 12, 131, 201
   (2) 133, 201, 202
   (3), (4) 122, 201
   (5), (6) 201
 11(1) 201
   (2) 202
 12 202

Hamburg Rules—*cont.*

Art. 13(1) 202
   (2)(a) 202
    (b) 202, 203
   (3) 202
   (4) 202, 203
 14(1)–(3) 203
 15(1)(a)–(g) 203
    (h), (j) 204
    (k) 204, 205
    (l)–(o) 204
   (2), (3) 204
 16 204
   (1) 204, 205
   (2) 204
   (3), (4) 205
 17 205
   (1) 125, 205, 206
   (2), (3) 205, 206
   (4) 206
 18 206
 19(1)–(5) 206
   (6)–(8) 207
 20 .... 207, 211
   (1)–(5) 207
 21 .... 208, 211
   (1) 202, 208
    (a)–(d) 208
   (2) 202, 208
    (a) 208, 209
    (b) 208
   (3) 208
   (4)(a), (b) 208
    (c) 209
   (5) 209
 22 .... 209, 211
   (1)–(3) 209
   (4) 209, 211
   (5), (6) 209
 23 210
   (1) 123, 124, 210
   (2) 210
   (3) 204, 210
   (4) 210
 24(1) 210
   (2) 211
 25 211
   (1) 110, 211
   (2)–(5) 211
 26 .... 199, 212
   (1)–(3) 212, 214

Hamburg Rules—*cont.*

Art. 26(4) 212

    27 213

Arts 28, 29 213

Art. 30 213

    (1) 213, 214

    (2), (3) 213

    31 213

    (1) 213, 214

    (2)–(4) 214

    32 214

    33(1) 214

    (2) 214, 215

    (3)–(6) 215

    34 215

Annex II 216

International Convention for the Unification of Certain Rules of Law relating to Bills of Lading, 1924 (Brussels). *See* **Hague Rules**

International Convention for the Unification of Certain Rules relating to the Limitation of Liability of the Owners of Seagoing Vessels, 1924 (Brussels). *See* **Limitation Convention, 1924**

International Convention on Civil Liability for Oil Pollution Damage, 1969 ...... 25, 26, 27, 160

Art. 3(b) 30

International Convention on Tonnage Measurement of Ships, 1969 ...... 50, 52, 53, 175

Annex I 167

International Convention relating to the Limitation of the Liability of Owners of Sea-Going Ships, 1957. *See* **Limitation Convention 1957**

Limitation Convention, 1924 (Brussels) 1, 5, 82, 84

Limitation Convention, 1957 ..... 1, 2, 5, 8, 9, 31, 41, 47, 58, 70, 82, 84, 109

Art. 1 19

    (1) 18, 20, 77

Limitation Convention, 1957—*cont.*

Art. 1(1)(b), (c) 21

    (4)(b) 28

    (5) 42, 43

    (6) 39, 73

    2 64

    (1) 58

    (3) 66

    (4) 70

    3 .... 48, 49

    (2) 68

    (3) 68, 69

    (4) 69

    (5) 78

    4(a) 26

    5 72

    6(2) 12

    (3) 13

Arts 7, 8 77

Limitation Convention, 1976 .. 1, 2, 7–84, 89, 90, 100, 104, 108, 109, 124, 132, 135, 136, 144, 159–168, 172, 175, 180, 217

Art. 1 .... 7–17, 29, 35, 36, 42, 76, 89, 104, 159, 165

    (1) 9, 10, 11, 49, 159

    (2) 9, 10, 11, 13, 16, 57, 77, 131, 159, 163, 166

    (3) 11, 159

    (4) 9, 10, 12, 13, 119, 131, 132, 133, 134, 159

    (5) 159

    (6) .. 14, 15, 16, 36, 72, 159

    (7) 62, 159

    2 .... 7, 17–25, 26, 36, 37, 119, 159

    (1) 17, 18, 20, 21, 24, 40, 159, 160, 166

    (a) 17, 19, 20, 24, 26, 109, 135, 160, 170

    (b) 17, 20, 135, 160

    (c) 17, 21, 160

    (d) 7, 18, 21, 22, 23, 25, 26, 49, 82, 84, 159, 160, 166

    (e) 7, 18, 22, 23, 82, 84, 159, 160

Limitation Convention, 1976—
cont.

Art. 2(1)(f) 7, 18, 23,
24, 159, 160
(2) .. 18, 21, 22, 24, 29, 160
3 .... 17, 25–30,
40, 159, 160
(a) 25, 26, 29, 160
(b) 25, 26, 27, 160, 166
(c) 25, 27, 30, 160, 166
(d) 25, 28, 30, 160
(e) 25, 28, 29, 30, 160
4 .... 2, 14, 17, 30–42, 54,
74, 101, 118, 122, 128,
129, 145, 159, 161, 169
5 .... 42–44, 161
6 .... 25, 44–45, 46,
47–53, 57, 63, 65,
67, 78, 79, 80, 83
(1) 44, 47–48, 57,
63, 104, 161, 164
(a) 44, 45, 48,
49, 161, 162
(b) 44, 46, 48,
49, 162, 169
(2) 8, 44, 46,
48–49, 63, 162, 164
(3) 8, 44, 46, 49, 63, 162
(4) 44, 49–50
(5) 44, 50
7 .... 45, 46, 53–57, 63,
65, 67, 78, 80, 83, 104,
161, 162, 163, 164, 167
(1) 45, 46, 54,
55, 162, 164, 167
(2) 45, 53, 104,
105, 162, 164, 167
(a), (b) 45, 162
8 ..... 45, 46, 47, 48, 57, 162
(1) 45, 46, 62, 162, 167
(2) 45, 48, 83
(a) 45, 46
(b), (c) 46
(3), (4) 46, 48
9 .... 57–59, 67, 99, 163
(1) 57, 163
(a)–(c) 57, 63,
72, 163, 164
(2) 57, 63, 72, 163, 164
10 .... 59–63, 163
(1) 59, 163

Limitation Convention, 1957—
cont.

Art. 10(2), (3) 59, 60, 163
11 .... 59, 63, 64, 65–67,
70, 71, 73, 75, 76, 163,
164, 165, 167, 168,
169
(1) 63, 65, 67, 72,
74, 163
(2) 63, 66, 164
(3) 63, 67, 164
12 .... 59, 60, 63–64, 65,
67–70, 75, 76,
163, 164, 168, 169
(1) 63, 67, 164
(2) 63, 68, 69, 164
(3), (4) 63, 69, 164
13 .... 62, 64, 67,
70–75, 76, 164
(1) 64, 66, 70–72,
75, 164, 165
(2) 64, 72–75, 165, 168
(a)–(d) 64, 165
(3) 64, 75, 165
14 .... 64, 65, 68,
69, 75–76, 165
15 .... 17, 76–81, 165
(1) 16, 76, 77
(2) 16, 76, 77, 78, 80
(a), (b) 76
(3) 76, 79
(4) 76, 79
(a), (b) 76
(5) 11, 17, 77, 79–81
(a) 77
(b) 77
16 .... 46, 81
(1)–(3) 81
17 81
(1) 81, 84
(2), (3) 81
(4) 82
18 82
(1) 82, 84
(2), (3) 82
19(1)–(3) 82
20 .... 82, 83
(1)–(3) 82
21(1)–(4) 83
22(1)–(3) 83
23 83

London Convention. *See* Limitation Convention, 1976

Paris Convention of 29 July 1960 on Third Party Liability in the field of Nuclear Energy as amended by Additional Protocol of 28 January 1964 .... 105, 155, 211

Protocol of 23 February 1968 to amend the International Convention for the Unification of Certain Rules relating to Bills of Lading 1924 (Brussels) 214

Protocol to the Athens Convention, 1976 .... 97, 177, 180, 182, 221

Protocol to the Athens Convention, 1990 98

United Nations Convention on the Carriage of Goods by Sea, 1978. *See* Hamburg Rules

Vienna Convention of 21 May 1963 on Civil Liability for Nuclear Damage 105, 155, 211

Warsaw Convention, 1929 .. 33, 34, 38, 40, 129

Art. 22 32
    (2)(a), (4) 68
    25 .... 32, 37, 39, 129

CHAPTER 1

INTRODUCTION

The International Conference on the Limitation of Liability for Maritime Claims took place in London between 1 and 19 November 1976 under the auspices of the International Maritime Organisation (IMO). It was generally accepted by those attending the conference that the rules relating to the limitation of liability for maritime claims enshrined in the 1924 and 1957 Limitation Conventions required updating. It was agreed at the conference that the limitation figures contained in the 1957 Convention needed to be increased and that the new limitation figures should be accompanied by a mechanism to accommodate problems of inflation. It was also agreed that the circumstances in which the right to limit should be forfeit needed reviewing.

It was recognised that the previous system of limitation had given rise to too much litigation and there was a desire that this should be avoided in future. There was agreement that a balance needed to be struck between the desire to ensure on the one hand that a successful claimant should be suitably compensated for any loss or injury which he had suffered and the need on the other hand to allow shipowners, for public policy reasons, to limit their liability to an amount which was readily insurable at a reasonable premium.

The solution which was finally adopted to resolve the competing requirements of claimant and defendant was (a) the establishment of a limitation fund which was as high as a shipowner could cover by insurance at a reasonable cost, and (b) the creation of a virtually unbreakable right to limit liability.

The text of the 1976 Convention finally adopted by the conference therefore represents a compromise. In exchange for

1

the establishment of a much higher limitation fund claimants would have to accept the extremely limited opportunities to break the right to limit liabiliy. Thus the right to limit liability can no longer be lost as a result of negligence on the part of the person seeking to limit. Under the 1976 Convention the right to limit liability is lost only when the claimant can prove wilful intent or recklessness on the part of the person seeking to limit (Article 4).

International Conventions have no independent life of their own. They require adoption as part of the national law of participating countries before they become effective. The 1976 Convention itself provides that certain of its provisions are optional insofar as adoption is concerned. It follows that when problems of limitation arise in practice it will always be essential to consult the national legislation which gives domestic effect to the Convention in the country concerned.

Thus the 1957 Limitation Convention was given domestic effect in the United Kingdom by the Merchant Shipping (Liability of Shipowners and Others) Act 1958 (the 1958 Act). By virtue of section 17 of the Merchant Shipping Act 1979 (the 1979 MSA), the 1976 Limitation Convention (as set out in Schedule 4, Part I, of the 1979 MSA) applies in the United Kingdom subject to the reservations mentioned in Part II of the same Schedule.

In accordance with the provisions of the Merchant Shipping Act 1979 (Commencement No. 10) Order 1986 (SI 1986/1052) the terms of the 1976 Limitation Convention came into force in the United Kingdom on 1 December 1986. By virtue of section 19(4) of the 1979 MSA the new limitation regime applies to liability arising out of post 1 December 1986 occurrences. By virtue of section 19(1) the provisions of six other statutes are amended as from 1 December 1986 in the manner specified in Schedule 5 to the 1979 MSA.

The main purpose of this book is to compare the new limitation regime with the old by reference to the changes wrought by the 1976 Convention and to examine how the new regime applies in the United Kingdom. Some space is also devoted to considering how the provisions of the 1976 Convention relate to the limitation provisions contained in the Athens Convention and the Hague, Hague–Visby and Hamburg Rules.

The 1974 Convention relating to the Carriage of Passengers and Their Luggage by Sea (the Athens Convention) was given domestic effect in the United Kingdom by the Merchant Shipping Act 1979. Section 14 of that Act provides that the Convention as set out in Part I of Schedule 3 shall have the force of law in the United Kingdom. Part I of the Schedule takes effect subject to the provisions of Part II and the "modifications" of Part III of Schedule 3.

In accordance with the terms of the Merchant Shipping Act 1979 (Commencement No. 11) Order 1987 (SI 1987/635) the terms of the Athens Convention came into force in the United Kingdom on 30 April 1987.

The Hague Rules were given domestic effect in the United Kingdom, primarily in relation to exports, by the Carriage of Goods by Sea Act 1924. That Act was repealed in 1971 and the Carriage of Goods by Sea Act 1971 gave instead the force of law to the Hague–Visby Rules in the United Kingdom in the circumstances set out in section 1 of the Act and Article X of the Rules as set out in the Schedule to the Act.

The Hamburg Rules will come into force internationally on 1 November 1992 and comment is made on the provisions of the Rules by way of comparison with the Hague and Hague–Visby Rules.

CHAPTER 2

HISTORY OF LIMITATION IN THE UNITED KINGDOM

Earlier legislation in the United Kingdom relating to limitation of liability for maritime claims was drawn together in section 503 of the Merchant Shipping Act 1894. The United Kingdom was a signatory to the 1924 and 1957 International Limitation Conventions and adopted many of the provisions of those Conventions. This was done not by incorporating the Conventions *en bloc* into domestic legislation but by amending section 503 of the 1894 Act. Thus the Merchant Shipping (Liability of Shipowners and Others) Act 1958 incorporated into United Kingdom law many of the provisions of the 1957 Limitation Convention and this was achieved by amending section 503 of the 1894 MSA. This "patchwork" approach has produced a number of problems in the United Kingdom over the years because the amendments made to section 503 have not always accurately mirrored the Convention provisions on which they were based.

The *en bloc* adoption by the United Kingdom of the 1976 Limitation Convention (by section 17 of the Merchant Shipping Act 1979) to replace the much amended provisions of section 503 of the 1894 MSA should at least ensure that issues of limitation will, as between the United Kingdom and countries adopting the Convention, receive uniform treatment (subject to "reservations" which will be discussed and the probability that the courts of different countries will produce their own highly individual interpretations of the Convention wording).

The United Kingdom has also recognised that those engaged in the carriage of goods and passengers by sea should be entitled to limit their liability on a per claim basis.

5

In 1924 the United Kingdom gave effect to the Hague Rules in relation to exports from this country by virtue of the Carriage of Goods by Sea Act. With the adoption of the Hague–Visby Rules in the late 1960s this Act was repealed and replaced by the Carriage of Goods by Sea Act 1971 which gave effect to the Hague–Visby Rules.

In 1974 the Athens Convention relating to the Carriage of Passengers and Their Luggage by Sea was signed but did not come into force internationally until 28 April 1987. The Athens Convention had been given effect in limited circumstances in the United Kingdom under Statutory Instrument 1980 No 1092 but was given full effect on 30 April 1987 by virtue of section 14 of the Merchant Shipping Act of 1979.

CHAPTER 3

THE 1976 LIMITATION CONVENTION

EXPLANATORY NOTE

There follows the full text of the 1976 Limitation Convention together with comments on each Article. The Convention itself is incorporated into the law of the United Kingdom by section 17 of the Merchant Shipping Act 1979 (the 1979 MSA) and the text of the Convention itself is set out in Part I of Schedule 4 to that Act. *However there are certain provisions in the Convention which do not appear in Schedule 4. The omissions are identified* by the provision being set in *italic*. The text of the Convention is set in a different typeface.

CHAPTER I—THE RIGHT OF LIMITATION

Article 1: Persons entitled to limit liability

1. Shipowners and salvors, as hereinafter defined, may limit their liability in accordance with the rules of this Convention for claims set out in Article 2.

2. The term "shipowner" shall mean the owner, charterer, manager and operator of a seagoing ship.

3. Salvor shall mean any person rendering services in direct connection with salvage operations. Salvage operations shall also include operations referred to in Article 2, paragraph 1(d), (e) and (f).

4. If any claims set out in Article 2 are made against any person for whose act, neglect or default the shipowner or salvor is responsible, such person shall be entitled to avail himself of the limitation of liability provided for in this Convention.

5. In this Convention the liability of a shipowner shall include liability in an action brought against the vessel herself.

6. An insurer of liability for claims subject to limitation in accordance with the rules of this Convention shall be entitled to the benefits of this Convention to the same extent as the assured himself.

7

7. The act of invoking limitation of liability shall not constitute an admission of liability.[1]

Comment follows below on the different categories of "persons" who are entitled to limit their liability under the 1976 Convention.

(a) Shipowners

Under section 503(1) of the Merchant Shipping Act 1894 (in its unamended form) only the owners of a ship were entitled to limit their liability. However, the right to limit applied to a "registered" or a "beneficial" owner and applied whether the ship was British or foreign.

As time has passed and new legislation and international Conventions have come into force the definition of "owner" has been extended and other persons have been added to the list of those entitled to limit their liability.

The 1957 Brussels Convention extended the class of persons entitled to limit liability. Thus Article 6, paragraph 2, provides:

"Subject to paragraph 3 of this Article, the provisions of this Convention shall apply to the charterer, manager and operator of the ship, and to the master, members of the crew and other servants of the owner, charterer, manager or operator acting in the course of their employment, in the same way as they apply to an owner himself . . ."

The primary reason for extending the class of persons entitled to limit was to overcome the problem first encountered in the case of The "Himalaya",[2] namely, attempts by a claimant, in order to circumvent the effects of limitation of liability, to bring a claim against some person other than the owner, for example, the master of the vessel.

The Merchant Shipping (Liability of Shipowners and Others) Act 1958 sought to give domestic effect to the 1957 Convention in this country. The class of persons whose liability could be limited is set out in section 3 of the Act. Section 3(1) provided that the persons entitled to limit liability "included any charterer and any person interested in or in possession of

1. See pp. 60–61, below.
2. [1954] 2 Lloyd's Rep. 267.

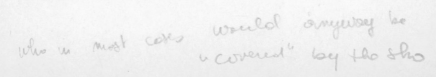
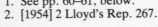

the ship, and, in particular, any manager or operator of the ship."

It is not clear what, if any, restriction is to be placed on the interpretation of the words—"person interested in . . . the ship". But clearly a shipbuilder or ship repairer or even a mortgagee in possession was by reason of these words entitled to limit his liability. As to the types of "managers" who could limit under the Act it may well be that the Act was restricted in its application to managers who were actually operating the vessel—the point was never tested in court. The words "manager" and "operator" appear together and may simply be particular examples of "any person interested in or in possession of the ship". If this interpretation is wrong and the expression "person interested in . . . the ship" is to be given a liberal interpretation it could extend the class of persons entitled to limit to any person who has or has had dealings with the vessel. The writers have never favoured this liberal interpretation.

Looking at the definition of "shipowner" in paragraph 2 of Article 1 of the 1976 Convention it would appear that certain classes of person who under the 1957 Convention and 1958 Act were entitled to limit their liability, such as persons merely in possession but not operating the vessel, e.g. a ship-repairer or shipbuilder or mortgagee, are no longer able to limit unless they can show that one of the class of persons who can limit under Article 1(1) was "responsible" for their "act, neglect or default" so as to bring themselves within paragraph 4 of Article 1. Unfortunately there is still no clarification as to the types of "managers" who may limit liability. Although the word "manager" itself is not qualified as it is in the 1958 Act by the words "person interested in . . . the ship", the remainder of the persons named in paragraph 2 are those who would normally operate the ship.

Slot charterers

Article 1(2) provides that a "charterer . . . and operator . . . of a seagoing ship" can limit his liability. However, an interesting question arises whether these words are sufficient to afford the right to limit to a "slot charterer", that is to say a party who has the right to use a specified part [but not the whole] of the cargo carrying capacity of a vessel on a particular voyage and who often issues his own bills of lading. Such a party is described in common parlance as a "charterer" and it is not straining language to say that he is an "operator". However, he is arguably not a charterer or operator of the whole ship but merely of a *part* of the ship.

All the other parties referred to in Article 1(2) have an interest in the whole ship and the limit of their liability is calculated with reference to the tonnage of the whole ship. There is no provision which allows a slot charterer to limit his liability proportionately to the space which he has chartered and accordingly the choice would seem to be between allowing the slot charterer to limit his liability according to the full tonnage of the vessel despite the fact that his contract allows him to use merely part of it or not allowing him to limit at all on the basis that he is not a charterer or operator of "a ship". The authors prefer the former view as this is more in keeping with the professed aim of the 1976 Convention.[3] Furthermore, it is true to say that whilst the slot charterer's contract limits the cargo space which is available to him he is in fact paying for the use of the rest of the vessel to ensure the safe carriage of "his" cargo to the discharge port.

(b) Salvors

The most significant innovation introduced by Article 1 of the 1976 Convention is the extension of the benefit of limitation to salvors (Article 1(1) and (3)) and to any person for whose act, neglect or default a salvor is responsible (Article 1(4)).

This extension was made in response to pressure from international salvage interests following the decision of the English House of Lords in The *"Tojo Maru"*.[4] In that case it was held that a salvor was not entitled to limit his liability in respect of damage caused by the negligent act of a diver who, although assisting in the salvage, was working away from the salvor's

3. See the comments of Steyn J. in The *"European Enterprise"* [1989] 2 Lloyd's Rep. at page 191.
4. [1971] 1 Lloyd's Rep. 341.

vessel at the time the damage occurred. The House of Lords held that the diver's negligent act was not an act done "in the management" of the salvor's tug nor an act done "on board" that tug.

By Article 1, the benefit of limitation is now conferred on salvors engaged in direct connection with salvage services, which services are defined in Article 1(3) as including in addition to salvage as strictly defined, wreck or cargo removal or other services described in Article 2(1)(d)[5] (e) and (f).

(c) Seagoing ships and hovercraft[6]

Article 1(2) of the 1976 Convention is similar in effect to Article 1(1) of the 1957 Convention in that it confers the right to limit in respect of "a seagoing ship". However, section 503 of the 1894 Act granted the right to limit in the United Kingdom to ships whether seagoing or not. In other words, the courts of the United Kingdom have since 1894, recognised the right of the owner of a ship, whether seagoing or not, to limit his liability.

Paragraphs 2 and 12 of Part II to Schedule 4 and section 17(1) of the 1979 MSA make it clear that in the United Kingdom the limitation provisions of the 1976 Convention are to continue to be applied in relation to any ship whether seagoing or not and that the word "ship" shall include "any structure (whether completed or in the course of completion) launched and intended for use in navigation as a ship or part of a ship".[7]

Article 15(5) provides that the Convention shall not apply to "aircushion vehicles" (hovercraft). However, this provision does not appear in Schedule 4, Part I, to the 1979 MSA and, therefore, does not have the force of law in the United Kingdom. By the Hovercraft (Civil Liability) Order 1986 certain provisions of the Convention are made applicable to hovercraft in the United Kingdom. (For details see commentary on Article 15 on pp. 77 *et seq.*)

---

5. But see reservation in paragraph 3(1) of Schedule 4, Part II, of the 1979 MSA.

6. See pages 77–78, below.

7. See page 168.

(d) Other persons

Article 1(4) of the 1976 Convention extends the right to limit to "any person for whose act, neglect or default the shipowner or salvor is responsible". (See (a) Shipowners, above.)

This wording appears to extend the class of those entitled to limit liability. Whereas Article 6(2) of the 1957 Limitation Convention and section 3(2) of the 1958 Act afforded the right to limit to the "Master, members of the crew and other *servants* of the Owner . . . acting in the course of their employment", Article 1(4) of the 1976 Convention is apparently wide enough to encompass agents and independent contractors such as stevedores provided that the shipowner is responsible for their actions as a matter of law.[8]

It is by no means clear what is meant by the word "responsible". Given a restricted interpretation it could mean that, for example, a stevedore must show, contrary to The *"White Rose"*,[9] that he is a "servant" of the shipowner before he can establish an independent right to limit.[10] Given a wider interpretation it may only be necessary for the stevedore to show that the shipowner was "responsible" for him being involved.

In the context of claims for damage to cargo, Article III, rule 1, of the Hague–Visby Rules places an obligation on the shipowner before and at the beginning of the voyage to exercise due diligence to make the ship seaworthy. In The *"Muncaster Castle"*[11] the House of Lords held that, as far as this obligation is concerned, the shipowner is liable if the vessel was unseaworthy as a result of the acts or omissions of independent contractors whom he has engaged. It would seem to follow that an independent contractor who renders a ship unseaworthy by his act, neglect or default will be able, if he is sued by the owners of the damaged cargo, to limit his liability under the 1976 Convention.

Similarly, in the context of the Hamburg Rules, Article 10(1) provides expressly that:

8. See the discussion on pages 130–134 in relation to the Hague–Visby and Hamburg Rules.
9. [1969] 2 Lloyd's Rep. 52.
10. See, for example, *McDermid* v. *Nash Dredging & Reclamation Co. Ltd.* [1986] 2 Lloyd's Rep. 24.
11. [1961] 1 Lloyd's Rep. 57.

"The carrier is responsible in relation to the carriage performed by the actual carrier, for the acts and omissions of the actual carrier and of his servants and agents acting within the scope of their employment."

However, the wording of Article 1(4) may in one respect reduce the class of persons who were entitled to limit their liability under the 1958 Act. Thus section 3(1) of the 1958 Act refers to any "persons interested in or in possession of a ship". Mortgagees in possession do not normally "operate" their ship and may not therefore, qualify under Article 1(2) of the 1976 Convention. Further, it is doubtful whether a shipowner could be said to "be responsible" (within the meaning of Article 1(4)) for the acts of a mortgagee in possession who does not operate the ship. It may well be therefore, that, the mortgagee in possession has inadvertently lost the right to limit under the 1976 Convention and the 1979 MSA.

(e) Owner/master

Article 6(3) of the 1957 Convention provides that, where the master or member of the crew is at the same time the owner, charterer, manager or operator of the vessel, such person will only be entitled to limit his liability if he commits the act, neglect or default in his capacity as Master or as a member of the crew.

This point arose in the United Kingdom in *The "Annie Hay"*.[12] The Owner of the *Annie Hay* was acting as master and in sole charge of navigation when the vessel was in collision with a yacht. The yacht was so damaged that it sank. There was no dispute that the cause of the collision was, in the main, the negligence of the owner/master.

The owner claimed to be entitled to limit his liability under section 3(2) of the 1958 Act (which enacted Article 6(3) of the 1957 Convention) on the ground that the claim arose out of his negligence in his capacity as master. It was held that he was so entitled.

There is no equivalent express provision in the 1976 Convention. However, Article 1 gives the shipowner a general

12. [1968] 1 Lloyd's Rep. 141.

entitlement to limit his liability which is only restricted by the provisions of Article 4 (conduct barring limitations). Thus, the prospects for a master/owner seeking to limit liability seem to have been improved by the 1976 Convention and the 1979 MSA since, subject to the provisions of Article 4, it would not seem to be relevant under the new regime whether at the relevant time the act in question was committed in the individual's capacity as master or as owner.

(f) Liability insurer

Article 1(6) of the 1976 Convention introduces an innovation in that where a person entitled to limit liability is insured, the insurer is entitled to the benefits of the Convention *"to the same extent"* as the assured himself. There is no such provision in either the 1957 Convention or the 1958 Act.

The intention of this provision appears to be to place the liability insurer in no worse position than the assured, insofar as limitation is concerned, should a direct action be brought against the liability insurer. It follows that the liability insurer should not be able to limit his liability if the assured cannot.

This provision raises an interesting question under the law of the United Kingdom. A direct action can be brought in certain circumstances by a third party against the insurer in the United Kingdom under the Third Parties (Rights Against Insurers) Act 1930. Thus where the assured has failed to satisfy a judgment and has been wound up the unsatisfied creditor "steps into the shoes" of the assured and takes over whatever rights the assured has against the insurer under the liability policy. Such "rights" are likely to be restricted either by the terms of the policy itself or by those of the Marine Insurance Act 1906 which provides *inter alia* that the insurer is not liable if the assured is in breach of an express or implied warranty in the policy, "whether it be material to the risk or not".[13]

It was held by the House of Lords in The *"Fanti"/The "Padre Island"*[14] that a third party claimant stepping into the

13. S.33(3).
14. [1990] 2 Lloyd's Rep. 191.

shoes of the assured under the 1930 Act and thereby taking over the assured's rights under the P&I policy could not recover from the P&I insurer under the Act unless and until the assured had complied with the Club's Rules and first paid the claim (which would, of course, have rendered the third party's claim against the insurer unnecessary). The third party claimant's rights under the Act were, therefore, held to be restricted by the express provisions of the insurance cover.

However, it is arguable that the terms of Article 1(6) of the 1976 Convention have inadvertantly prejudiced the liability insurer's rights in this respect. The conduct necessary to debar the shipowner from liability may well also be conduct which would prevent him from successfully prosecuting a claim against his liability underwriter under the Club Rules or section 55(2) of the Marine Insurance Act. However, by virtue of section 17(1) of the 1979 MSA the terms of the 1976 Convention are given the force of law in the United Kingdom. Therefore, if the insurer by Article 1(6) is afforded the right to limit "to the same extent" as the assured he may not be entitled to rely upon those provisions of the policy or the Marine Insurance Act 1906 which have the effect of restricting his liability to the assured and may have to meet the claim of the third party claimant in full if the assured has forfeited his right to limit liability.

Such result cannot have been intended by the drafters of the Convention or by the United Kingdom legislature since it flies in the face of the Convention's declared aim that the new limitation regime should be based on a foundation of stable affordable insurance cover.

A way round the problem may lie in the wording of section 1(1) of the 1930 Act itself which provides that:

" . . . his (the assured's) rights against the insurer under the contract in respect of the liability shall, *notwithstanding anything in any act or rule of law to the contrary* be transferred to and vest in the third party to whom the liability was so incurred."

It is therefore possible to argue, if the assured is fully liable to the third party, that notwithstanding the provisions of the 1979 MSA, it is only those limited rights which the assured has against the insurer under the liability policy which are to be transferred to the third party under the 1930 Act. In other words, the 1930 Act defines the liability of the insurer to the third party and Article 1(6) of the 1976 Convention only comes into play when that liability has been determined.

(g) Summary

The persons entitled to limit their liability are:

(1) Owners
(2) Charterers
(3) Managers
(4) Operators

of a *seagoing* ship (in UK not restricted to seagoing)

(5) any person for whose act, neglect or default the parties identified in 1–4 inclusive is responsible.
(6) Salvors.
(7) any person for whose act, neglect or default the salvor is responsible.
(8) Insurers of liability of the parties identified in 1–7 inclusive.

Excluded persons/excluded vessels

(i) Non-seagoing ships (Article 1(2)). However, state parties may under Article 15(2) of the 1976 Convention make specific provisions of national law regulating the system of limitation to be applied to vessels which, according to law of that state, are ships intended for navigation on inland waterways. In the case of the United Kingdom, the legislature has decreed by paragraph 2 of Part II of Schedule 4 and section 17 of the 1979 MSA that the provisions of the 1976 Convention shall have the force of law in the United Kingdom in relation to any ship whether seagoing or not.[15]

(ii) Article 15(1) of the 1976 Convention accords the right to State Parties to exclude wholly or partially from the application of the Convention any person referred to in Article 1 who does not, at the time when the rules of the Convention are invoked,

15. See page 11, above and 77, below.

habitually reside in or have his principal place of business in a State Party and any ship which does not fly the flag of a State Party. However, the United Kingdom does not seem to have made any such reservation in this respect and the relevant part of Article 15(1) is not included in Part I of Schedule 4 to the 1979 MSA.

(iii) Article 15(5) provides that the Convention shall *not* apply to:

(a) aircushion vehicles;
(b) floating platforms constructed for the purpose of exploring or exploiting the natural resources of the seabed or the subsoil thereof.[16]

Article 15(5) is not included in Part I of Schedule 4 to the 1979 MSA and therefore does not have the force of law in the United Kingdom. Therefore, so far as the United Kingdom is concerned, aircushion vehicles and floating platforms[17] are, prima facie, entities to which the provisions of the 1976 Convention do apply. In the case of hovercraft section 48 of the 1979 MSA envisages that the 1976 Convention will apply to hovercraft and the necessary orders will be made. (For details of the Order in relation to hovercraft, see the commentary in relation to Article 15.[18])

Article 2: Claims subject to limitation

1. Subject to Articles 3 and 4 the following claims, whatever the basis of liability may be, shall be subject to limitation of liability:

(a) Claims in respect of loss of life or personal injury or loss of or damage to property (including damage to harbour works, basins and waterways and aids to navigation), occurring on board or in direct connection with the operation of the ship or with salvage operations, and consequential loss resulting therefrom;
(b) Claims in respect of loss resulting from delay in the carriage by sea of cargo, passengers or their luggage;
(c) Claims in respect of other loss resulting from infringement of rights

16. See pages 79–81, below.
17. But see Part II, para. 12 of Schedule 4 to the 1979 MSA where the definition of "ship" is extended to cover "any structure . . . launched and intended for use in navigation as a ship . . . ", which limits the type of floating platform in respect of which the right to limit applies.
18. See pages 77–81, below.

other than contractual rights, occurring in direct connection with the operation of the ship or salvage operations;

(d) Claims in respect of the raising, removal, destruction or the rendering harmless of a ship which is sunk, wrecked, stranded or abandoned, including anything that is or has been on board such ship;

(e) Claims in respect of the removal, destruction or the rendering harmless of the cargo of the ship;

(f) Claims of a person other than the person liable in respect of measures taken in order to avert or minimise loss for which the person liable may limit his liability in accordance with this Convention, and further loss caused by such measures.

2. Claims set out in paragraph 1 shall be subject to limitation of liability even if brought by way of recourse or for indemnity under a contract or otherwise. However, claims set out under paragraph 1(d), (e) and (f) shall not be subject to limitation of liability to the extent that they relate to remuneration under a contract with the person liable.

The range of claims in respect of which the right to limit liability is available has been extended by the 1976 Convention to a significant degree.

Before analysing the Article and its subsections in detail it is worth highlighting the two principal changes introduced by the 1976 Convention. These are:

(1) Claims now qualify for limitation whatever the basis of liability may be.

(2) Claims now qualify for limitation if they arise on board or in direct connection with the operation of the ship or with salvage operations.

ARTICLE 2(1)

Article 2(1) of the 1976 Convention applies to " . . . claims whatever the basis of liability may be . . . ". Article 1(1) of the 1957 Convention applied to " . . . *claims* arising from . . . " a list of specified "occurrences". However, the position in the United Kingdom has always been that the right to limit liability is restricted to claims for which the shipowner is liable in *damages*. (See section 503(1) of the 1894 MSA as amended by the 1958 Act.) For example in The *"Stonedale No. 1"*[19] it was held that an owner could not limit his liability for wreck

19. [1956] A.C. 1.

removal expenses payable under statute since such expenses were in the nature of a debt rather than damages. Similarly in the case of *The "Kirknes"*[20] it was held that the owners of a towed vessel could not limit their liability for damage caused to the tug since the tow's liability arose not from any breach of contract or duty but from the strict covenant in the towage contract to indemnify the tug. In other words, the tow was not liable in "damages".

The effect of the 1976 Convention and the 1979 MSA is to remove altogether the requirement that the claim must sound in damages. Limitation is now available in respect of claims "whatever the basis of liability may be . . . even if brought by way of recourse or for indemnity under a contract or otherwise . . . ", subject to certain exclusions.

ARTICLE 2(1)(a)

Under the previous limitation regime the benefit of limitation was available in respect of injury or damage caused to a person or to property on board, or if they were not on board, only if such injury or damage was caused by a person on board or by a person not on board in the course of specific activities which were laid down by Article 1 of the 1957 Convention and which were enacted into English law by section 2 of the 1958 Act.

Thus, limitation was restricted to acts or omissions done by a person on board or in the navigation or management of the ship, or in the loading, carriage or discharge of its cargo, or in the embarkation, carriage or disembarkation of its passengers.

These restrictions have, from time to time, resulted in unfortunate decisions such as that in *The "Tojo Maru"*[21] where the House of Lords held that the salvors were not entitled to limit their liability since the negligent act of the diver was not an act done either in the "management" of or "on board" the tug.

The 1976 Convention seeks to deal with this problem by replacing the list with a wider definition of claims which are subject to limitation. The Convention refers in Article 2(1)(a) to

20. [1956] 2 Lloyd's Rep. 651.
21. [1971] 1 Lloyd's Rep. 341.

events occurring "on board or in direct connection with the operation of the ship, or with salvage operations, and conse- quential loss resulting therefrom".

The extent to which the right to limit has been extended by this wording will doubtless be the subject of much litigation. It should, for example, have the effect of enabling a shipowner to limit his liability in respect of claims for personal or property damage caused by a person for whose act, neglect or default he is responsible in a situation where the vessel is in drydock and the damage is caused by such a person whilst ashore in the per- formance of an act directly connected with the operation of the ship. It might encompass external repair and maintenance work and would probably cover the provision of bunkers or supplies since such services would be directly connected with the operation of the ship.

It is also noteworthy that unlike the other subsections of Article 2(1), Article 2(1)(a) expressly allows claims for conse- quential losses to qualify for limitation purposes. It is not clear how far (if at all) the wide wording of this provision will be restricted in the United Kingdom by the doctrine of remote- ness of damage. Thus in recent years there has been a trend towards allowing claims for damages for psychiatric injuries where the claimant has witnessed a disaster (or its aftermath) in which a close relative has been killed or injured. It is sub- mitted that if the disaster in question was a maritime one there would be a right to limit liability in respect of a claim of this nature on the basis that it is a claim for "personal injury . . . occurring . . . in direct connection with the operation of the ship . . . " and is a "consequential loss resulting from . . . " such operation.

ARTICLE 2(1)(b)

A further apparent innovation introduced by this subsection is the extension of the benefit of limitation to claims resulting from delay in the carriage of cargo, passengers or their lug- gage. However the innovation may be more apparent than real in that a claim for recoverable financial loss consequent on delay would in any event be a "claim" within Article 1(1) of the 1957 Convention or "damages" within section 503(1) of the

1894 MSA as amended by the 1958 Act and thus subject to the right to limit under the old regime.

ARTICLE 2(1)(c)

Both Article I(1)(b) of the 1957 Convention and section 2(1) of the 1958 Act allowed the benefit of limitation where "rights" had been "infringed". The draftsmen of the 1976 Convention preserved this right but restricted the scope of limitation to non-contractual "rights". They may have had in mind circumstances in which a claimant had a statutory right of easement which was capable of being damaged by a ship. One example of such a right is the wayleave or right of passage enjoyed by a railway company over a bridge spanning a river.[22]

So long as the right being infringed is not contractual the precise legal nature of the right and the nature of the legal liability incurred by its infringement does not seem to be relevant in view of the wording of the introductory paragraph to Article 2(1).

ARTICLE 2(1)(d)

This subsection confers the right to limit in the case of claims for the cost of removal or destruction of wrecks except where the claims relate to remuneration under a contract with the person liable (Article 2(2)).

As *The "Stonedale No. 1"*,[23] referred to above[24] demonstrated, a shipowner could not limit in the United Kingdom in respect of a claim for wreck removal expenses put forward by a harbour authority which had raised a wreck pursuant to statutory powers. With the intention of giving a shipowner the right to limit in such circumstances the 1957 Convention extended the right to limit to "liability imposed by any law relating to removal of wreck" (Article 1(1)(c)). This provision was incorporated into the 1958 Act as section 2(2)(a). However section 2(5) of the 1958 Act provided that section 2(2)(a) would not

---

22. See *Gypsum Carriers Inc.* v *The Queen* (1978) 78 D.L.R. 175 Fed. Crt. and [1978] 4 *Current Law* para 706.
23. [1956] A.C. 1.
24. See page 18, above.

come into force in the United Kingdom until such day as the Secretary of State might appoint by statutory instrument. No date has ever been appointed and accordingly this provision has never been effective in the United Kingdom.

Article 2(1)(d) of the 1976 Convention includes provisions confirming the right to limit in respect of claims for the raising, removal or destruction of a ship which is sunk, wrecked, stranded or abandoned including *anything on board* such ship. It also extends the right to any obligation or liability relating to the rendering harmless of a ship which has been sunk, stranded, abandoned or wrecked, and to *anything* that is *or has been* on board the ship. Therefore if, after sinking, a part of the ship or her cargo[25] escapes or breaks loose and steps are taken to recover it or render it harmless it seems that the shipowner can limit his liability for such costs.

However in keeping with its policy of unlimited liability for wreck removal expenses the United Kingdom has, by paragraph 3 of Schedule 4, Part II, and section 17 of the 1979 MSA, made a reservation in respect of Article 2(1)(d) of the 1976 Convention. Consequently, liability for claims for the cost of wreck removal remains unlimited insofar as the operation is performed pursuant to statutory powers. (Indeed it appears that as a result of the wording in the introductory paragraph to Article 2, to the effect that the subsequent claims are to be the subject of limitation "whatever the basis of liability," the reservation exercised by the United Kingdom may have inadvertently taken out of limitation in the United Kingdom any claims (whether statutory or otherwise) relating to wreck removal, provided that the liability does not relate to remuneration under a contract with the person liable.)

ARTICLE 2(1)(e)

By virtue of Article 2(1)(e) of the 1976 Convention, limitation is expressly available in respect of certain claims relating to the salvage of cargo except where such claims relate to remuneration under a contract with the person liable (Article 2(2)). Conflicts may therefore arise between the provisions of Articles

25. See Article 2(1)(e) and page 23, below.

2(1)(d) and 2(1)(e). Under Article 2(1)(d) the expression "anything that is or has been on board such ship" could include cargo. But limitation is not available under 2(1)(d)[26] in the United Kingdom. It may therefore be that in the United Kingdom, claims in respect of cargo removal, qualify for limitation before the ship is sunk, wrecked, stranded or abandoned but not after any such event has occurred.

ARTICLE 2(1)(f)

This subsection as originally submitted to the 1976 Conference by the Drafting Sub-Committee read as follows:

> "(f) claims in respect of measures taken in order to avert or minimise loss for which the person liable may limit his liability in accordance with this Convention and further loss caused by such measures."

The effect of this original draft wording seems clear; if the shipowner (the person liable) would be able to limit his liability in respect of a particular category of loss, he is also entitled to limit his liability in respect of claims made against him by third parties for expenses incurred in taking measures to avert or minimise that loss. This right is extended to claims for further loss caused in the course of taking those measures to avert or minimise. For example, if there is a threat of chemical pollution following a stranding and measures are taken by third parties to minimise the damage caused thereby, the subsequent claim against the shipowner (the person liable) to recover the cost of taking such measures will be subject to limitation; and if in the course of taking those measures further loss is caused, claims arising will also be subject to limitation.

Examination of the Official Records of the 1976 Conference suggests that the delegates' principal concern regarding the subsection as originally drafted, was that a contractor brought in by the shipowner (the person liable) to effect measures to avert or minimise the loss, could find himself faced with a plea of limitation when submitting his account. This problem was

---

26. Paragraph 3 of Schedule 4, Part II, of the 1979 MSA and page 21, above.

overcome by inserting the rider in Article 2(2) to the effect that the person limiting cannot limit against his own contractor. Of further significance is the introduction by Conference delegates in line 1 of subsection (f) of the words " . . . of a person other than the person liable . . . ". The introduction of these extra words appears to emphasise the fact that the right to limit arises solely in relation to a claim made against a shipowner (the person liable) to recover the costs of steps taken by a third party to prevent or minimise a loss.

Thus the combined effect of subsections 2(1)(f) and 2(2) can be summarised as follows:–

1. The loss in respect of which the measures to avert or minimise are taken must be one in respect of which the right to limit liability arises.
2. The claim must be in respect of either (i) expenses incurred by persons *other than the shipowner* (the person liable) to avert or minimise loss or (ii) further loss caused by the taking of such measures.
3. Where the claim is in respect of measures taken by a third party by virtue of a contract with the shipowner (the person liable) such claim is not subject to limitation (rider in Article 2(2)).

ARTICLE 2(2)

The intention of this subsection is to ensure that the claims listed in 2(1) at all times maintain their character. To take one possible example of how this might work in practice: assume that a tug which is towing a barge comes into collision with another vessel and is found liable to that vessel. If under the terms of the tug and tow contract, the tow is to indemnify the tug such indemnity claim would retain its character as a liability in damages in respect of which limitation can be claimed (under Article 2(1)(a)) and the barge owner would be entitled to limit. Accordingly, the claim remains a claim for collision damages and does not become a mere claim in contract.

The intention of the second sentence of Article 2(2) is to prevent the shipowner (or the person liable) seeking to limit his liability to his own contractor. Thus, although a shipowner can limit in respect of a claim for wreck removal costs incurred by a third party (e.g. a harbour authority) under Article 2(1)(d),[27] he could not limit his liability to pay the invoice of his own contractor employed to remove the wreck.

Loss of or damage to valuables; loss or damage by fire[28]

By virtue of section 18(1) of the 1979 MSA the owners of a *British ship* still have the right originally granted in section 502 of the 1894 MSA to exclude their liability *totally* in the United Kingdom in certain circumstances where there has been a fire on board or loss of valuables by theft. Under section 502 this right only existed if the loss did not result from the actual fault or privity of the person seeking to limit. However, since by virtue of section 18 the conduct now necessary to defeat the right to limit is wilful intent or recklessness rather than fault or privity, this right is now even more valuable to a British shipowner.

Article 3: Claims excepted from limitation

The rules of this Convention shall not apply to:

(a) Claims for salvage or contribution in general average;
(b) Claims for oil pollution damage within the meaning of the International Convention on Civil Liability for Oil Pollution Damage, dated November 29th 1969 or of any amendment or Protocol thereto which is in force;
(c) Claims subject to any international convention or national legislation governing or prohibiting limitation of liability for nuclear damage;
(d) Claims against the shipowner of a nuclear ship for nuclear damage;
(e) Claims by servants of the shipowner or salvor whose duties are connected with the ship or salvage operations, including claims of their heirs, dependants or other persons entitled to make such claims, if under the law governing the contract of service between the shipowner or salvor and such servants the shipowner or salvor is not entitled to limit his liability in respect of such claims, or if he is by such law only permitted to limit his liability to an amount greater than that provided for in Article 6.

27. But not in the United Kingdom, see page 21.
28. For further discussion see page 41, below.

ARTICLE 3(a)

This subsection of the 1976 Convention retains the provisions of Article 4(a) of the 1957 Convention insofar as it excludes application to claims for salvage and contribution in general average. However, it should be remembered that, if a cargo interest pays his salvage or general average contribution he may seek to claim such contribution back from the ship by way of damages if it is proved that the incident resulted from breach of the contract of carriage by the shipowner. In such circumstances the shipowner may have the right to limit his liability under Article 2 because Article 3(a) excludes the right to limit merely in respect of a direct claim by a salvor or a direct claim by a party who has incurred a general average loss or sacrifice. However, the shipowner will still have to establish that the claim is one in respect of which he is entitled to limit under one of the specific provisions of Article 2. Therefore, if the salvage services arose but there was no "loss of or damage to cargo" there may be no right to limit under Article 2(1)(a).[29] Furthermore, even if the ship was "stranded or abandoned" before being salved there would be no right to limit in the United Kingdom under Article 2(1)(d) since this provision is not given effect by section 17 of the 1979 MSA.[30]

ARTICLE 3(b)

It is assumed the draftsman intended simply that a shipowner's right of limitation for oil pollution claims should remain governed by the 1969 Civil Liability Convention (CLC), and not by the 1976 Convention. It seems likely, however, that Article 3(b) has a wider effect than intended: provided that the claim is of its nature for "oil pollution damage" as defined in the CLC, then irrespective of whether the claim is actually made under the CLC, and irrespective of whether it is made against the shipowner (who is the only party entitled to limit under CLC) or some other party, no right of limitation will exist under the 1976 Convention. This could mean that where pollution claims

29. However, a right to limit may still exist under the Hague and Hague–Visby Rules (see pages 128–129).
30. See pages 21–22.

are brought against parties other than a shipowner neither the CLC nor the 1976 Convention will provide any right of limitation. This is recognised as a defect in the Convention which needs to be addressed in the domestic legislation which incorporates the Convention. In the United Kingdom this problem is addressed by paragraph 4(1) of Part II of Schedule 4 to the MSA 1979 which provides that:

"The claims excluded from the Convention by paragraph (b) of Article 3 are claims in respect of *any liability incurred* under section 1 of the Merchant Shipping (Oil Pollution) Act 1971."[31]

The words in italic make it clear that for the purposes of English law, Article 3(b) applies only to liabilities actually incurred under CLC. Furthermore, it does not exclude a claim for limitation of liability for oil pollution liability by any person other than the owner (e.g. a charterer or salvor). Indeed, this provision is intended to dovetail with section 7 of the Merchant Shipping (Oil Pollution) Act 1971 (which incorporates the CLC into the law of the United Kingdom) which envisages that proceedings can be taken against a person other than a shipowner for oil pollution liability incurred otherwise than under section 1 of the Merchant Shipping (Oil Pollution) Act 1971 and that such person may be entitled to limit his liability in connection with the ship by virtue of the MSA 1979.

ARTICLE 3(c)

This subsection excludes liability for claims which are the subject of an international convention or national legislation governing or prohibiting limitation of liability for nuclear damage. Thus, if there is no relevant convention or other legislation as to limitation, limitation will, prima facie be available. By virtue of section 17 and paragraph 4(2) of Schedule 4, Part II, of the 1979 MSA, the United Kingdom legislature has provided that the claims which are to be excluded from the Convention as applied in the United Kingdom are those claims "made by virtue of any of sections 7 to 11 of the Nuclear Installations Act 1965". This does not represent any change in the

31. Emphasis added.

law in the United Kingdom since section 14(1) of the Nuclear Installations Act 1965 itself expressly excluded the right to limit contained in section 503 of the 1894 MSA. (The Nuclear Installations Act 1965 itself has provisions allowing limitation in certain circumstances—section 16.)

ARTICLE 3(d)

This subsection excludes any claim for *nuclear* damage caused by a *nuclear* ship. Whilst liability for such damage cannot therefore be limited under the 1976 Convention, the Convention on the Liability of Operators of Nuclear Ships 1962 has provisions allowing limitation for such damage.

ARTICLE 3(e)

This subsection provides that the limits set out in the 1976 Convention shall not be available in respect of claims arising under certain contracts of service where the law governing the particular contract of service imposes a higher financial limit than those set out in the 1976 Convention or provides that there shall be no right to limit at all. It is also noteworthy that the exclusion applies only if the *law governing the contract of service* imposes a higher limit; the exclusion does not necessarily apply merely because the *contract itself* provides for a higher limit. The subsection therefore follows the basic principles set out in the 1957 Convention and the 1958 Act. However, the wording of Article 3(e) of the 1976 Convention is, on the face of it, more restrictive than the wording of either Article 1(4)(b) of the 1957 Convention (" . . . claims by the Master, by members of the crew, by any servants of the Owner on board the ship or by servants of the Owner whose duties are connected with the ship . . . ") or section 2(4) of the 1958 Act (" . . . any liability in respect of loss of life or personal injury caused to, or loss of or damage to any property or infringement of any right of, a person who is on board or employed in connection with the ship . . . "). Nevertheless, since in all cases it is claims arising under a contract of employment which are excluded it does not seem that the change in terminology will be of material effect.

Article 3(e) of the 1976 Convention does however, introduce an innovation in that it expressly extends the exclusion of the right to limit to claims by or on behalf of the servants of *salvors* under a contract of service between them and the salvors. This express exclusion is necessary as a result of the inclusion of salvors as "persons entitled to limit liability" in Article 1 of the 1976 Convention.

The position in the United Kingdom insofar as claims arising under contracts of employment are concerned is covered by section 35 of the 1979 MSA. This section provides that if the contract of service is governed by the law of any part of the United Kingdom *and* the liability arises from an occurrence which takes place after section 35(2) comes into force liability is unlimited. Section 35(2) came into force except in relation to fishing vessels on 30 April 1987[32] and in relation to fishing vessels on 10 November 1989.[33]

Summary

The claims which are exempted from limitation are:

(1) Direct claims by salvors for salvage remuneration—Article 3(a).

(2) Direct claims for general average contribution by a party incurring a general average expenditure or sacrifice—Article 3(a).

(3) Contractual claims for remuneration by a third party engaged in the raising, removal, destruction or the rendering harmless of a ship which is sunk, wrecked, stranded or abandoned including anything that is or has been on board such ship—Article 2(2).

(4) Contractual claims for remuneration by a party engaged in the removal, destruction or the rendering harmless of cargo on a ship—Article 2(2).

(5) Contractual claims for remuneration by a third party engaged in attempts to avert or minimise a loss in respect of which the person liable could limit his liability—Article 2(2).

(6) Claims for oil pollution damage within the meaning of

---

32. See S.I. 1987/719. Merchant Shipping Act 1979 (Commencement No. 12) Order 1987.
33. See S.I. 1989/1881.

the International Convention on Civil Liability for Oil Pollution Damage—Article 3(b). (In the case of the United Kingdom the excluded claims are those for "any liability incurred" under the Merchant Shipping (Oil Pollution) Act 1971—paragraph 4(1) of Schedule 4, Part II, of 1979 MSA.)

(7) Claims subject to any international convention or national legislation governing or prohibiting limitation of liability for nuclear damage—Article 3(c). (In the case of the United Kingdom the excluded claims are those arising under sections 7–11 of the Nuclear Installations Act 1965—paragraph 4(2) of Schedule 4, Part II, of 1979 MSA.)

(8) Claims for nuclear damage against the owner of a nuclear ship—Article 3(d).

(9) Claims by or on behalf of servants of shipowners or salvors under contracts of service where limitation is either denied or limited to an amount higher than that set out in the 1976 Convention by the law governing the contract of service—Article 3(e). (In the case of the United Kingdom section 35(2) of the 1979 MSA excludes claims arising under contracts of service which are governed by the law of any part of the United Kingdom *and* where the liability arises from an occurrence which took place after section 35(2) came into effect.)

N.B.: In the case of the United Kingdom claims (*quaere* all claims) in respect of the raising, removal, destruction or the rendering harmless of a ship which is sunk, wrecked or abandoned including anything that is or has been on board such ship are exempted from limitation until a fund is established by the Secretary of State—paragraph 3 of Schedule 4, Part II, of the 1979 MSA.

Article 4: Conduct barring limitation

A person liable shall not be entitled to limit his liability if it is proved that the loss resulted from his personal act or omission, committed with the intent to cause such loss, or recklessly and with knowledge that such loss would probably result.

I. The effect of Article 4

Article 4 of the 1976 Convention is a product of the most radical change in the philosophy underlying the concept of a shipowner's right to limit the extent of his liability for his acts and those of his servants.

Under the 1957 Convention limitation was available in accordance with the provisions of the Convention except where "the occurrence giving rise to the claim resulted from the actual fault or privity of the owner".

The meaning of "actual fault or privity of the owner" has been the subject of much litigation before the courts in the United Kingdom.

The primary problem has been to establish who, in law, constituted the "owner". This was a particularly difficult question where the vessel concerned was owned by a company. The problem was solved in most countries that adopted the Convention by the development of the concept of the *"alter ego"*. This concept first saw light of day in the United Kingdom in the *Lennard's Carrying Co.* case[34] where the court was required to consider the problem in the context of the Merchant Shipping Act 1894.

The court held that, upon the true construction of section 503 of the MSA 1894, the "fault or privity" must be the fault or privity of somebody who is not merely a servant or agent for whom the company is liable but somebody for whom the company is liable because his action is the very action of the company itself.

In *The "Lady Gwendolen"*,[35] the assistant managing director of a brewing company who, although not specifically authorised by resolution to act in the board's name, was ultimately responsible for the traffic department, was held to be the alter ego of the company in matters of ship management. Consequently, the failure by the traffic department to train the vessel's master in the use of radar and in particular a failure to check the master's compliance with the Collision Regulations and to warn him that radar would not permit him to travel safely at full speed in fog, were omissions for which the assistant managing director and hence the company was responsible. It followed that, the collision, which resulted from the vessel's excessive speed in fog, did not take place without the actual

34. [1915] A.C. 705.
35. [1965] 1 Lloyd's Rep. 335.

fault or privity of the owner and that the owning company was barred from limiting its liability.

Similarly, in The "Marion",[36] the ship's managers failed to ensure that the ship was equipped only with adequate up-to-date charts on board. In consequence of using an obsolete chart which had been allowed to remain on board, the vessel's anchor fouled an oil pipeline on the seabed. It was held that the managers were at fault and that that fault was, as a matter of law, the actual fault of the shipowners. Again, the shipowners could not show that the damage occurred without their "actual fault" and therefore they were not entitled to limit their liability.

The meaning of "privity" has been considered in the context of the Marine Insurance Act 1906, section 39(5). The "Eurysthenes"[37] was entered with a P. & I. Club for Class 1 risks and suffered a stranding in the course of a voyage. The P. & I. Club alleged that the vessel was unseaworthy and further that the club was not obliged to indemnify the shipowner if it could be shown that the vessel was sent to sea in an unseaworthy condition with the privity of the shipowner within section 39(5) of the Marine Insurance Act 1906. The Court of Appeal held that, in this context, "privity" meant "with knowledge and consent".

Under the 1976 Convention the test no longer involves the actual fault or privity of the owner. The new definition requires proof of loss resulting from the "personal act or omission" of the person liable for the loss which was "committed with the intent to cause such loss, or recklessly and with knowledge that such loss would probably result".

Whilst the words of Article 4 have been derived from and bear a distinct resemblance to the words of other Conventions, they differ in small but material respects.

Article 25 of the Warsaw Convention 1929 as amended by Article 13 of the Hague Protocol 1955 provides that:

"The limits of liability specified in Article 22 shall not apply if it is proved that the damage resulted from an act or omission of the carrier, his servants or agents done with intent to cause damage or recklessly and with knowledge that damage would probably result;

36. [1984] 2 Lloyd's Rep. 1.
37. [1976] 2 Lloyd's Rep. 171.

provided that, in the case of such act or omission of a servant or agent, it is also proved that he was acting within the scope of his employment."

Article 13 of the Athens Convention provides that:

"The Carrier shall not be entitled to the benefit of the limits of liability prescribed in Articles 7 and 8 and paragraph 1 of Article 10 if it is proved that the damage resulted from an act or omission of the carrier done with intent to cause such damage, or recklessly and with knowledge that such damage would probably result."[38]

Article IV Rule 5(e) of the Hague–Visby Rules provides that:

"Neither the carrier nor the ship shall be entitled to the benefit of the limitation of liability provided for in this paragraph if it is proved that the damage resulted from an act or omission of the carrier done with intent to cause damage or recklessly and with knowledge that damage would probably result."[39]

Article 8 Rule 1 of the Hamburg Rules provides that:

"The Carrier is not entitled to the benefit of the limitation of liability provided for in Article 6 if the loss, damage or delay resulted from an act or omission of the carrier done with intent to cause such loss damage or delay or recklessly and with knowledge that such loss damage or delay would probably result."[40]

Article 4 of the 1976 Convention provides that:

"A person liable shall not be entitled to limit his liability if it is proved that the loss resulted from his personal act or omission committed with the intent to cause such loss, or recklessly and with knowledge that such loss would probably result."

The following differences seem to exist:

(a) The 1976 Convention speaks of the "personal" act or omission of the person liable. The Athens Convention, Hague–Visby and Hamburg Rules merely speak of the act or omission of "the Carrier" whilst the Warsaw Convention speaks of the acts or omissions of "the Carrier, his servants or agents".

(b) The Warsaw Convention, the Athens Convention, the Hague–Visby Rules and the Hamburg Rules speak of the "carrier" being unable to limit liability

38. See pages 100–101.
39. See pages 127–130.
40. See page 130.

whereas the 1976 Convention speaks of the "person liable" being unable to limit liability. However, each of the other Conventions and Rules have definitions of "Carrier" and in some instances the "Carrier" includes parties who would be "persons liable" under the 1976 Convention.

(c) The Warsaw Convention, the Athens Convention and the Hague–Visby Rules speak of "damage" caused by the act or omission of the carrier. The Hamburg Rules speak of "loss, damage or delay" so caused whilst the 1976 Convention speaks only of "loss".

(d) The Warsaw Convention and the Hague–Visby Rules, when speaking of the intent to cause "damage" or of acts done "recklessly" and with knowledge of "damage", refer to "damage" in the abstract whereas the Athens Convention, the Hamburg Rules and the 1976 Convention speak in each case of "such" damage (Athens Convention), "such" loss, damage or delay (Hamburg Rules) or "such" loss (1976 Convention).

In *The "European Enterprise"*,[41] Steyn J commented upon the different wording of the Warsaw Convention and the Hague–Visby Rules. He used the fact that the Warsaw Convention refers expressly to the acts of "the Carrier, his servants or agents" as an aid to construction in determining that the use of the mere word "Carrier" in the Hague–Visby Rules illustrated that it was only the personal acts of the carrier which would debar his right to limit under those rules.

However, in *The "Lion"*[42] Hobhouse J. stated that

"In my judgment it is clearly important and correct that there should be a consistent approach to the construction of similar Maritime Conventions using similar terms and expressing similar ideas."

The court will therefore attempt wherever possible to give a consistent construction. Nevertheless, there may be circumstances where this is not possible and consideration is now given to different words and phrases:

41. [1989] 2 Lloyd's Rep. at page 192.
42. [1990] 2 Lloyd's Rep. at page 149.

(a) "Personal" act or omission

The Athens Convention, Hague–Visby Rules, Hamburg Rules and the 1976 Convention differ fundamentally from the Warsaw Convention since the latter provides expressly that misconduct on the part of the carrier's servants or agents acting within the course of their employment will result in the loss of the right to limit.

The Athens Convention, Hamburg Rules and Hague–Visby Rules on the other hand speak blandly of "acts or omissions of the carrier" defeating the right to limit without further reference. It seems from the *travaux préparatoires* to these Conventions that it is only misconduct on the part of the carrier himself which is meant to defeat the right to limit.[43] This interpretation has now been accepted by the English court in The *"European Enterprise"*[44] in relation to the Hague–Visby Rules and in The *"Lion"*[45] in relation to the Athens Convention and it is likely that the Hamburg Rules would be construed in a similar manner.[46]

The 1976 Convention expressly provides that it is only the "personal" act or omission of the person liable which will defeat the right to limit. However, it is still necessary to consider in the case of corporations whose act or omission will be treated as the "personal" act or omission which may defeat the right to limit.

Thus it seems that the concept of the *alter ego* co-opted from the law developed from the limitation provisions of the 1894 MSA will have to be applied in order to ascertain whose "action is the very action of the company itself".

(b) The "person liable"

Article 4 of the 1976 Convention speaks of the "personal" act or omission of a "person liable" which term presumably encompasses all the various parties identified in Article 1 which

---

43. See Diamond [1978] LMCLQ 225, 244–245 and p. 21 of Diamond on Hamburg Rules (lecture for Lloyd's of London Press on 28 September 1978).
44. [1989] 2 Lloyd's Rep. 195.
45. [1990] 2 Lloyd's Rep. 144.
46. See the dictum of Hobhouse J. in The *"Lion"* [1990] 2 Lloyd's Rep. at pages 149–150.

is headed: "Persons entitled to limit liability". Therefore a "person liable" could be the shipowner, the charterer, manager, operator, salvor or liability insurer of the vessel or a further class of person defined as "any person for whose act, neglect or default the shipowner or salvor is responsible".

Whose "personal" act will therefore defeat the right to limit? Presumably the personal act of any one of the different persons identified in Article 1 will prevent him from limiting his *own liability* in the event of a *claim against him* but will not necessarily defeat the right to limit of any other "persons" in the same group in the event of a claim against them. Therefore, if, for example, loss arose as a result of the personal act of a ship's manager he would not be able to limit liability in the event of a successful claim against him whereas the shipowner might be able to limit since the act or omission would not necessarily be "personal" to him. However, bearing in mind the close relationship which frequently exists between the management and ownership structures the distinction may not be so clear cut since the *alter ego* of both "persons" might well be the same.

In view of the express provisions of Article 1(6) the right of a liability insurer to limit liability is presumably debarred not so much by "personal" misconduct on his part as by "personal" misconduct on the part of his assured. However interesting arguments could well arise in the case of P. & I. insurance where an owner, demise charterer and manager are frequently entered members in respect of the same ship. It may be that in such circumstances one assured is able to limit liability whereas another is not. Then the right of the P. & I. insurer to limit may depend on which member is sued.[47]

(c) "Loss"

Article 2 of the 1976 Convention refers in various places to loss of life, personal injury, loss of or damage to property etc., whereas Article 4 speaks merely of "loss". Whilst this is not particularly happy drafting it is submitted that the word "loss"

47. For a discussion of the link between the liability insurer's rights under Article 1(6) and his rights under the Third Parties (Rights Against Insurers) Act 1930, see pages 14–16.

is plainly intended to encompass all the various types of loss or damage or injury or expense to which Article 2 refers.[48]

(d) (i) "Such loss"

The provisions of the Warsaw Convention and the Hague–Visby Rules would seem to suggest that the carrier's right to limit liability is lost if he intended to cause *any* damage or acted recklessly and with knowledge that *any* damage would probably result whether or not the intended or foreseeable damage was the same as the damage actually inflicted.[49]

This was the view adopted by Chapman J. at first instance in the case of *Goldman* v. *Thai Airways International Ltd.*[50] when construing the provisions of the Warsaw Convention as amended by the Hague Protocol. He concluded that so long as a pilot envisaged that a glass of wine would be spilled as a result of his act or omission the carrier could not limit liability if the damage actually suffered by the plaintiff was personal injury. However, on appeal to the Court of Appeal[51] all three members of the court, namely Eveleigh, O'Connor and Purchas L.JJ. held that this was incorrect. Despite the use of the general word "damage" rather than the more specific words "the damage", the Court of Appeal held that:

" . . . the Article requires the plaintiff to prove the following (1) that the damage resulted from an act or omission; (2) that it was done with intent to cause damage; (3) that it was done when the doer was aware that damage would probably result but he did so regardless of that probability; (4) that the damage complained of is the kind of damage known to be the probable result." (p. 698)

However, Eveleigh L.J. who delivered the leading judgment went on to say at p. 700 that:

48. Article IV, Rule 5(e), of the Hague–Visby Rules speaks merely of "damage" and it is submitted that such usage is far more restrictive than the use of the word "loss" in Article 4 of the 1976 Convention. See page 128. By way of contrast the mere use of the word "damage" in Article 13 of the Athens Convention can probably be construed in a far more liberal fashion, see pages 100–101.

49. Contrast the Athens Convention, Hamburg Rules and 1976 Convention all of which have the prefix "such".

50. *The Times*, 2 April 1981.

51. [1983] 3 All E.R. 693.

"It is with rather less confidence that I have said that the damage anticipated must be of the same kind of damage as that suffered. I have reached my conclusion because Article 25 is designed to cover cases of damage both to the person, in other words, injury, and to property."[52]

It is submitted that similar considerations apply to the 1976 Convention. Not only does the Convention apply to both physical loss and personal injury (as does the Warsaw Convention) but more importantly, the use of the words "such loss" in Article 4 seem to underline the fact that the right to limit is barred *only* if the type of loss intended or envisaged by the "person liable" is the actual loss suffered by the claimant.[53] Indeed, it is arguable that the use of the words "such loss" imports an added safeguard to the "person liable". Whereas under the fourth limb of the test set down by Eveleigh L.J. in *Goldman* v. *Thai Airways*, it must be proved that the damage complained of is *the kind* of damage known to be the probable result, the use of the words "such loss" suggests that in order to defeat the right to limit under the 1976 Convention it must be proved that the damage complained of is the *same* damage known to be the probable result.

(d) (ii) "Intent to cause such loss"

It is clear from these words that in order to deprive the "person liable" of the right to limit, it must be proved that the "person liable" had the subjective intent (or *mens rea*) to cause the loss. It is not sufficient to prove that a reasonably competent person could not have failed to conclude that his act or omission would cause the loss. It must be shown that the "person liable" himself actively intended the loss.

(d) (iii) "Or recklessly and with knowledge that such loss would probably result"

The meaning of the word "recklessly" or "recklessness" has been construed by the courts in the United Kingdom in a

---

52. Query, therefore, whether a similar construction would be afforded to the similar words in Article IV, Rule 5(e), of the Hague–Visby Rules, since those Rules do not cover injury to the person. See pages 129–130.

53. Similar considerations apply to Article 13 of the Athens Convention.

number of cases such as *R.* v. *Caldwell*[54] and *R.* v. *Lawrence Stephen.*[55] It connotes either carelessness or utter heedlessness of consequence with the result that the perpetrator is deemed to have considered neither the probability or even the possibility of a likely result. However, in *Goldman* v. *Thai Airways*[56] Eveleigh L.J. cautioned against the dangers of proceeding on the basis of constructions drawn from English statutes when construing an international convention drawn up in a number of languages.

The Court of Appeal in the *Goldman* case emphasised that the word "recklessly" had to be construed in Article 25 of the Warsaw Convention in conjunction with the words "and with knowledge that damage would probably result". Eveleigh L.J. stated at p. 700 that:

"An act may be reckless when it involves a risk, even though it cannot be said that the danger envisaged is a probable consequence. It is enough that it is a possible consequence, although there comes a point when the risk is so remote that it would not be considered reckless to take it. We look for an element of recklessness which is perhaps more clearly indicated in the French term 'temerairement'. Article 25 however, refers not to possibility, but to the probability of resulting damage. Thus something more than a possibility is required. The word 'probable' is a common enough word. I understand that to mean something is likely to happen. I think that is what is meant in Article 25. In other words, one anticipates damage from the act or omission."

II. Onus of proof under Article 4

Under Article 1(6) of the 1957 Convention the onus of proving the facts necessary to defeat the right to limit of the person seeking to limit liability was to be determined in accordance with the law of the court considering the matter (*lex fori*). In the case of the United Kingdom the onus of proof was on the person who sought to limit his liability.[57]

The "Working Group on Basic Issues relating to the

54. [1982] A.C. at 354.
55. [1982] A.C. at 520.
56. [1983] 3 All E.R. 693.
57. *The "Empire Jamaica"* [1955] 2 Lloyd's Rep. 109 (C.A.); *The "Norman"* [1960] 1 Lloyd's Rep 1 (H.L.).

Limitation System" submitted a report to the 1976 Limitation
Conference suggesting that a provision should be included in
Article 4 making it clear that the determination of who should
have the burden of proof should continue to be made in
accordance with the *lex fori* (see p. 134 of the Official
Records). However, the suggestion does not seem to have
been accepted and there is no provision in the 1976 Convention
decreeing how the onus of proof is to be determined. Nevertheless, Article 2(1) of the 1976 Convention stipulates that:
"Subject to Articles 3 and 4 the following claims . . . *shall be*
subject to limitation of liability."

These words reflect the basic philosophy underlying the new
system to the effect that the right to limit applies automatically
unless evidence is produced proving that the party claiming
limitation is guilty of conduct barring limitation within the
terms of Article 4.

Additionally the wording of Article 4 itself makes it plain
that the right to limit exists unless the person challenging the
right to limit proves conduct barring limitation.

It is clear from the decision of the Court of Appeal in *Goldman* v. *Thai Airways*[58] that the onus of proving the facts
necessary to debar the carrier's right to limit liability in the case
of the Warsaw Convention lies on the plaintiff. Similar views
have been expressed in respect of the relevant provisions of the
Hague–Visby Rules[59] and the Athens Convention.[60] The
authors consider it likely that a consistent approach will be
adopted in the case of the 1976 Convention and the onus will
be placed upon the person challenging the right to limit.[61]

III. The overall effect of the changes

The effect therefore of the 1976 Convention is to completely
transform the law in relation to the rights of shipowners (and

---

58. [1983] 3 All E.R. 693.
59. See Diamond [1978] LMCLQ at 245.
60. *The "Lion"* [1990] 2 Lloyd's Rep. 144.
61. See the comments of Hobhouse J. in *The "Lion"* [1990] 2 Lloyd's Rep.
at pages 149–150. In *The "Bowbelle"* [1990] 3 All E.R. 476 Sheen J. held that
the court is not obliged to investigate whether or not the person liable has
been guilty of conduct barring limitation when that person commences a limitation action.

others) to limit liability. Under the 1957 Convention, a successful plaintiff was entitled to full reimbursement of his claim unless the party limiting was able to prove his right to limit liability by satisfying the court that there was no "fault or privity" on his part. As a result of the 1976 Convention, the party limiting appears to be *entitled* to limit his liability *unless* the person challenging the right to limit proves that the "person liable" is guilty of "conduct barring limitation" under Article 4.

A person seeking to limit liability who is guilty of "conduct barring limitation" loses the benefits of limitation. He may also lose the benefits of his liability insurance cover. Section 55(2)(a) of the Marine Insurance Act 1906 provides that: "The insurer is not liable for any loss attributable to the wilful misconduct of the assured." (It is generally accepted that in this context the word "wilful" means "reckless".)

It would seem that the combined effect of Article 4 of the 1976 Convention and the Marine Insurance Act[62] is that where there has been wilful intent or recklessness the right to limit will be lost along with the right to make any recovery from liability insurers.

IV. Vestiges of section 502 of the MSA 1894

This section provided in effect that the owner of a *British* ship was *not to be liable* for *any* loss or damage to property caused by a fire on board ship or to valuables by reason of theft where the nature and value of the valuables was not declared to the owner at the time of shipment, in each case provided that the loss or damage did not result from his actual fault or privity.

Whilst section 502 of the 1894 Act has been repealed by Part 1 of Schedule 7 to the 1979 Act, the wording of section 502 is substantially restated in section 18 of the 1979 MSA. However by virtue of section 18(3) the conduct which was formerly necessary to defeat the shipowner's right to deny liability

---

62. "Conduct barring limitation" may also enable insurers to deny liability under s.39(5) of the Marine Insurance Act 1906. (See *The "Eurysthenes"* [1976] 2 Lloyd's Rep. 171 and pages 14–16, above.)

(namely fault and privity) is replaced by the conduct barring limitation as set out in Article 4 of the 1976 Convention.

Therefore, in the case of loss or damage to *property* (not death or personal injury) caused by fire on board or theft of valuables the right of an owner of a *British* ship to escape liability *totally* seems to have been further improved.[63] However, this provision does not enable such an owner to escape liability which he incurs under the Athens Convention as incorporated into the municipal legislation of the United Kingdom.[64]

Article 5: Counterclaims

Where a person entitled to limitation of liability under the rules of this Convention has a claim against the claimant arising out of the same occurrence, their respective claims shall be set off against each other and the provisions of this Convention shall only apply to the balance, if any.

This Article is very similar in terms and effect to the equivalent provision of the 1957 Convention (Article 1(5)). Thus it remains the case that claims and counterclaims arising out of the same occurrence must be set off against each other and limitation is to be applied only to the balance, if any, payable.

The only change is in the identity of the persons to whom the provision applies. The phrase " . . . owner of a ship . . . " in Article 1(5) of the 1957 Convention is replaced in Article 5 of the 1976 Convention by the phrase " . . . person entitled to limitation of liability under the rules of this Convention . . . ".

Persons entitled to limit liability by Article 1 of the 1976 Convention now include salvors as well as charterers, managers and operators of ships. It is tempting therefore to assume that one of the aims of this extension is to deal with the situation where a shipowner has a counterclaim against a salvor

---

63. Article VIII of the Hague and Hague–Visby Rules states that nothing in the Rules "affects the rights and obligations of the carrier under any statute for the time being in force relating to the limitation of the liability of owners of sea-going ships". S. 6(1) of COGSA 1924 (giving effect to the Hague Rules and now repealed) and s.6(4) of COGSA 1971 (giving effect to the Hague–Visby Rules) provide that this right of the British shipowner is to be treated as a "provision relating to the limitation of liability".

64. Paragraph 12 of Part II of Schedule 3 to the 1979 MSA.

for negligence in the performance of salvage services. If Article 5 applied it would have the effect of enabling the salvor to set off his claim for remuneration for salvage services against the shipowner's counterclaim for negligence before applying his right to limit liability to any balance due to the shipowner.

However, if that was the intention it may not have been achieved by the wording adopted in Article 5. Article 5 refers to "a claim . . . arising out of the same occurrence". This covers a claim and counterclaim arising, for example, out of a collision. However, it is difficult to see how it can be said that a salvor's claim for salvage remuneration arises out of "the same occurrence" as that which gives rise to the shipowner's claim for negligence. The shipowner's claim arises out of the salvor's negligent act—the salvor's claim for remuneration arises out of a quite separate salvage contract or engagement.

The problem of the negligent salvor, his right to limit liability and to set off his claim for salvage remuneration against counterclaims for negligence arose in acute form in the United Kingdom in the case of The "Tojo Maru".[65]

In that case the arbitrator (who found erroneously that the salvors were entitled to limit their liability) held that limitation was to be applied after set-off. In contrast, Willmer L.J. (who found that there was no right of limitation) expressed the opinion that the arbitrator was wrong. The Court of Appeal held that if limitation were available, which it was not, then limitation would have to be applied before set-off. The House of Lords did not find it necessary to express an opinion on the issue but Lord Reid commented that he was not convinced that the courts below had reached a correct conclusion on this matter.

Article 1(5) of the 1957 Convention was not considered at any stage in The "Tojo Maru" because that particular Article was never incorporated in the 1958 Act. Even if it had been, it would not, it is submitted, have affected the outcome of that case because, for reasons explained above, the claim and counterclaim did not arise out of "the same occurrence." Should another "Tojo Maru" case arise in the United Kingdom the

65. [1971] 1 Lloyd's Rep. 341.

courts may well find that Article 5 of the 1976 Convention does not solve that particular problem.

CHAPTER II—THE LIMITS OF LIABILITY

Article 6: The general limits

1. The limits of liability for claims other than those mentioned in Article 7, arising on any distinct occasion, shall be calculated as follows:

    (a) in respect of claims for loss of life or personal injury,

        (i) 333,000 Units of Account for a ship with a tonnage not exceeding 500 tons,

        (ii) for a ship with a tonnage in excess thereof, the following amount in addition to that mentioned in (i):

        for each ton from 501 to 3,000 tons, 500 Units of Account;

        for each ton from 3,001 to 30,000 tons, 333 Units of Account;

        for each ton from 30,001 to 70,000 tons, 250 Units of Account; and

        for each ton in excess of 70,000 tons, 167 Units of Account.

    (b) In respect of any other claims,

        (i) 167,000 Units of Account for a ship with a tonnage not exceeding 500 tons,

        (ii) for a ship with a tonnage in excess thereof the following amount in addition to that mentioned in (i):

        for each ton from 501 to 30,000 tons, 167 Units of Account;

        for each ton from 30,001 to 70,000 tons, 125 Units of Account; and

        for each ton in excess of 70,000 tons, 83 Units of Account.

2. Where the amount calculated in accordance with paragraph 1(a) is insufficient to pay the claims mentioned therein in full, the amount calculated in accordance with paragraph 1(b) shall be available for payment of the unpaid balance of claims under paragraph 1(a) and such unpaid balance shall rank rateably with claims mentioned under paragraph 1(b).

3. However, without prejudice to the right of claims for loss of life or personal injury according to paragraph 2, a State Party may provide in its national law that claims in respect of damage to harbour works, basins and waterways and aids to navigation shall have such priority over other claims under paragraph 1(b) as is provided by that law.

4. The limits of liability for any salvor not operating from any ship or for any salvor operating solely on the ship to, or in respect of which he is rendering salvage services, shall be calculated according to a tonnage of 1,500 tons.

5. For the purpose of this Convention the ship's tonnage shall be the gross tonnage calculated in accordance with the tonnage measurement rules contained in Annex I of the International Convention on Tonnage Measurements of Ships, 1969.

Article 7: The limit for passenger claims

1. In respect of claims arising on any distinct occasion for loss of life or personal injury to passengers of a ship, the limit of liability of the shipowner thereof shall be an amount of 46,666 Units of Account multiplied by the number of passengers which the ship is authorised to carry according to the ship's certificate, but not exceeding 25 million Units of Account.

2. For the purpose of this Article "claims for loss of life or personal injury to passengers of a ship" shall mean any such claims brought by or on behalf of any person carried in that ship:

(a) under a contract of passenger carriage, or
(b) who, with the consent of the carrier, is accompanying a vehicle or live animals which are covered by a contract for the carriage of goods.

Article 8: Unit of Account

1. The Unit of Account referred to in Articles 6 and 7 is the Special Drawing Right as defined by the International Monetary Fund. The amounts mentioned in Articles 6 and 7 shall be converted into the national currency of the State in which limitation is sought, according to the value of that currency at the date the limitation fund shall have been constituted, payment is made, or security is given which under the law of that State is equivalent to such payment. *The value of a national currency in terms of the Special Drawing Right, of a State Party which is a member of the International Monetary Fund, shall be calculated in accordance with the method of valuation applied by the International Monetary Fund in effect at the date in question for its operations and transactions. The value of a national currency in terms of the Special Drawing Right, of a State Party which is not a member of the International Monetary Fund, shall be calculated in a manner determined by that State Party.*

2. *Nevertheless, those States which are not members of the International Monetary Fund and whose law does not permit the application of the provisions of paragraph 1 may, at the time of signature without reservation as to ratification, acceptance or approval or at the time of ratification, acceptance, approval or accession or at any time thereafter, declare that the limits of liability provided for in this Convention to be applied in their territories shall be fixed as follows:*

(a) *in respect of Article 6, paragraph 1(a) at an amount of:*
(i) *5 million monetary units for a ship with a tonnage not exceeding 500 tons;*

    (ii) for a ship with a tonnage in excess thereof the following amount in addition to that mentioned in (i):

    for each ton from 501 to 3,000 tons, 7,500 monetary units;

    for each ton from 3,001 to 30,000 tons, 5,000 monetary units;

    for each ton from 30,001 to 70,000 tons, 3,750 monetary units; and

    for each ton in excess of 70,000 tons, 2,500 monetary units; and

  (b) in respect of Article 6, paragraph 1(b), at an amount of:

    (i) 2.5 million monetary units for a ship with a tonnage not exceeding 500 tons;

    (ii) for a ship with a tonnage in excess thereof, the following amount in addition to that mentioned in (i):

    for each ton from 501 to 30,000 tons, 2,500 monetary units;

    for each ton from 30,001 to 70,000 tons, 1,850 monetary units; and

    for each ton in excess of 70,000 tons, 1,250 monetary units; and

  (c) in respect of Article 7, paragraph 1, at an amount of 700,000 monetary units multiplied by the number of passengers which the ship is authorised to carry according to its certificate, but not exceeding 375 million monetary units.

Paragraphs 2 and 3 of Article 6 apply correspondingly to sub-paragraphs (a) and (b) of this paragraph.

   3. The monetary unit referred to in paragraph 2 corresponds to sixty-five and a half milligrammes of gold of millesimal fineness nine hundred. The conversion of the amounts referred to in paragraph 2 into the national currency shall be made according to the law of the State concerned.

   4. The calculation mentioned in the last sentence of paragraph 1 and the conversion mentioned in paragraph 3 shall be made in such a manner as to express in the national currency of the State Party as far as possible the same real value for the amounts in Articles 6 and 7 as is expressed there in units of account. State Parties shall communicate to the depositary the manner of calculation pursuant to paragraph 1, or the result of the conversion in paragraph 3, as the case may be, at the time of the signature without reservation as to ratification, acceptance or approval, or when depositing an instrument referred to in Article 16 and whenever there is a change in either.

The 1976 Convention follows the existing law in that it treats:

   (a) loss of life or personal injury claims, and

   (b) any other claims;

on a separate but interlinked basis.

   It also maintains the system whereby the quantum of the fund is calculated by reference to the vessel's tonnage.

However, it differs from the old regime in many important ways.

Article 6: The general limits

ARTICLE 6(1)

Whereas the 1957 Convention established a flat rate for each ton of the vessel's tonnage, there is under the 1976 Convention a sliding scale with various layers of limitation depending on the vessel's tonnage. (See pages 56–57, below.) Under the new regime small ships pay comparatively more per ton than large ships. The Convention itself provides for a minimum fixed level of limitation for all ships up to 500 tons. However by virtue of paragraph 5 of Schedule 4, Part II, and section 17 of the 1979 MSA, there is a lower minimum fixed level of limitation in the United Kingdom for vessels of less than 300 tons.

Whereas the 1957 Convention expressed the limitation amounts in Poincaré francs (which units were then converted into the national currency of the country concerned) the 1976 Convention provides in Article 8 that the unit of account is to be the Special Drawing Right (SDR), the value of which is to be determined in terms of national currencies at the date the limitation fund is constituted, payment is made or security is given (whichever is relevant).

Paragraph 7 of Schedule 4, Part III, and section 17 of the 1979 MSA provide, so far as the United Kingdom is concerned, that the sterling value of the SDR is to be the value fixed by the International Monetary Fund (IMF). The introduction of the SDR was not an innovation insofar as the law in the United Kingdom is concerned, since under the existing law, the value of the Poincaré franc was already expressed for limitation purposes in terms of SDR which were in turn converted into sterling (section 1 of MSA 1981).

The changing value of the SDR in relation to most major currencies can be monitored daily on the currency page of the *Financial Times*. The rate published in the F.T. is that prevailing at close of business in Washington on the working day preceding publication.

In the case of states which are not members of the IMF

specific provisions are made in Article 8[66] allowing for the replacement of the SDR as the unit of account for limitation purposes by a monetary unit corresponding to 65.5 milligrammes of gold of millesimal fineness 900 (i.e. 1 Poincaré franc) which unit is in turn to be converted into the national currency of the state in question. (The relationship between the SDR and the Poincaré franc is 1 SDR: 15 Poincaré francs as will be seen from a comparison between the limitation figures appearing in Articles 6 and 8.)

ARTICLE 6(2)

Article 3 of the 1957 Convention (section 503(1)(d)(i) and (ii) of the 1894 MSA (as amended)) provided different limits (a) for loss of life and personal injury claims either alone or together with property claims (francs 3,100) and (b) for property claims alone (francs 1,000). It is specifically provided that where the occurrence gives rise to both personal and property claims the fund is limited to the aggregate figure of francs, 3,100 per ton of which francs 2,100 is reserved exclusively for personal claims. Where the fund reserved exclusively for personal claims is insufficient to satisfy all the claims the unpaid balance of such claims ranks rateably with the property claims against the property fund.

Under Article 6 of the 1976 Convention the problem is approached somewhat differently. Separate limitation funds are provided for the two categories of claim. However, where the event gives rise to *both* death and/or personal injury claims and property claims and the fund calculated under Article 6(1)(a) for loss of life or personal injury claims is not sufficient to satisfy such claims in full then the fund calculated under Article 6(1)(b) ("other claims") is available to meet the unsatisfied balance of the loss of life or personal injury claims. However, in so doing the balance of the loss of life or personal injury claims rank rateably with the "other claims" (Article 6(2)).

---

66. Article 8(1) (apart from the first sentence thereof) (2) (3) and (4) are not included in Schedule 4, Part I, to the MSA 1979 as provisions of the 1976 Convention which "have the force of law" in the United Kingdom by virtue of section 17(1) of that Act.

The intention of the Convention seems to have been to allow the balance of death or personal injury claims (to the extent that they exceed the fund available in Article 6(1)(a)) to be levied against the fund for "other claims" in Article 6(1)(b) only where the occurrence has given rise to *both* death or personal injury claims *and* other claims. However, Article 6(2) does not say that and is capable of being construed to the effect that the balance of personal injury claims left unsatisfied by the fund in Article 6(1)(a) can be levied against the fund established by Article 6(1)(b) even if the occurrence did not give rise to "other claims". In such circumstances the reference to such claims ranking rateably with "other claims" applies *only if and when* there are "other claims". The wording of the 1976 Convention is in this respect not so clear as that of Article 3 of the 1957 Convention.

ARTICLE 6(3)

It is to be observed in passing that Article 6(3) of the 1976 Convention has not been incorporated into the law of the United Kingdom by the 1979 MSA (see Schedule 4, Part I). This Article preserves the right of State Parties to legislate to give priority in respect of claims for damage to harbour works etc. over "other claims" (Article 6(1)(b)). A State Party may not, however, grant priority to such claims over loss of life and personal injury claims (Article 6(1)(a)). The assumption must be that the United Kingdom legislature has no intention of taking advantage of this saving (but see Article 2(1)(d)[67]).

ARTICLE 6(4)

The 1976 Convention provides by Article 1(1) that salvors may limit their liability and Article 6(4) provides that a salvor who is "not operating from any ship" or who is "operating solely on the ship to or in respect of which, he is rendering salvage services" shall be entitled to calculate the limit of his liability by reference to a deemed tonnage of 1,500 tons. Interesting questions will arise when damage is caused by salvage personnel as to whether or not they are "operating from a vessel" or, if so,

---

67. See pages 21–22, above.

from which vessel (if there is a salvage flotilla), since the applicable limit of liability will depend on the conclusion reached.

ARTICLE 6(5)

Under the old regime the tonnage of a vessel for the purposes of limitation was to be her "registered tonnage" with the addition of any engine room space "deducted for the purpose of ascertaining that tonnage". By virtue of Article 6(5) of the 1976 Convention the tonnage of a vessel for purposes of limitation under the new regime is to be calculated in accordance with the tonnage measurement rules contained in Annex 1 of the International Convention on Tonnage Measurement of Ships 1969.

Article 6(5) is not included in Schedule 4, Part I, of the 1979 MSA and therefore does not have "the force of law" in the United Kingdom by virtue of section 17(1) of that Act. However, paragraphs 5(2) and (3) of Schedule 4, Part II, and Section 17 of the 1979 MSA provide that similar rules are to be applied in the United Kingdom.

Calculation of limitation tonnage

Article 6(5) of the 1976 Convention provides:

"For the purposes of this Convention, the ship's tonnage shall be the gross tonnage calculated in accordance with the tonnage measurement rules contained in Annex I of the International Convention on Tonnage Measurement of Ships, 1969."

(For the position in the United Kingdom see paragraphs 5(2) and (3) of Schedule 4, Part II, and section 17 of the 1979 MSA).

The International Convention on Tonnage Measurement of Ships 1969 was implemented in England by the Merchant Shipping (Tonnage) Regulations 1982, S.I. 1982 No. 841. These regulations came into operation on 18 July 1982 replacing the Merchant Shipping (Tonnage) Regulations 1967. As from that date, all United Kingdom registered vessels of more than 24 metres in length which are new and older vessels which, through modification, suffer a "substantial variation in their existing gross tonnage", must be measured according to the new regulations. Ships built before that date can be re-measured according to the new regulations at the owners' request and with effect from 18 July 1994 all ships, whenever built, *must* be measured according to the new regulations. In the meantime the tonnage of existing ships shall continue at figures calculated in accordance with 1967 Tonnage Regulations (Regulations 3 and 13).

Under the new Tonnage Regulations every ship will be assigned a gross tonnage and a net tonnage. Unlike the previous method of tonnage measurement the gross tonnage will give a realistic indication of the ship's size. Calculation is based on the moulded volume of the entire ship (hull, deck structures and all enclosed spaces) and there are no deductions, exemptions or special allowances. On the other hand, the net tonnage is intended to give a general indication of the ship's earning capacity. The net tonnage is in fact derived from a formula based upon the moulded volume of the cargo spaces, the moulded depth of the ship, the summer draught and, in the case of passenger carrying vessels, the number of passengers which can be carried.

The regulations contain special provisions for segregated ballast oil tankers and vessels carrying deck cargoes.

Insofar as vessels (including pleasure yachts and fishing boats) of less than 24 metres in length are concerned, the pre-1982 system of measurement remains in force (regulation 12, MSA (Tonnage) Regulations 1982).

It is only possible to generalise regarding the effect which remeasurement will have on the gross (limitation) tonnage. Thus single deck ships, e.g. tankers and bulk carriers, will find their tonnage very largely unchanged whereas the effect on ro-ro ships will be to increase the gross tonnage substantially.

For example, a tanker which under the old regulations had a gross tonnage of 36,825 will have a gross tonnage of 35,017 under the new regulations. On the other hand a vehicle carrier of 14,480 tons gross will find her gross tonnage increased to 53,800.

The new Tonnage Regulations and the Convention upon which they are based contemplate the issue of International Tonnage Certificates by the governments of contracting states.

It is further contemplated that such International Tonnage Certificates will be accepted as valid by the governments of other contracting states.

TRANSITIONAL PROVISIONS

Paragraph 2(1) of the Merchant Shipping (Liability of Ship-owners and Others) (Calculation of Tonnage) Order 1986 (S.I. 1986 No. 1040) which came into effect on 1 December 1986 (the same day as the 1976 Limitation Convention came into force in the United Kingdom) provided that for the purposes of Article 6 of the Limitation Convention "the gross tonnage of the ship be calculated in accordance with regulations 4 to 6 of the Merchant Shipping (Tonnage) Regulations 1982". Paragraph 2(2) of the statutory instrument provides that:

"In the case of a ship of which, at the time when limitation is claimed, the tonnage has not been and cannot be ascertained in accordance with paragraph (1) above, the best evidence available of the measurements of the ship shall be used in calculating the tonnage of the ship according to those regulations."

As indicated above the Tonnage Convention and the Limitation Convention both came into effect on 1 December 1986 though it is not until July 1994 that all vessels are required to have been re-measured. There will be incidents between now and July 1994 to which the 1976 Limitation Convention applies involving vessels in respect of which the "gross tonnage" cannot be ascertained from her tonnage certificate because she has not been re-measured.

The safe rule of thumb during this transitional period is that for all incidents prior to 1 December 1986 the old limitation provisions and the old tonnage regulations apply and for all incidents after 1 December 1986 the new limitation provisions and the new tonnage regulations apply.

Where the limitation tonnage has to be "ascertained" in accordance with paragraph 2(2) of the statutory instrument the "best evidence" will be used. This will normally be a job for a surveyor or naval architect and may be taken as a convenient opportunity to have the vessel re-measured in anticipation of the July 1994 deadline for re-measurement.

(In the current *Lloyd's Register of Ships* where the gross tonnage of a vessel appears in bold type this indicates that the ship has been measured in accordance with the old tonnage regulations. Where the tonnage is recorded in italics this indicates that the tonnage has been ascertained in accordance with the 1969 Tonnage Convention.)

Article 7: The limit for passenger claims

The 1976 Convention introduces by virtue of Article 7 a completely separate limitation fund for claims for loss of life or personal injury to passengers as defined in Article 7(2). This limitation fund is not calculated by reference to the vessel's tonnage but by reference to the number of passengers which the ship is *certificated to carry*. (As to the relevant certificate in the United Kingdom see paragraph 6(1) of Schedule 4, Part II, and section 17 of the 1979 MSA.) This special fund applies *on any distinct occasion* and is subject to a maximum of 25,000,000 SDR. It must be emphasised that this separate limitation fund applies only when there are claims for loss of life or personal injury to passengers.

The International Convention on the Carriage of Passengers and their Luggage, Athens 1974 (the Athens Convention) came into force internationally on 28 April 1987 and was given the force of law in the United Kingdom by virtue of section 14 of the Merchant Shipping Act 1979 and is annexed as Schedule 3 to that Act. Section 14 brought the Convention into force in the United Kingdom on 30 April 1987.[68] (Prior to that date the United Kingdom gave the Convention the force of law domestically with effect from 1 January 1981.[69])

A summary of the limitation aspects of the Athens Convention will be found on pages 96–101 and 218–219.

Article 7(1) of the Athens Convention provides that:

"The liability of the carrier for the death of or personal injury to a passenger shall in no case exceed 700,000 francs per carriage."

By virtue of a protocol of 19 November 1976 the limit of

68. Merchant Shipping Act 1979 (Commencement No. 11) Order 1987 (S.I. No 635).
69. S.I. 1980 No. 1092.

700,000 francs [70] referred to in Article 7(1) is to be substituted by the limit of 46,666 SDR which is the same figure as is found in Article 7(1) of the 1976 Convention. Furthermore, Article 13 of the Athens Convention provides that the conduct which will debar the right to limit under that Convention is the same as the conduct which will debar the right to limit under Article 4 of the 1976 Convention.

However, despite these apparent similarities the provisions of the Athens Convention and the 1976 Convention differ in the following respects:

(a) The limit of 46,666 SDR in Article 7(1) of the Athens Convention is to apply to *each passenger claiming*. Therefore the limit of liability in the Athens Convention will vary depending on the number of passengers claiming. In the case of a catastrophe involving the death of or personal injury to all the passengers, the maximum exposure may be calculated by multiplying 46,666 SDR by the number of passengers *actually on board*. However, the limit of liability set out in Article 7(1) of the 1976 Convention is *fixed* at an amount calculated by multipying 46,666 SDR by the *number of passengers which the vessel is certificated to carry*. Therefore, the limit of liability under the 1976 Convention is not related to the number of passengers claiming or the number of passengers actually on board.

(b) The limit fixed by Article 7(1) of the Athens Convention applies per "carriage" which is defined in Article 1(8) as the whole period during which the passenger is being transported. The limit fixed by Article 7(1) of the 1976 Convention applies "on any distinct occasion". Therefore, if a passenger is injured twice during the course of a voyage, the type of limitation of liability set out in Article 7(1) of the Athens Convention would only apply once whereas the type of limi-

70. In the United Kingdom this figure was increased to 1,525,000 francs with effect from 1 June 1987 (S.I. 1987 No 855) and with effect from 10 November 1987 for the figure of 1,525,000 francs 100,000 SDR is substituted (S.I. 1989 No. 1830).

tation of liability set out in Article 7(1) of the 1976 Convention would probably apply twice as there would be two "distinct occasion(s)".

There will be cases in which the passenger limitation provisions of both the 1976 Convention and the Athens Convention apply. Where injuries have been serious the claimants may find that the per passenger limits under the Athens Convention are insufficient to meet their claims in full whereas a global fund calculated in accordance with the provisions of Article 7 of the 1976 Convention would be sufficiently large to enable all claimants to be paid in full. In this connection the terms of Articles 14 and 19 of the Athens Convention are important. Article 14 of the Athens Convention provides that:

"No action for damages for the death of or personal injury to a passenger, or for loss of damage to luggage, shall be brought against a carrier or performing carrier otherwise than in accordance with this Convention."

Article 19 of the Athens Convention provides that:

"This Convention shall not modify the rights or duties of the carrier, the performing carrier, and their servants or agents provided for in international conventions relating to the limitation of liability of Owners of seagoing ships."

It is submitted that the combined effect of these two articles is to require all passengers to present their claims in accordance with the provisions of the Athens Convention when this is applicable to the incident giving rise to the claims. On the other hand it gives the Carrier the right to *further* limit his liability where the total amount payable to all claimants after application of the limitation provisions of the Athens Convention exceeds the global fund calculated in accordance with the terms of Article 7 of the 1976 Convention.

The position in the United Kingdom

Paragraph 13 of Part II of Schedule 3 to the 1979 MSA provides that:

"It is hereby declared that nothing in the Convention (the Athens Convention) affects the operation of Section 503 of the Merchant

Shipping Act 1894 or Section 17 of this Act (which limit a shipowner's liability in certain cases of loss of life, injury or damage)."

This provision appears to be no more than a restatement of Article 19 of the Athens Convention but including specific reference to the limitation provisions of the 1976 Convention (as incorporated into United Kingdom law) which are not to be modified by the operation of the limitation provisions of the Athens Convention.

Summary of Limits

FOR LOSS OF LIFE/PERSONAL INJURY CLAIMS ONLY

Tonnage not exceeding 500 tons*		333,000 SDR
Tonnage between 501 tons and 3,000 tons	Extra	500 SDR *per ton*
Tonnage between 3,001 tons and 30,000 tons	Extra	333 SDR *per ton*
Tonnage between 30,001 tons and 70,000 tons	Extra	250 SDR *per ton*
Tonnage in excess of 70,000 tons	Extra	167 SDR *per ton*
Salvor not operating from any ship or operating solely on ship being salved (fixed tonnage of 1,500 tons)		833,000 SDR

OTHER CLAIMS

Tonnage not exceeding 500 tons*		167,000 SDR
Tonnage between 501 tons and 30,000 tons	Extra	167 SDR *per ton*
Tonnage between 30,001 tons and 70,000 tons	Extra	125 SDR *per ton*
Tonnage in excess of 70,000 tons	Extra	83 SDR *per ton*
Salvor not operating from any ship or operating solely on ship being salved (fixed tonnage of 1,500 tons)		334,000 SDR

TOTAL POTENTIAL EXPOSURE WHERE THERE ARE PERSONAL AND PROPERTY CLAIMS

Tonnage not exceeding 500 tons*		500,000 SDR
Tonnage between 501 tons and 3,000 tons	Extra	667 SDR *per ton*
Tonnage between 3,001 tons and 30,000 tons	Extra	500 SDR *per ton*
Tonnage between 30,001 tons and 70,000 tons	Extra	375 SDR *per ton*
Tonnage in excess of 70,000 tons	Extra	250 SDR *per ton*
Salvors not operating from any ship or operating solely on ship being salved (fixed tonnage of 1,500 tons)		1,167,000 SDR

*N.B. In the United Kingdom this first tranche which applies to vessels not exceeding 500 tons is split into two sections: (i) vessels with a tonnage not exceeding 299 tons and (ii) vessels with a tonnage between 300 and 500. For all vessels within section (i), regardless of tonnage, the limit for loss of life/ personal injury claims is 166, 667; for "other claims" the limit is 83,333 SDR and where both types of claim are involved the limit is 250,000 SDR.

PASSENGER CLAIMS

For each passenger which a ship is certifi-
cated to carry: 46,666 SDR
subject to a maximum of: 25,000,000 SDR

Article 8: Unit of Account

It is *only* the first two sentences of Article 8(1) which are included in Part I of Schedule 4 of the 1979 MSA and which accordingly have the force of law in the United Kingdom.

For further comment on this Article see the discussion on pages 47–48, above, in relation to Article 6(1).

Article 9: Aggregation of claims

1. The limits of liability determined in accordance with Article 6 shall apply to the aggregate of all the claims which arise on any distinct occasion:

   (a) against the person or persons mentioned in paragraph 2 of Article 1 and any person for whose act, neglect or default he or they are responsible; or
   (b) against the shipowner of a ship rendering salvage services from that ship and the salvor or salvors operating from such ship and any person for whose act, neglect or default he or they are responsible; or
   (c) against the salvor or salvors who are not operating from a ship or who are operating solely on the ship to, or in respect of which, the salvage services are rendered and any person for whose act, neglect or default he or they are responsible.

2. The limits of liability determined in accordance with Article 7 shall apply to the aggregate of all claims subject thereto which may arise on any distinct occasion against the person or persons mentioned in paragraph 2 of Article 1 in respect of the ship referred to in Article 7 and any person for whose act, neglect or default he or they are responsible.

Whilst the provisions for aggregation of claims in the 1976 Convention are lengthy by reason of the need to incorporate special rules to govern claims against salvors and by passengers they in fact introduce no changes of substance.[71] The equivalent provision in the 1957 Convention is Article 2(1) the terms of which were incorporated into the law of the United Kingdom by section 8(2) of the 1958 Act.

A shipowner is entitled to limit his liability in respect of the aggregate of all claims which arise on any "distinct occasion". The 1976 Convention differs from the 1957 Convention in that whereas the 1957 Convention refers in general terms to " . . . the aggregate of personal claims and property claims . . . ", the 1976 Convention expressly lists the types of claims which are to be aggregated on each "distinct occasion".

The meaning of "distinct occasion" has often been the subject of litigation in the United Kingdom. An example of a finding that two collisions were not "one distinct occasion" is to be found in the case of The "Lucullite".[72] The Lucullite had been negligently moored alongside another vessel in heavy weather. The rough seas caused the Lucullite to range against the other vessel causing serious damage to that vessel. The Lucullite cast off and, in the course of manoeuvring, struck another vessel which sank. The owners of the Lucullite asserted that the damage to the two vessels arose on one distinct occasion. The court held that the second collision was not the necessary consequence of the first and that, therefore, the two collisions arose on two distinct occasions and that the two claimants could not be required to prove their claims against one limitation fund.

On the other hand in The "Harlow"[73] a tug, with five barges in tow, collided with the vessel Dalton in the River Thames due to the negligent navigation of the Harlow. The Dalton sustained serious damage. The collision caused the Harlow's steering gear to jam and, with her engines still running at full speed, she attempted to make a turn in the river. In so doing she collided with a second vessel. The court held that the second collision occurred on the same occasion as the first and,

71. But see pages 67 and 71–72, below.
72. (1929) 33 Ll.L. Rep. 186.
73. (1922) 10 Ll.L. Rep. 66.

accordingly, both claims for damages would have to be proved against the same limitation fund.

INTRODUCTION TO ARTICLES 10–14

These Articles deal with the practical aspects of limitation.

By express reservation and by implication much is left to the individual state parties to arrange on a domestic basis. In the High Court of England and Wales Order 75 of the Rules of the Supreme Court has been amended to accommodate the changes to the practical aspects of limitation. In the comments which follow the terms of the 1976 Convention are examined in the light of Order 75 as amended.

Article 10: Limitation of liability without constitution of a limitation fund

1. Limitation of liability may be invoked notwithstanding that a limitation fund as mentioned in Article 11 has not been constituted.

However, a State Party may provide in its national law that, where an action is brought in its courts to enforce a claim subject to limitation, a person liable may only invoke the right to limit liability if a limitation fund has been constituted in accordance with the provisions of this Convention or is constituted when the right to limit liability is invoked.

2. If limitation of liability is invoked without the constitution of a limitation fund, the provisions of Article 12 shall apply, correspondingly.

3. Questions of procedure arising under the rules of this Article shall be decided in accordance with the national law of the State Party in which action is brought.

ARTICLE 10(1)

This subsection provides that a person may invoke limitation of liability notwithstanding that a limitation fund has not been established. However, it also goes on to provide that a State Party may opt to provide by its national law that where an action is brought in its courts to enforce a claim "subject to limitation" a fund must be established if limitation is to be invoked.

ARTICLE 10(2)

This subsection provides that the terms of Article 12 (which deals with distribution of the fund) are to apply even if limitation of liability is invoked without the constitution of a fund.

ARTICLE 10(3)

This subsection provides that rules of procedure to be applied where limitation is invoked without the constitution of a fund are to be laid down by the national law of the country where the action is brought.

The position in the United Kingdom

The second sentence of Article 10(1) does not appear in Schedule 4, Part 1, to the 1979 MSA and does not therefore have the force of law in the United Kingdom by virtue of section 17(1) of the Act. The implication is therefore, that the United Kingdom Government does not intend to place restrictions on a person's right to invoke limitation of liability without constitution of a fund. This is further suggested by reference to RSC, Order 75, rule 37A(1), in the *Supreme Court Practice* which is phrased in permissive rather than mandatory terms, viz. "The plaintiff *may* constitute a limitation fund. . . ."

Under the law of England and Wales as it existed prior to the coming into force of the 1976 Convention a person could invoke limitation in two ways:

(a) Pleaded by way of defence in an action.[74] In such a case where the damages which would otherwise be recoverable exceed the limit of liability, judgment is given for the limit.[75] If limitation is invoked in this manner it has never been necessary for any limitation fund to be constituted before judgment. The reason for this is that if, the person liable is adjudged entitled to limit his liability, the judgment does not establish his right to limit as regards all claims in respect of that occurrence but merely establishes his right against the plaintiff in that particular action.[76] It is therefore possible that if another claimant

---

74. See Order 18, Rule 22, of the RSC 1985.
75. *Beauchamp* v. *Turrell* [1952] 2 Q.B. 207; *Wheeler* v. *London & Rochester Trading Co. Ltd.* [1957] 1 Lloyd's Rep. 69.
76. See Atkin's *Court Forms 3 (Admiralty/Affidavits)*, 2nd ed., p. 50.

brings a further action in respect of loss or damage arising out of the same occurrence for a sum in excess of the limit of liability, the person liable would effectively have to pay the limit again (assuming he could again prove his right to limit in the further action).[77]

.It is submitted that nothing in the 1976 Convention or the 1979 MSA varies a person's right to limit liability by way of defence in the manner outlined above.

(b) By commencing a limitation action, which action, if successful, entitles the person liable to limit his liability against "all and every person or persons whatsoever claiming or being entitled to claim in respect of damage or loss" resulting from the particular incident.

It has not been necessary in England and Wales when *commencing* a limitation action to deposit the fund with the court. The English Rules of the Supreme Court (RSC)[78] proceeded on the premise that a person liable is not entitled to limit his liability until he proves his right so to do to the satisfaction of the court.[79] Accordingly, the *obligation* to constitute a limitation fund arose only after the Admiralty Registrar or judge had decreed that the person liable was entitled to limit his liability and had calculated the quantum of the fund.

Whilst the *obligation* to constitute a fund did not arise in the United Kingdom until a later stage in the proceedings, it was often desirable for a person seeking to limit his liability to pay the amount of his limitation fund into court at an early stage after invoking limitation. If he did not, and between the date of invoking limitation and the date of the decree the limitation

---

77. In *The "Waltraud"* [1991] 1 Lloyd's Rep. 389 Sheen J gave summary judgments in two separate actions by various cargo claimants. He observed that it would be sensible for the defendants to commence a limitation action rather than plead limitation by way of defence in two separate actions where the total damages might well exceed the 1976 limitation fund. On an application for interim payments the plaintiffs, relying on this paragraph, argued that the court should order interim payments up to the limitation fund in each action. Mr Justice Sheen rejected this argument and ordered interim payments in both actions not exceeding the global tonnage limitation of the vessel.

78. See Order 75, Rules 37–43, of RSC 1985.

79. See Atkin's *Court Forms 3 (Admiralty/Affidavits)*, 2nd ed., p. 52.

unit suffered one of its periodic revaluations, the amount which he was ultimately ordered to pay into court could be higher than the sum he would have been obliged to pay at any earlier date.

The position appears to be the same under the 1976 Convention, thus:

(i) Under Article 8(1) of the 1976 Convention the value of the SDR is fixed "at the date the limitation fund shall have been constituted, payment is made or security is given . . . "[80] The person liable therefore runs the risk that the quantum of his limitation fund will increase the longer he waits;

(ii) the various rights contained in Article 13 designed to protect the other assets of the person invoking limitation apply *only after* "a limitation fund has been constituted".

In consequence the "person liable" will still have to reach an informed decision as to whether he should constitute the limitation fund at an early stage and thereby (a) protect himself against subsequent increases in the fund and (b) obtain the benefit of the rights afforded by Article 13 or wait until the claims have been proved.

It is noteworthy that Article 1(7) of the 1976 Convention has clarified a principle of law which has hitherto been unclear in the United Kingdom. The traditional view[81] was that a person could commence a limitation action *before* admitting liability but that liability had effectively to be admitted before a limitation decree could be made.[82] However, this was doubted by Sir C. Butt in The "Karo".[83] Article 1(7) of the 1976 Convention now provides that "the *act of invoking limitation* of liability shall not constitute an admission of liability". However, this still leaves open the question whether liability has to be

---

80. Under the Hague–Visby Rules the relevant date for calculating the value of the SDR is the date of judgment—s.2(5) of the Merchant Shipping Act 1981.

81. The "Amalia" (1863) B. & L. 151; The "Sisters" (1876) 2 Asp. M.C. 589.

82. See Temperley, The Merchant Shipping Acts, 7th ed., p. 181, Note 1.

83. (1888) 13 P.D. 24.

admitted before a decree of limitation can be made. It is submitted that liability has to be admitted at that stage since the decree pronounces that *liability* is limited.

CHAPTER III—THE LIMITATION FUND

Article 11: Constitution of the fund

1. Any person alleged to be liable may constitute a fund with a Court or other competent authority in any State Party in which legal proceedings are instituted in respect of claims subject to limitation. The fund shall be constituted in the sum of such of the amounts set out in Articles 6 and 7 as are applicable to claims for which that person may be liable, together with interest thereon from the date of the occurrence giving rise to the liability until the date of the constitution of the fund. Any fund thus constituted shall be available only for the payment of claims in respect of which limitation of liability can be invoked.

2. A fund may be constituted, either by depositing the sum, or by producing a guarantee acceptable under the legislation of the State Party where the fund is constituted and considered to be adequate by the Court or other competent authority.

3. A fund constituted by one of the persons mentioned in paragraph 1(a), (b) or (c) or paragraph 2 of Article 9 or his insurer shall be deemed constituted by all persons mentioned in paragraph 1(a), (b) or (c) or paragraph 2, respectively.

Article 12: Distribution of the fund

1. Subject to the provisions of paragraph 1, 2 *and* 3 of Article 6 and of Article 7, the fund shall be distributed among the claimants in proportion to their established claims against the fund.

2. If, before the fund is distributed, the person liable, or his insurer, has settled a claim against the fund such person shall, up to the amount he has paid, acquire by subrogation the rights which the person so compensated would have enjoyed under this Convention.

3. The right of subrogation provided for in paragraph 2 may also be exercised by persons other than those therein mentioned in respect of any amount of compensation which they may have paid, but only to the extent that such subrogation is permitted under the applicable national law.

4. Where the person liable or any other person establishes that he may be compelled to pay, at a later date, in whole or in part any such amount of compensation with regard to which such person would have enjoyed a right of subrogation pursuant to paragraphs 2 and 3 had the compensation been paid before the fund was distributed, the Court or other competent authority of the State where the fund has been constituted may order that a sufficient

sum shall be provisionally set aside to enable such person at such later date to enforce his claim against the fund.

Article 13: Bar to other actions

1. Where a limitation fund has been constituted in accordance with Article 11, any person having made a claim against the fund shall be barred from exercising any right in respect of such claim against any other assets of a person by or on behalf of whom the fund has been constituted.

2. After a limitation fund has been constituted in accordance with Article 11, any ship or other property, belonging to a person on behalf of whom the fund has been constituted, which has been arrested or attached within the jurisdiction of a State Party for a claim which may be raised against the fund, or any security given, may be released by order of the Court or other competent authority of such State. However, such release shall always be ordered if the limitation fund has been constituted:

   (a) at the port where the occurrence took place, or, if it took place out of port, at the first port of call thereafter; or
   (b) at the port of disembarkation in respect of claims for loss of life or personal injury; or
   (c) at the port of discharge in respect of damage to cargoes; or
   (d) in the State where the arrest is made.

3. The rules of paragraphs 1 and 2 shall apply only if the claimant may bring a claim against the limitation fund before the Court administering that fund and the fund is actually available and freely transferable in respect of that claim.

Article 14: Governing law

Subject to the provisions of this Chapter the rules relating to the constitution and the distribution of a limitation fund, and all rules of procedure in connection therewith, shall be governed by the law of the State Party in which the fund is constituted.

Article 2 of the 1957 Convention provides that when the aggregate of claims exceeds the limits of liability the total sum representing such limits may be constituted as one distinct limitation fund. However, the 1957 Convention gave no guidance as to how and where the fund was to be constituted. This was all left to the domestic law of each country.[84] The 1976 Convention, on the other hand, provides in Articles 11 and 12 detailed guidelines for the constitution and distribution of the

---

84. See for example *The "Abadesa" (No. 2)* [1968] 1 Lloyd's Rep. 493.

fund and it is only where the guidelines are not specific to certain situations that reference is to be made to the national law of the State Party where the fund is constituted (Article 14).

The specific provisions of Articles 11 and 12 of the 1976 Convention follow generally the rules which were applied in England and Wales before the coming into force of the 1976 Convention in relation to the constitution and distribution of the fund. These rules are contained in Order 75, Rules 37–43, of the Rules of the Supreme Court (RSC). In particular, the terms of Article 11 have been expressly incorporated in a new rule 37A.[85]

Article 11: Constitution of the fund

ARTICLE 11(1)

This provision establishes that a fund may be constituted with the court or other competent authority of a State Party[86] in which legal proceedings are instituted in respect of claims subject to limitation. In the case of England and Wales the fund is to be constituted with the Admiralty Court.[87] The amount of the fund is the total of such of the amounts set out in Article 6 (loss of life, injury and property claims) and Article 7 (passenger claims) as are applicable to the claims against them and is to include (in accordance with the traditional practice in England and Wales[88]) interest from the date of the occurrence giving rise to the liability until the date of constitution of the fund.

The Convention does not stipulate the rate at which interest is payable; that is left to national legislation. In the case of England and Wales the necessary machinery is set out in Paragraph 8 of Schedule 4, Part II, to the 1979 MSA which provides

85. This rule was given effect by RSC (Amendment) 1985 (S.I. 1985 No. 69).

86. Defined in the United Kingdom for the purposes of the 1979 MSA by para 13, Schedule 4, Part II, to the 1979 MSA.

87. See para. 11 of Schedule 4, Part II, to the 1979 MSA and s. 20(1)(*b*) and (3)(*c*) of the Supreme Court Act 1981.

88. See *The "Funabashi"* [1972] 1 Lloyd's Rep. 371. But see also *The "Garden City"* (*No. 2*) [1984] 2 Lloyd's Rep. 37.

that the Secretary of State may prescribe the rate of interest to be applied.[89]

The provision finally restates Article 2(3) of the 1957 Convention to the effect that the fund so constituted shall be available only for payment of claims in respect of which limitation can be invoked. The effect of this provision seems to be that if a claimant has a claim in respect of which the person liable cannot limit, the claimant cannot participate in the limitation fund. His claim is entirely separate. However it is possible that if he makes such a claim against the fund he may run the risk of being unable to enforce his claim against the other assets of the person liable.[90]

ARTICLE 11(2)

This subsection provides that the fund may be constituted in the form of cash or by a guarantee acceptable under the *legislation* of the State Party[91] where the fund is constituted and considered to be adequate by the court or other competent authority. Prior to the coming into force of the 1976 Convention, the law of England and Wales[92] did not allow for constitution of a fund other than by a cash deposit and there is nothing in the 1979 MSA to indicate that this situation will change. However, most other jurisdictions will accept either a cash deposit or a guarantee. Therefore, whilst the courts of England and Wales may still require cash deposits in future when funds are constituted it will nevertheless (since the Convention has the "force of law" in the United Kingdom by virtue of section

89. The rate of 12% is prescribed in the Merchant Shipping Act (Liability of Shipowners and Others) (Rate of Interest) Order 1986 (S.I. 1986 No. 1932).

90. See Article 13(1), pages 70–72, below. The wording of Article 13(1) suggests that so long as a limitation fund has been constituted and the claimant has "made a claim against the fund" that claimant is estopped from pursuing his claim against any other asset of the person seeking to limit even if the claim is disallowed on the limitation proceedings. It would seem to be wise for a person who has a claim which does not qualify for limitation purposes not to submit his claim against the limitation fund if he wishes to pursue the claim against any other asset of the person liable.

91. See footnote 86 on page 65.

92. See Order 75, Rule 24, and Order 22, Rule 1, of the RSC 1985.

17(1) of the 1979 MSA) have to accept as sufficient a fund constituted in another State Party[93] by deposit of a guarantee acceptable to the court or other competent authority of the State Party (Article 13).

ARTICLE 11(3)

The fund may be constituted by "any person alleged to be liable" who is entitled to the benefit of limitation (Article 11(1)). Where the fund is constituted by any one of the several persons mentioned in Article 9 or by an insurer of one of those persons, the fund will be regarded as having been constituted "by all persons mentioned" in Article 9. The wording of Article 11(3) is curious in this respect since, despite the fact that the fund may be set up by an insurer on behalf of an assured, the fund is not on the face of it deemed to have been constituted on behalf of the insurer himself (the insurer not being "a person mentioned" in Article 9[94]).

Article 12: Distribution of the fund

ARTICLE 12(1)

This subsection provides that "the fund" is to be distributed among the claimants in proportion to their established claims against the "fund". "The fund" as strictly construed is that referred to in the second and third sentences of Article 11(1), namely, the total of the applicable sums set out in Articles 6 and 7 "together with interest thereon from the date of the occurrence . . . until the date of the constitution of the fund". There is nothing therefore in Article 12(1) to indicate whether interest earned by the fund *after* its constitution is to be distributed among the claimants. However, in the case of England and Wales there is authority[95] to the effect that interest earned on a fund paid into court is divisible between the claimants against that fund and it is probable, in view of the provisions

---

93. See footnote 86 on page 65, below.
94. See page 57, above and page 77, below.
95. *The "Garden City" (No. 2)* [1984] 2 Lloyd's Rep. 37.

of Article 14 that this rule will continue to be applied after the 1976 Convention is in force.[96]

This subsection echoes Article 3(2) of the 1957 Convention and emphasises that the fund is distributed in proportion to "established" claims. In other words, the subsection restates the existing rule that the fund is not distributed in proportion to the quantum of claims as submitted but in proportion to the quantum of claims as ultimately allowed by the court. This function is exercised in London by the Admiralty Registrar under Order 75, Rules 41–43, of the Rules of the Supreme Court (RSC), and on the continent by adjusters appointed by the court.

ARTICLE 12(2)

This subsection restates in different wording Article 3(3) of the 1957 Convention. It provides in effect that if a person liable (or his insurer) settles a claim before the fund is distributed he acquires by subrogation the rights which the person compensated would otherwise have had to share in distribution of the limitation fund under the 1976 Convention. In other words if the person liable settles a claim for £100 when for contractual or other legal reasons the claim would only prove at £80 before the court in which the fund is constituted his subrogated right to prove against the fund is limited to £80.[97]

96. In *Swiss Bank Corp.* v. *Brink's-MAT Limited* [1986] *2 All E. R. 188* Bingham J. (a judge of the English Commerical Court) held in the context of a claim arising under the Warsaw Convention that the limit on liability imposed by Article 22(2)(a) of that Convention was all-embracing and that interest could not be awarded *in addition* to the sum calculated under Article 22(2)(a). However, it is plain from the report that Bingham J. was much influenced by the fact that Article 22(4) of the Warsaw Convention expressly provided that the limits imposed by Article 22 did not prevent the relevant court from awarding costs *in addition* to the said limits. He argued therefore that Article 22(4) was unnecessary unless there was a presumption that the sum calculated under Article 22(2)(a) would otherwise have been all-embracing. But for Article 22(4) it seems that the judge would have followed the "inclination" of "any English judge" to award interest in addition to the limit. There is no provision in the 1976 Convention similar to that of Article 22(4) of the Warsaw Convention and it is submitted that the decision in the *Swiss Bank Corp.* case will not be followed in England and Wales in cases arising under the 1976 Convention.

97. *The "World Mermaid"* see *The "Giacinto Motta"* [1977] 2 Lloyd's Rep. 221.

ARTICLE 12(3)

This subsection extends the right of subrogation in Article 12(2) to persons other than those mentioned in 12(2) (that is, to persons other than "the person liable or his insurer") but only to the extent that such right of subrogation is permitted by "the applicable national law". This subsection is an innovation and is presumably intended to apply to payments made by persons who are not "liable" for a claim in the strict sense but are nevertheless not volunteers in that they are allowed the right of subrogation by "the applicable national law".

It is also unclear whether the "applicable national law" is a reference to the law of the country where the fund is constituted or the law of the country which has jurisdiction in respect of the transaction giving rise to the right of subrogation. Article 3(3) of the 1957 Convention refers in a slightly different context to the "national law of the State where the fund has been constituted". It is submitted that in view of the different wording of Article 14 the reference in 12(2) may be to the law of the country which has jurisdiction in respect of the transaction giving rise to the right of subrogation.

ARTICLE 12(4)

This subsection restates the rules set out in Article 3(4) of the 1957 Convention and section 7(1) of the 1958 Act. It is designed to protect a person who contemplates an additional future liability and does not wish to be prejudiced by the distribution of the fund before the future liability materialises. The addition of the words "or any other person" in the first line seems to be intended to protect the persons referred to in Article 12(3).

Liens or other rights in respect of any ship or property—effect on distribution

In the case of the United Kingdom, paragraph 9 of Schedule 4, Part II, to the 1979 MSA (which is given the force of law by virtue of section 17 of that Act) provides that no lien or other right in respect of any ship or property shall affect the proportions in which the fund is distributed among several claimants.

This provision restates section 17(2) of the 1958 Act and is intended to override the decision in *The "Countess"*[98] where the House of Lords held that if one claimant had a possessory lien over the ship, effect had to be given to his superior right even to the extent of depriving other claimants of all right of recovery against the limitation fund.

Article 13: Bar to other actions

The intention of this Article is to ensure that when a limitation fund has been constituted under the 1976 Convention the other assets of a "person liable" should not be exposed to separate action in respect of claims arising out of the occurrence in respect of which the fund has been constituted which are also "subject to limitation" under the 1976 Convention. In this respect, the 1976 Convention follows the philosophy underlying the 1957 Convention which is also reflected in the MSA 1958 in the United Kingdom.

ARTICLE 13(1)

This subsection substantially restates Article 2(4) of the 1957 Convention which was in turn reflected in slightly different terms in the United Kingdom in section 6 of the 1958 Act. Subsection 13(1) provides that where:

  (a) a limitation fund has been constituted *"in any State Party"*[99] in accordance with Article 11 of the 1976 Convention; and
  (b) a person *has "made a claim"* against the fund;

he is debarred from "exercising any right" in respect of *that same claim* against any *other assets* of a person by or on behalf of whom the fund has been constituted.

In *The "Bowbelle"*[100] Sheen J made the point that ". . . common sense dictates that there should be some machinery by which warning can be given to would-be arrestors that they

---

98. [1923] A.C. 345.
99. For the position in the United Kingdom see para. 13 of Schedule 4, Part II, and section 17 of the 1979 MSA.
100. [1990] 3 All E.R. 476.

should not arrest any of the ships belonging to the owners of the *Bowbelle*" (because the owners had already set up a limitation fund). This has now been done by RSC, Order 75, rule 6(1A),[101] which requires the person who is seeking to limit his liability to file in the Supreme Court (Admiralty and Commercial Court) Registry a *praecipe* stating:

(a) that a limitation fund in respect of damage arising from the relevant incident has been constituted, and
(b) an undertaking to acknowledge service of any writ issued against the owners of the vessels in question.

Thereafter a caveat against the arrest of the vessels named in the *praecipe* is to be issued. Because of this procedure any individual seeking to arrest a vessel in England would be placed on notice by the existence of the caveat and, in theory, courts should not find themselves hearing applications to free a vessel from arrest where a limitation fund has already been constituted.

The aim of the subsection is therefore to protect the *assets* of the person seeking limitation; it does not on the face of it prevent a party from pursuing an action on the merits against the person seeking limitation. However, in the case of the United Kingdom, the legislature has decreed[102] that where a fund has been established in one of the courts of the United Kingdom[103] that court *may* (not "must") stay any proceedings relating to any claims arising out of that occurrence which are pending against the person by whom the fund has been constituted. This provision restates the discretion which the courts of the United Kingdom had enjoyed in slightly different circumstances since 1894 by virtue of section 504 of the 1894 Act.

It is not certain whether Article 13(1) has effectively prevented attachment of the assets of an insurer after a limitation fund has been established by that insurer on behalf of his assured. The subsection protects the assets of a "person" by or on behalf of whom the fund has been established under Article 11. Article 11(3) seems to say that even if a fund is constituted by an insurer on behalf of one of the "persons" mentioned in

101. Amended by RSC (Amendment No 2) 1990 (S.I. 1990 No. 1689).
102. Para. 8(2) of Schedule 4, Part II, and section 17 of the 1979 MSA.
103. Para. 11 of Schedule 4, Part II, and section 17 of the 1979 MSA.

Article 9(1)(a), (b) or (c) or (2) (which do not include an "insurer") the fund is nevertheless deemed to be constituted by all those "persons" but not by the insurer. This result can certainly not have been intended by those drafting the Convention but a possible answer to this problem lies in the wording of Article 1(6) which provides that an insurer "shall be entitled to the benefits of this Convention to the same extent as the assured himself". Alternatively, the insurer may seek to constitute a fund both on behalf of the assured *and* on his own behalf. (If he is "alleged to be liable" he is presumably entitled to establish the fund on his own behalf under Article 11(1).) He would therefore qualify as a person *by* whom the fund has been constituted for the purposes of Article 13(1).

ARTICLE 13(2)

(a) *General aims of the subsection.* This subsection is intended to ensure that when a limitation fund has been constituted under the 1976 Convention, the vessels or other property of the person on whose behalf the fund has been constituted should be protected from arrest or detention. The subsection essentially restates the rules set out in Article 5 of the 1957 Convention which principles had in turn been incorporated in slightly different language into the domestic legislation of the United Kingdom by section 5 of the 1958 Act. However, difficulties have arisen in the United Kingdom in relation to the wording of section 5 of the 1958 Act and the English court has held[104] that even if a limitation fund was established in another court, the English court would not release from arrest in the United Kingdom a vessel owned by a person who had established the foreign limitation fund unless that person could satisfy the English court that "there was no serious question to be tried in relation to absence of actual fault or privity on his part".

The difficulty arose as a result of a combination of two factors:

(i) the wording of section 5 of the 1958 Act (and also Article 5 of the 1957 Convention) provided that a

---

104. *The "Wladyslaw Lokietek"* [1978] 2 Lloyd's Rep. 520.

court could release a vessel after a limitation fund or security had been established *only* if the court was satisfied that the shipowner was entitled to limit his liability.

(ii) Article 1(6) of the 1957 Convention provided that the burden of proving whether or not the right to limit was available was to be determined by the *lex fori*.

In the United Kingdom the presumption was that a person could *not* limit his liability under section 503 of the 1894 MSA (as amended by the 1958 Act) *unless* he proved to the satisfaction of the court that there was no fault or privity on his part. This was extremely difficult to prove in interlocutory proceedings relating to an arrest and was normally not resolved until after a full hearing of the merits following full discovery.

These difficulties have been resolved by Article 13(2) of the 1976 Convention since the subsection provides expressly that the right (or obligation in certain circumstances) of the court to release a vessel or other property is triggered not so much by proof that the owner of the vessel or other property can limit his liability but by the establishment by or on behalf of such person of a limitation fund in accordance with Article 11 of the Convention.[105] Furthermore, the presumption which existed under the previous limitation regime that a person was *not entitled* to limit his liability *unless he* proved such entitlement has been displaced by the presumption that a person *is entitled* to limit his liability under the 1976 Convention *unless some other party* proves that he is guilty of the conduct described in Article 4.[106]

(b) *The mechanics of the subsection.* Article 13(2) is effectively in two parts:

(i) it sets out the factors which must be satisfied before the court can act to release a vessel or property which has been arrested in its jurisdiction. There are two factors:

105. See pages 71–72, above.
106. See page 39, above. In *The "Bowbelle"* [1990] 3 All E.R. 476 Sheen J. held that in an application for limitation the court is not required to investigate the question whether the shipowner has been guilty of conduct barring limitation.

(A) A limitation fund must have been established by or on behalf of the person to whom the ship or property arrested belongs in a *State Party*[107] in which legal proceedings have been instituted in respect of the claims in question. (This State Party does not have to be the same State Party as that in whose territory the ship or property has been arrested.)

(B) The vessel or property must have been arrested or attached for a claim which *may* be made against the limitation fund which has been established. Therefore the governing factor is the nature of the claim and it is not a requirement that the claim *has actually been made* against the limitation fund.

(ii) Once it is established that the court can act to release a vessel or property which has been arrested, the court has to determine whether circumstances exist in which it is *obliged* to release or whether the circumstances are such that it has a *discretion* whether to release:

(A) The court *must* release the vessel or property if the limitation fund has been constituted:

(1) at the place where the occurrence took place, or, if it took place out of port, at the first port of call thereafter; or

(2) at the port of disembarkation in respect of claims for loss of life or personal injury; or

(3) at the port of discharge in respect of damage to cargo; or

(4) in the State where the arrest is made.

(B) The court has a *discretion* whether to release the vessel or property in circumstances other than these set out in (A).

In the case of the United Kingdom, the legislature has decreed[108] that when an order is made by any court of the United Kingdom under Article 13(2) releasing a vessel or property from arrest, the person applying for such relief is deemed to

107. See Art. 11(1). For the position in the United Kingdom see para. 13 of Schedule 4, Part II, and s. 17 of 1979 MSA.
108. See para. 10 of Schedule 4, Part II, and s. 17 of the 1979 MSA.

have submitted to the jurisdiction of that court to adjudicate on the claim for which the ship or property was arrested or attached.

ARTICLE 13(3)

This subsection emphasises that the rights contained in Article 13(1) and (2) apply *only* where (a) the claimant *may* bring a claim against the limitation fund before the court administering that fund *and* (b) that fund is available and "freely transferable" in respect of that claim. The words "freely transferable" were not in the original draft articles submitted by the Legal Committee of the IMO and were introduced apparently[109] to ensure that the constitution of a limitation fund would only bar actions in other countries provided that currency regulations did not prevent transfer out of the State in question of any sums to be distributed from the fund.

Article 14: Governing law

This section establishes that to the extent that the provisions of Articles 11, 12 and 13 do not provide specific guidance, rules relating to the "constitution and distribution of a limitation fund and all rules of procedure in connection therewith" shall be governed by the law of the State Party in which the fund is constituted. Therefore, for example, the courts of the United Kingdom will probably, in the absence of specific guidance in Article 12, continue to rule that interest earned on a limitation fund after it has been established in the United Kingdom is to be distributed together with the fund.[110]

The reference to rules relating to the "constitution and distribution" of a limitation fund arguably restricts the application of the law of the state in which the fund has been established to matters contained in Articles 11 and 12 and not in Article 13 (see the headings to the various Articles). However, it is submitted that the earlier reference in Article 14 to the

109. See page 99 of the *Official Records of the International Conference 1976.*

110. *The "Garden City" (No. 2)* [1984] 2 Lloyd's Rep. 37. See page 65, above.

"provisions of this *chapter*" (which includes Article 13) and the use of the words "and all rules of procedure *in connection therewith*" are plainly intended to apply the law in question to matters contained in Articles 11, 12 and 13.

CHAPTER IV—SCOPE OF APPLICATION

Article 15

1. This Convention shall apply whenever any person referred to in Article 1 seeks to limit his liability before the Court of a State Party or seeks to procure the release of a ship or other property or the discharge of any security given within the jurisdication of any such State. *Nevertheless, each State Party may exclude wholly or partially from the application of this Convention any person referred to in Article 1, who at the time when the rules of this Convention are invoked before the Courts of that State does not have his habitual residence in a State Party, or does not have his principal place of business in a State Party, or any ship in relation to which the right of limitation is invoked or whose release is sought and which does not at the time specified above fly the flag of a State Party.*

2. A State Party may regulate by specific provisions of national law the system of limitation of liability to be applied to vessels which are:—

(a) according to the law of that State, ships intended for navigation on inland waterways;

(b) ships of less than 300 tons.

A State Party which makes use of the option provided for in this paragraph shall inform the depositary of the limits of liability adopted in its national legislation or the fact that there are none.

3. A State Party may regulate by specific provisions of national law the system of limitation of liability to be applied to claims arising in cases in which interests of persons who are nationals of other State Parties are no way involved.

4. The Courts of a State Party shall not apply this Convention to ships constructed for or adapted to, and engaged in, drilling:

(a) when that State has established under its national legislation a higher limit of liability than that otherwise provided for in Article 6; or

(b) when the State has become party to an international convention regulating the system of liability in respect of such ships.

In a case to which sub-paragraph (a) applies that State Party shall inform the depositary accordingly.

5. *This Convention shall not apply to:*

   (a) *aircushion vehicles;*
   (b) *floating platforms constructed for the purpose of exploring or exploiting the natural resources of the seabed or the subsoil thereof.*

ARTICLE 15(1)

This subsection substantially restates the position as it was under Article 7 of the 1957 Convention. Thus, the 1976 Convention applies whenever a person who is entitled to limit liability seeks to do so before a court of a state which is party to the Convention, or seeks the release of a ship or other property from arrest or the discharge of security within the jurisdiction of a State Party.

However, a State Party is entitled to exclude either wholly or partially from the application of the Convention any person who would otherwise be entitled to limitation if such person is not habitually resident or does not have his principal place of business in a State Party at the time when the right to limit is invoked. Similarly, any State Party may exclude a ship if it does not fly the flag of a State Party at the time when the right of limitation is invoked or its release from arrest is sought. It would appear that the United Kingdom has decided not to take advantage of these permitted reservations since the material parts of Article 15(1) do not appear in Schedule 4, Part I, to the 1979 MSA and do not therefore have the force of law in the United Kingdom by virtue of section 17(1) of that Act.[111]

ARTICLE 15(2)

This subsection entitles a State Party to make specific regulations in its national law in relation to the limit of liability of (a) non sea-going ships and (b) ships of less than 300 tons.

(a) *Non sea-going ships.* Article 1(1) of the 1957 Convention (like Article 1(2) of the 1976 Convention) provides that the Convention shall apply to sea-going ships. However, Article 8 of the 1957 Convention allowed a State Party to decide what

111. See pages 15–16, above.

"other classes" of ship could be treated in the same manner as sea-going ships for the purposes of the Convention.

Article 15(2) of the 1976 Convention gives a State Party more limited rights in this respect than it enjoyed under the 1957 Convention since the right to make specific national regulations is restricted to vessels which are, *according to the law of that state, intended* for navigation on inland waterways.

In the case of the United Kingdom, the new regime has introduced no change in this respect.[112] Both under section 503 of the 1894 MSA and paragraph 2 of Schedule 4, Part II, and Section 17(1) of the 1979 MSA, limitation is available to non sea-going ships in the United Kingdom.

(b) *Ships of less than 300 tons.* Some changes have been introduced by the 1976 Convention. Article 3(5) of the 1957 Convention provided for a minimum deemed tonnage of 300 tons for purposes of limitation in respect of all types of claim. However the Protocol of Signature of that Convention reserved to States the right to make specific provisions of national law in relation to ships of less than 300 tons. By virtue of Article 6 of the 1976 Convention there is a single minimum limitation fund for all ships not exceeding 500 tons, i.e. the fund is the same for a ship of 10 tons as it is for one of 500 tons. However, Article 15(2) preserves the right of a State Party to make specific national regulations in relation to ships of less than 300 tons.

In the case of the United Kingdom the principle of the deemed minimum tonnage of 300 tons was, by section 1(1) of the 1958 Act, applied only to loss of life or personal injury claims and did not apply to property claims. However, by virtue of paragraph 5 of Schedule 4, Part II, and section 17(1) of the 1979 MSA, there is a new minimum level of limitation for ships of less than 300 tons in respect of *all* claims within Article 6.[113] These provisions do not apply to passenger claims since by virtue of Article 7 of the 1976 Convention limitation of this type of claim is no longer regulated by the tonnage of the ship but by the number of passengers which the ship is certificated to carry.

112. See pages 7, 15 and 16, above.
113. See pages 56–57, above.

ARTICLE 15(3)

This subsection allows a State Party to make specific national regulations relating to limitation where no nationals of other states are involved. In the case of the United Kingdom, this provision does not appear in Schedule 4, Part I, to the 1979 MSA. It seems that the United Kingdom decided not to reserve to itself the right to make such specific regulations.

ARTICLE 15(4)

This subsection provides that the Convention shall not apply to ships which have either been constructed for or adapted to drilling *and* are engaged in drilling in the following circumstances:

(a) when the State Party has by its national legislation established a higher limit of liability than that in Article 6; or

(b) when the State has become party to an international convention regulating the system of liability in respect of such ships.

In the case of the United Kingdom, this provision does not appear in Schedule 4, Part I, of the 1979 MSA and therefore does not have the force of law in the United Kingdom by virtue of section 17(1) of that Act. Accordingly the implication is that such vessels are subject in the United Kingdom to the limitation provisions of the 1976 Convention provided they satisfy the definition of "ship" in paragraph 12 of Schedule 4, Part II, to the MSA 1979.

ARTICLE 15(5)

This subsection provides that the terms of the 1976 Convention shall not apply to:

(a) aircushion vehicles;

(b) floating platforms constructed for the purpose of exploring or exploiting the natural resources of the seabed or the subsoil thereof.

In the case of the United Kingdom this provision does not appear in Schedule 4, Part I, to the 1979 MSA and therefore does not have the force of law in the United Kingdom by virtue of section 17(1) of that Act. Accordingly the exclusions do not seem to apply in the United Kingdom. The Hovercraft (Civil Liability) Order 1986,[114] which came into force in the United Kingdom on the same date as the 1976 Limitation Convention (1 December 1986) provides that the limitation provisions of the 1976 Convention as incorporated in the 1979 MSA shall apply to:

(a) loss of life or personal injury connected with a hovercraft which is caused to persons not carried by the hovercraft;

(b) loss or damage connected with a hovercraft which is caused to property; and

(c) infringements of rights through acts or omissions connected with a hovercraft.

The Order further provides that the Limitation Convention shall not apply to claims in respect of loss of or damage to passengers' baggage or crew's property carried by the hovercraft. The rights of hovercraft passengers and their baggage are covered (as specified in section 3 of the Order) by the Carriage By Air Act 1961 as modified by Schedule 1 to the Order itself.

Schedule 3 of the Order sets out the modifications which it has been necessary to make to the 1976 Limitation Convention to accommodate hovercraft. It should be noted that the limitation fund of a hovercraft under Article 6 is calculated by reference to the "maximum operational weight" of the craft rather than the gross tonnage. Article 7 of the Convention, which deals with limitation of liability for passenger claims, is omitted since such claims and the carrier's right to limit in respect thereof are specifically dealt with by the Carriage By Air Act 1961 (section 3 of the Order).

There does not seem to be any specific provision in the 1979 MSA referring to floating platforms. Bearing in mind that the exclusion in Article 15(2) does not seem to be effective in the United Kingdom, floating platforms are prima facie subject to

114. S.I. 1986 No. 1305.

the new limitation regime in the United Kingdom. However, it is submitted that such platforms may not fall within the definition of "ship" in paragraph 12 of Schedule 4, Part II, of the 1979 MSA (i.e. "a structure . . . launched and intended for use in navigation as a ship or part of a ship"). If this interpretation is correct liability in respect of such platforms will be unlimited in the United Kingdom.

CHAPTER V—FINAL CLAUSES

Article 16: Signature, Ratification and Accession

1. This Convention shall be open for signature by all States at the head-quarters of the InterGovernmental Maritime Consultative Organisation (hereinafter referred to as "the Organisation") from February 1st 1977 until December 31st 1977, and shall thereafter remain open for accession.

2. All States may become parties to this Convention by:

(a) signature without reservation as to ratification, acceptance or approval; or
(b) signature, subject to ratification, acceptance or approval followed by ratification, acceptance or approval; or
(c) accession.

3. Ratification, acceptance, approval or accession shall be effected by the deposit of a formal instrument to that effect with the Secretary-General of the Organisation (hereinafter referred to as "the Secretary-General").

Article 17: Entry into force

1. This Convention shall enter into force on the first day of the month following one year after the date on which 12 States have either signed it without reservation as to ratification, acceptance or approval or have deposited the requisite instruments of ratification, acceptance, approval or accession.

2. For a State which deposits an instrument of ratification, acceptance, approval or accession, or signs without reservation as to ratification, acceptance or approval, in respect of this Convention after the requirements for entry into force have been met but prior to the date of entry into force, the ratification, acceptance, approval or accession or the signature without reservation as to ratification, acceptance or approval, shall take effect on the date of entry into force of the Convention or on the first day of the month following the 90th day after the date of signature or the deposit of the instrument, whichever is the later date.

3. For any State which subsequently becomes a Party to this Convention, the Convention shall enter into force on the first day of the month following the expiration of 90 days after the date when such State deposited its instrument.

4. In respect of the relations between States which ratify, accept, or approve this Convention or accede to it, this Convention shall replace and abrogate the International Convention relating to the Limitation of the Liability of Owners of Seagoing Ships, done at Brussels on October 10th 1957, and the International Convention for the Unification of certain Rules relating to the Limitation of Liability of the Owners of Seagoing Vessels, signed at Brussels on August 25th 1924.

Article 18: Reservations

1. Any State may, at the time of signature, ratification, acceptance, approval or accession, reserve the right to exclude the application of Article 2, paragraph 1(d) and (e). No other reservations shall be admissible to the substantive provisions of this Convention.

2. Reservations made at the time of signature are subject to confirmation upon ratification, acceptance or approval.

3. Any State which has made a reservation to this Convention may withdraw it at any time by means of a notification addressed to the Secretary-General. Such withdrawal shall take effect to the date the notification is received. If the notification states that the withdrawal of a reservation is to take effect on a date specified therein, and such date is later than the date the notification is received by the Secretary-General, the withdrawal shall take effect on such later date.

Article 19: Denunciation

1. This Convention may be denounced by a State Party at any time after one year from the date on which the Convention entered into force for that Party.

2. Denunciation shall be effected by the deposit of an instrument with the Secretary-General.

3. Denunciation shall take effect on the first day of the month following the expiration of one year after the date of deposit of the instrument, or after such longer period as may be specified in the instrument.

Article 20: Revision and Amendment

1. A Conference for the purpose of revising or amending this Convention may be convened by the Organisation.

2. The Organisation shall convene a Conference of the States Parties to this Convention for revising or amending it at the request of not less than one-third of the Parties.

3. After the date of the entry into force of an amendment to this Convention, any instrument of ratification, acceptance, approval or accession deposited shall be deemed to apply to the Convention as amended, unless a contrary intention is expressed in the instrument.

Article 21: Revision of the limitation amount and of Unit of Account or Monetary Unit

1. Notwithstanding the provisions of Article 20 a Conference only for the purposes of altering the amounts specified in Article 6 and 7 and in Article 8 paragraph 2, or of substituting either or both of the units defined in Article 8, paragraphs 1 and 2, by other units shall be convened by the Organisation in accordance with paragraphs 2 and 3 of this Article. An alteration of the amounts shall be made only because of a significant change in their real value.

2. The Organisation shall convene such a Conference at the request of not less than one fourth of the States Parties.

3. A decision to alter the amounts or to substitute the units by other Units of Account shall be taken by a two-thirds majority of the States Parties present and voting in such Conference.

4. Any State depositing its instrument of ratification, acceptance, approval or accession to the Convention, after entry into force of an amendment, shall apply to the Convention as amended.

Article 22: Depositary

1. This Convention shall be deposited with the Secretary-General.
2. The Secretary-General Shall:

(a) transmit certified true copies of this Convention to all States which were invited to attend the Conference on Limitation of Liability for Maritime Claims and to any other States which accede to this Convention;

(b) inform all States which have signed or acceded to this Convention of:

(i) each new signature and each deposit of an instrument and any reservation thereto together with the date hereof;

(ii) the date of entry into force of this Convention or any amendment thereto;

(iii) any denunciation of this Convention and the date on which it takes effect;

(iv) any amendment adopted in conformity with Articles 20 or 21;

(v) any communication called for by any Article of this Convention.

3. Upon entry into force of this Convention, a certified true copy thereof shall be transmitted by the Secretary-General to the Secretariat of the United Nations for registration and publication in accordance with Article 102 of the Charter of the United Nations.

Article 23: Languages

This Convention is established in a single original in the English, French, Russian and Spanish languages, each text being equally authentic.

DONE AT LONDON this nineteenth day of November one thousand nine hundred and seventy-six.

IN WITNESS WHEREOF the undersigned being duly authorised for that purpose have signed this Convention.

Article 17: Entry into force

Article 17(1). The Convention has now been ratified by 20 States[115] and came into force internationally on 1 December 1986.

In the case of the United Kingdom, those provisions to the 1976 Convention set out in Schedule 4, Part I, to the 1979 MSA and those provisions in Schedule 4, Part II, which have effect in connection therewith and which are given the force of law in the United Kingdom by virtue of section 17 came into force on 1 December 1986 by virtue of the Merchant Shipping Act 1979 (Commencement No. 10) Order 1986 [see Appendix].

Article 17(4). This subsection provides that when the 1976 Convention regulates the relations between certain states in relation to limitation, the 1976 Convention shall replace and abrogate the 1924 and 1957 Conventions· in respect of such relations.

Article 18: Reservations

Article 18(1). This subsection allows any state to reserve the right to exclude the application of Article 2(1)(d) or (e) but does not allow it to make any other reservation in relation to the "substantive provisions" of the 1976 Convention. The United Kingdom has made a reservation in respect of Article 2(1) (d) but not in respect of Article 2(1) (e).[116]

---

115. These are identified in Appendix IX.
116. See pages 21–23, above.

CHAPTER 4

LIMITATION: PASSENGER CLAIMS

THE PASSENGER CONTRACT: GENERAL PRINCIPLES

In most jurisdictions ordinary principles of the law of contract apply to a contract for the carriage of passengers by sea. Of particular importance in the United Kingdom are the common law principles dealing with the efficacy of contractual exclusion and limitation clauses. This is because tickets issued for passenger carriage invariably contain terms which attempt to exclude or limit the liability of the carrier. A passenger ticket is an unsigned contract document and the general common law principle is that any term which appears on the ticket will only form part of the contract if reasonable steps were taken to bring it to the attention of the passenger before or at the time the contract was entered into. This involves a consideration of a number of factors including the nature of the term and the steps taken to bring it to the attention of the other party at the time the contract was entered into.

In the United Kingdom, quite apart from the common law principles, as from 1 February 1978 any term attempting to exclude or limit liability must satisfy the terms of the Unfair Contract Terms Act 1977. The Act renders certain exclusion clauses absolutely void whereas others are only valid to the extent that they meet the reasonableness test.

THE ATHENS CONVENTION 1974[1]

This Convention, to which the United Kingdom is a party[2] came into force internationally on 28 April 1987. It has the force of law in the United Kingdom by virtue of section 14 of the Merchant Shipping Act 1979 and is annexed as Schedule 3 to that Act. Part I of Schedule 3 sets out the text of the Convention and Part II contains certain special provisions which have effect in connection with the Convention in the United Kingdom.

Section 14 of the Merchant Shipping Act 1979 did not come into force until 30 April 1987.[3] Prior to that date, in the exercise of its powers under section 16 of the 1979 Merchant Shipping Act, the United Kingdom, by S.I. 1980 No. 1092, gave the Convention the force of law in the United Kingdom as from 1 January 1981 until such time as it was possible to bring the Convention into force under section 14. Further, by S.I. 1980 No. 1125,[3a] in relation to any contract of carriage to which S.I. 1980 No. 1092 applied, a carrier was required to give notice to passengers of the application of the Convention and of some of its salient provisions.[4] Failure to comply with this requirement rendered the carrier guilty of an offence and liable on summary conviction to a fine. This penal provision is now embodied in S.I. 1987 No. 703[4a] which came into force on 30 April 1987. In *The "Lion"*[5] it was held that the shipowners were entitled to rely on the provisions of the Athens Convention notwithstanding the fact that they had failed to give notice as required by the provisions of S.I. 1980 No. 1125.

Article 1: Definitions

In this Convention the following expressions have the meaning hereby assigned to them:

1. The full title of the Convention is: Convention relating to the Carriage of Passengers and their Luggage by Sea.
2. Other states which have adopted the Convention are listed in Appendix IX.
3. Merchant Shipping Act 1979 (Commencement No. 11) Order 1987 (S.I. No. 635).
3a. Carriage of Passengers and their Luggage by Sea (Interim Provisions) (Notice) Order 1980.
4. Notice is normally given in the terms and conditions printed on the ticket.
4a. Carriage of Passengers and their Luggage by Sea (Notice) Order 1987.
5. [1990] 2 Lloyd's Rep. 144.

1.(a) "carrier" means a person by or on behalf of whom a contract of carriage has been concluded, whether the carriage is actually performed by him or by a performing carrier;

(b) "performing carrier" means a person other than the carrier, being the owner, charterer or operator of a ship, who actually performs the whole or part of the carriage;

2. "contract of carriage" means a contract made by or on behalf of a carrier for the carriage by sea of a passenger or of a passenger and his luggage, as the case may be;

3. "ship" means only a seagoing vessel, excluding an aircushion vehicle;

4. "passenger" means any person carried in a ship.
   (a) under a contract of carriage, or
   (b) who, with the consent of the carrier, is accompanying a vehicle or live animals which are covered by a contract for the carriage of goods not governed by this Convention;

5. "luggage" means any article or vehicle carried by the carrier under a contract of carriage, excluding:
   (a) articles and vehicles carried under a charter party, bill of lading or other contract primarily concerned with the carriage of goods, and
   (b) live animals;

6. "cabin luggage" means luggage which the passenger has in his cabin or is otherwise in his possession, custody or control. Except for the application of paragraph 8 of this Article and Article 8, cabin luggage includes luggage which the passenger has in or on his vehicle;

7. "loss of or damage to luggage" includes pecuniary loss resulting from the luggage not having been re-delivered to the passenger within a reasonable time after the arrival of the ship on which the luggage has been or should have been carried, but does not include delays resulting from labour disputes;

8. "carriage" covers the following periods:
   (a) with regard to the passenger and his cabin luggage, the period during which the passenger and/or his cabin luggage are on board the ship or in the course of embarkation or disembarkation, and the period during which the passenger and his cabin luggage are transported by water from land to the ship or vice-versa, if the cost of such transport is included in the fare or if the vessel used for the purpose of auxiliary transport has been put at the disposal of the passenger by the carrier. However, with regard to the passenger, carriage does not include the period during which he is in a marine terminal or station or on a quay or in or on any other port installation;
   (b) with regard to cabin luggage, also the period during which the passenger is in a marine terminal or station or on a quay or in or on any other port installation if that luggage has been taken over by the carrier or his servant or agent and has not been re-delivered to the passenger;

(c) with regard to other luggage which is not cabin luggage, the period from the time of its taking over by the carrier or his servant or agent onshore or on board until the time of its re-delivery by the carrier or his servant or agent;

9. "international carriage" means any carriage in which, according to the contract of carriage, the place of departure and the place of destination are situated in two different States, or in a single State if, according to the contract of carriage or the scheduled itinerary, there is an intermediate port of call in another State;

(a) Carrier/performing carrier

The Convention places liability on the carrier and the performing carrier. Carrier is defined as "a person by or on behalf of whom a contract of carriage has been concluded, whether the carriage is actually performed by him or by a performing carrier". This wide definition of carrier will include tour operators, ferry companies and cruise companies. A performing carrier is defined as "a person other than the carrier, being the owner, charterer or operator of a ship, who actually performs the whole or part of the carriage. It follows that if a ship owned by A has been chartered to B who issues his own passenger ticket, B is the carrier and A is the performing carrier.

During the performing carrier's sector of the voyage, the carrier will remain liable for the acts or omissions of the performing carrier and his servants and agents. The performing carrier himself will be liable jointly and severally with the carrier and may seek to rely upon the terms of the Convention.[6] The fact that there is joint and several liability is an advantage to the claimant.

Where a sub-contractor to the carrier does not come within the definition of "performing carrier", a claimant's right of recourse will be restricted to his rights against the carrier who will be liable for the acts of the sub-contractor but may have a right over against the sub-contractor.

(b) Contract of carriage

Where the carriage does not take place under a contract, or where it is gratuitous, the provisions of the Convention will not

6. See Article 4.

apply and the carrier will not have the benefits of the limits of liability provided in the Convention. However, provided that he is a person entitled to limit his liability in accordance with Article 1 of the 1976 Limitation Convention, his right to rely upon the global limit under that Convention would be retained.

Paragraph 9 of Part II of Schedule 3[7] provides that in any contract for the carriage of passengers to which the law of the United Kingdom applies, "any reference in the Convention to a Contract of Carriage excludes a contract of carriage which is not for reward". A similar provision was contained in the United Kingdom's interim provisions contained in S.I. 1980 No. 1092. It is not clear how these words should be interpreted. Do they signify that the "reward" must substantially reflect the costs incurred by the carrier in carrying the passenger? This might have been relevant to one class of passengers on board the "*Herald of Free Enterprise*" who had "purchased" tickets through the Sun newspaper for a nominal fare of £1. But for the special wording of S.I. 1980 No. 1092 (and paragraph 9 of Part II of Schedule 3), that would normally have presented no difficulty since, under English contract law, consideration must be sufficient, though it need not be adequate. The point was never tested before the courts.

(c) Ship

The Convention only applies if the carriage is performed on a sea-going vessel.[8] In giving effect to the 1976 Convention in the United Kingdom, it is provided in Schedule 4, Part II, paragraph 2,[9] that the right to limit shall apply in relation to "any ship whether seagoing or not". No such amendment applies in relation to the Athens Convention which, therefore, only applies to sea-going vessels. It is suggested that this inconsistency between the application of the Athens Convention and the 1976 Convention in the United Kingdom results from a legislative error. This error has the unfortunate result that

7. See Appendix III.
8. See consideration of the meaning of "sea-going" in the context of the 1976 Convention, page 11.
9. See Appendix IV.

where, as in the case of the 1989 *Marchioness* Thames disaster, a pleasure-craft is involved, the Athens Convention will not apply because the vessel concerned is not "sea-going". On the other hand, because of the amendment to the 1976 Limitation Convention as it operates in the United Kingdom, the passenger limitation provisions of the 1976 Convention will apply to such an incident. The fund available under the 1976 Convention is a global fund calculated by reference to the number of passengers which the vessel is licensed to carry. The availability of a global fund may in practice be of advantage to claimants.

Aircushion vehicles are excluded from the Convention.[10]

(d) Passenger

A passenger is defined as any person carried on a ship either under a contract of carriage or one who is with the consent of the carrier accompanying a vehicle or live animals which are carried under a contract for the carriage of goods not covered by the Convention. This would, for example, cover drivers accompanying commercial vehicles.

Some practical problems may arise from this definition. For example, in the case of the *Marchioness* disaster of August 1989, the boat had been hired by an individual for the purpose of celebrating his birthday. None of those whom he invited to attend the party had purchased or been issued with tickets and it must be a matter of debate whether they were strictly speaking passengers within the definition of the Convention. It may, however, be sufficient that the individual who hires the boat has entered into a contract for the carriage of his guests. This point was never tested.

(e) Luggage/cabin luggage

Luggage is any article or vehicle carried under a contract of passenger carriage but excludes articles or vehicles carried

---

10. For special provisions relating to the limitation of liability for claims arising from the operation of aircushion vehicles, see page 80.

under a charterparty or bill of lading and also excludes live animals.

Cabin luggage on the other hand, means the passenger's personal effects in his cabin, in his vehicle or in his personal possession. The distinction between luggage and cabin luggage is relevant in the context of limitation of liability under Article 8 of the Athens Convention. The distinction between luggage and cabin luggage is also relevant in the context of the period of time during which the carrier is responsible for loss or damage (See definition of carriage, below.)

(f) Loss of or damage to luggage

The introduction of the word "pecuniary" in this definition may have the effect of extending the carrier's liability to pay damages which would otherwise be regarded as too remote. If, for example, the passenger's luggage contains vital documents the loss of which prevents the passenger concluding a beneficial deal, it is arguable that the pecuniary loss which he suffers thereby is recoverable. However, it is the authors' view that questions of remoteness will continue to be governed by the domestic law of the country in which the claim is pursued and if such a loss is too remote, the wording of the Convention alone would not make the loss recoverable. In the event, the luggage limitation figures are so small that in practice the distinction will be unimportant.

(g) Carriage

In respect of a passenger and his cabin luggage, the period of the carrier's liability runs from embarkation to disembarkation including any periods of transport by water from land to the ship or *vice-versa*, if either the cost of such transport is included in the fare or if the vessel used for such transport has been put at the disposal of the passenger by the carrier. However, although luggage is covered from the moment the carrier has taken charge of it (normally at the terminal/quay), the Convention does not apply whilst the passenger himself is in a marine terminal or station or on a quay or other port installation.

(h) International carriage

International carriage is carriage where, according to the terms of the contract of carriage, the places of departure and of destination are in two different states, or in the same state if there is an intermediate port of call in another state. However, in the United Kingdom, in order to maintain the position which existed under the interim provisions of S.I. 1980 No. 1092, the Carriage of Passengers and their Luggage by Sea (Domestic Carriage) Order, 1987[11] (which came into effect on 30 April 1987), provides that the Athens Convention shall continue to apply to contracts for the carriage of passengers where the places of departure and destination are within the United Kingdom, Channel Islands and the Isle of Man and under which there is no intermediate port of call outside that area.[12]

Article 2: Application

1. This Convention shall apply to any international carriage if:
   (a) the ship is flying the flag of or is registered in a State Party to this Convention, or
   (b) the contract of carriage has been made in a State Party to this Convention, or
   (c) the place of departure or destination, according to the contract of carriage, is in a State Party to this Convention.
2. Notwithstanding paragraph 1 of this Article, this Convention shall not apply when the carriage is subject, under any other international convention concerning the carriage of passengers or luggage by another mode of transport, to a civil liability regime under the provisions of such convention, in so far as those provisions have mandatory application to carriage by sea.

Comment

Having defined "International Carriage" in Article 1 (9), Article 2 defines the circumstances in which the Convention will apply provided the carriage is international as defined. Thus, if a carrying vessel is registered in or flies the flag of a Convention country, the Convention will apply, and likewise it

11. S.I. 1987 No. 670
12. It is not clear whether, if a passenger misses his ship and then joins her in another port situated in a country which is not a State Party, the Convention still applies because the port of departure/destination as stated in the ticket is in a State Party.

will apply if the contract of carriage in question is made within a Convention country or the place of departure or destination named in that contract of carriage is within a Convention country.

Article 2 (2) deals with a situation where the contract of carriage may be subject to other Conventions which are mandatorily applicable.

Article 3: Liability of the carrier

1. The carrier shall be liable for the damage suffered as a result of the death of or personal injury to a passenger and the loss of or damage to luggage if the incident which caused the damage so suffered occurred in the course of the carriage and was due to the fault or neglect of the carrier or of his servants or agents acting within the scope of their employment.

2. The burden of proving that the incident which caused the loss or damage occurred in the course of the carriage, and the extent of the loss or damage, shall lie with the claimant.

3. Fault or neglect of the carrier or of his servants or agents acting within the scope of their employment shall be presumed, unless the contrary is proved, if the death of or personal injury to the passenger or the loss of or damage to cabin luggage arose from or in connection with the shipwreck, collision, stranding, explosion or fire, or defect in the ship. In respect of loss of or damage to other luggage, such fault or neglect shall be presumed, unless the contrary is proved, irrespective of the nature of the incident which caused the loss or damage. In all other cases the burden of proving fault or neglect shall lie with the claimant.

Article 4: Performing carrier

1. If the performance of the carriage or part thereof has been entrusted to a performing carrier, the carrier shall nevertheless remain liable for the entire carriage according to the provisions of this Convention. In addition, the performing carrier shall be subject and entitled to the provisions of this Convention for the part of the carriage performed by him.

2. The carrier shall, in relation to the carriage performed by the performing carrier, be liable for the acts and omissions of the performing carrier and of his servants and agents acting within the scope of their employment.

3. Any special agreement under which the carrier assumes obligations not imposed by this Convention or any waiver of rights conferred by this Convention shall affect the performing carrier only if agreed by him expressly and in writing.

4. Where and to the extent that both the carrier and the performing carrier are liable, their liability shall be joint and several.

5. Nothing in this Article shall prejudice any right of recourse as between the carrier and the performing carrier.

Article 5: Valuables

The carrier shall not be liable for the loss of or damage to monies, negotiable securities, gold, silverware, jewellery, ornaments, works of art, or other valuables, except where such valuables have been deposited with the carrier for the agreed purpose of safe-keeping in which case the carrier shall be liable up to the limit provided for in paragraph 3 of Article 8 unless a higher limit is agreed upon in accordance with paragraph 1 of Article 10.

Article 6: Contributory fault

If the carrier proves that the death of or personal injury to a passenger or the loss of or damage to his luggage was caused or contributed to by the fault or neglect of the passenger, the court seized of the case may exonerate the carrier wholly or partly from his liability in accordance with the provisions of the law of that court.

Articles 3–6

The basis of liability under the Convention is set out in Articles 3–6.

Article 3 defines the basis of the carrier's liability, but does not restrict the right of recovery to passengers. Claims may be pursued by any person "for damage suffered as a result of a passenger's death, personal injury or the loss or damage to luggage". This wording appears to open the door to third-party claims for consequential loss and as Article 3 states that the carrier "shall be liable" this liability may not depend on whether the domestic law of the country in which the claim is pursued would recognise such a claim.

Article 3 (1) also provides that in the case of death or personal injury to a passenger and loss or damage to luggage, the carrier shall be liable if the incident was "due to the fault or neglect" of the carrier or his servant or agent acting within the scope of their employment. The burden is on the claimant to prove:

(i) that the incident occurred in the course of the carriage;

(ii) that it was due to the fault or neglect of the carrier or of his servants or agents acting within the scope of their employment, and,

(iii) the extent of the loss or damage.

However, where death or personal injury or loss or damage to
cabin luggage arises from or in connection with a shipwreck,
collision, stranding, explosion, fire or from a defect in the ship,
then fault or neglect on the part of the carrier is presumed
"unless the contrary is proved". In other words the burden is
upon the carrier to prove that there was no fault or neglect on
his part or on the part of those for whom he is responsible.

"Shipwreck, collision, stranding, explosion and fire" are
dramatic and easily recognised events all of which would trig-
ger a presumption of fault on the part of the carrier under
Article 3 (3). However, "a defect in the ship" is less easily
recognised. Physical faults which make the ship unseaworthy
would presumably qualify but inadequate manning or maintenance would probably not unless they cause physical defects in
the ship.

As regards loss or damage to "other luggage" (as opposed to
"cabin luggage"), fault or neglect is presumed in all cases
unless the contrary is proved.

Where the carrier can prove the death or personal injury or
loss of or damage to luggage was caused or contributed to by
the passenger, then the court may relieve the carrier wholly or
partly from his liability in accordance with the provisions of the
law of that court.[13]

Whereas the carrier is liable throughout the carriage, the
performing carrier is liable for incidents occurring during "the
part of the carriage performed by him". Where both the carrier
and the performing carrier are liable for the same occurrence,
their liability is joint and several. The carrier is liable for the
acts and omissions of his own servants and agents and for the
acts of the servants and agents of the performing carrier. However, strangely, there is no express provision which states that
the performing carrier is responsible for the acts and omissions
of his own servants and agents, but this surely must have been
intended. Support for this proposition may possibly be found
in the last sentence to Article 4(1), but, arguably, the words
used are not sufficiently precise.

Article 5 provides that the carrier is not liable for the loss of

13. Schedule 3, Part II, para. 3, provides that in the context of Article 6 in
the United Kingdom, the law in relation to contributory negligence is to be
found in the Law Reform (Contributory Negligence) Act 1945.

or damage to monies, negotiable securities, gold, silverware, jewellery and other valuables unless they were deposited with the carrier for the agreed purpose of safekeeping, in which case, unless a higher limit is agreed, the carrier shall not be liable beyond the limits stated in Article 8 of the Convention.

Article 7: Limit of liability for personal injury

1. The liability of the carrier for the death of or personal injury to a passenger shall in no case exceed 700,000 francs per carriage. Where in accordance with the law of the court seized of the case damages are awarded in the form of periodical income payments, the equivalent capital value of those payments shall not exceed the said limit.

2. Notwithstanding paragraph 1 of this Article, the national law of any State Party to this Convention may fix, as far as carriers who are nationals of such State are concerned, a higher *per capita* limit of liability.

Article 8: Limit of liability for loss of or damage to luggage

1. The liability of the carrier for the loss of or damage to cabin luggage shall in no case exceed 12,500 francs per passenger, per carriage.

2. The liability of the carrier for the loss of or damage to vehicles including all luggage carried in or on the vehicle shall in no case exceed 50,000 francs per vehicle, per carriage.

3. The liability of the carrier for the loss of or damage to luggage other than that mentioned in paragraphs 1 and 2 of this Article shall in no case exceed 18,000 francs per passenger, per carriage.

4. The carrier and the passenger may agree that the liability of the carrier shall be subject to a deductible not exceeding 1,750 francs in the case of damage to a vehicle and not exceeding 200 francs per passenger in the case of loss of or damage to other luggage, such sum to be deducted from the loss or damage.

Article 9: Monetary unit and conversion

1. The franc mentioned in this Convention shall be deemed to refer to a unit consisting of 65.5 milligrams of gold of millesimal fineness 900.

2. The amounts referred to in Articles 7 and 8 shall be converted into the national currency of the State of the court seized of the case on the basis of the official value of that currency, by reference to the unit defined in paragraph 1 of this Article, on the date of the judgment or the date agreed upon by the parties.

Article 10: Supplementary provisions on limits of liability

1. The carrier and the passenger may agree, expressly and in writing, to higher limits of liability than those prescribed in Articles 7 and 8.

2. Interest on damages and legal costs shall not be included in the limits of liability prescribed in Articles 7 and 8.

Articles 7–10

Articles 7 and 8 set out the maximum amounts per contract of carriage for which the carrier may be liable. In summary these are:

Death or personal injury passenger	46,666 SDR[14]
Loss/damage to cabin luggage per passenger (excluding luggage in or on a vehicle)	833 SDR
Loss/damage to a vehicle including luggage in or on it (per vehicle)	3,333 SDR
Loss/damage to other luggage per passenger	1,200 SDR

(By Article 8(4), the carrier and the passenger can agree to a deductible not exceeding 117 SDR for damage to a vehicle and 13 SDR per passenger for loss of or damage to luggage.)

The above are minimum limits and the carrier may not stipulate for any lower limits. However, if they so wish, the carrier and the passenger may agree to higher limits provided such agreement is express and in writing (Article 10). These higher limits may not be binding on the performing carrier unless "agreed by him expressly and in writing" — see Article 4 (3).

Schedule 3, Part II, paragraph 4,[15] empowers the Secretary of State to substitute different limits for those stated in Article 7(1) (in respect of death or personal injury) for a carrier whose principal place of business is in the United Kingdom. This power was exercised following the *Herald of Free Enterprise* disaster and the limit for death or personal injury was set in the United Kingdom at Fr. 1,525,000 (£80,009) with effect from 1 June 1987. This higher limit only applies to carriers whose ordinary place of business is in the UK.[16]

14. The 1976 Protocol to the Convention which came into force on 30 April 1989, states limits in SDR's as opposed to the Gold Francs used in the original text. The value of the SDR in the national currency shall be calculated at the date of judgment or at the date agreed by the parties (Article 9).

15. See Appendix III.

16. S.I. 1987 No. 855 Carriage of Passengers and their Luggage by Sea (United Kingdom Carriers) Order 1987—£80,000 is the limit applicable to the carriage of passengers by UK airlines.

At an IMO Conference held in London in March 1990, a new Protocol was approved to "enhance compensation" and "establish a simplified procedure for updating limitation amounts". When the Protocol comes into force (90 days after being ratified by ten States), the limits will be increased as follows:

Death or personal injury passenger	175,000 SDR
Loss/damage to cabin luggage per passenger (excluding luggage in or on a vehicle)	1,800 SDR
Loss/damage to a vehicle including luggage in or on it (per vehicle)	10,000 SDR
Loss/damage to other luggage per passenger	1,200 SDR

(The deductible that may be agreed between carrier and passenger will be increased to 300 SDR for damage to a vehicle and 135 SDR per passenger for loss of or damage to luggage.)

The Protocol sets out procedures to allow amendments to these limits, without having to convene a further IMO Conference: the limits can be amended by a two-thirds majority of the Contracting States. However, no limit can be increased to exceed three times the previous limit nor should it exceed the above limits increased by 6 per cent per year, calculated on a compound basis from the date the Protocol was opened for signature.

Article 11: Defences and limits for carriers' servants

If an action is brought against a servant or agent of the carrier or of the performing carrier arising out of damage covered by this Convention, such servant or agent, if he proves that he acted within the scope of his employment, shall be entitled to avail himself of the defences and limits of liability which the carrier or the performing carrier is entitled to invoke under this Convention.

Article 12: Aggregation of claims

1. Where the limits of liability prescribed in Articles 7 and 8 take effect, they shall apply to the aggregate of the amounts recoverable in all claims arising out of the death of or personal injury to any one passenger or the loss of or damage to his luggage.

2. In relation to the carriage performed by a performing carrier, the aggregate of the amounts recoverable from the carrier and the performing carrier and from their servants and agents acting within the scope of their employ-

ment shall not exceed the highest amount which could be awarded against either the carrier or the performing carrier under this Convention, but none of the persons mentioned shall be liable for a sum in excess of the limit applicable to him.

3. In any case where a servant or agent of the carrier or of the performing carrier is entitled under Article 11 of this Convention to avail himself of the limits of liability prescribed in Articles 7 and 8, the aggregate of the amounts recoverable from the carrier, or the performing carrier as the case may be, and from that servant or agent, shall not exceed those limits.

Articles 11 and 12

Article 11 provides that the servant or agent of the carrier or of the performing carrier can limit his liability for death of or personal injury to a passenger, or for loss of or damage to luggage or vehicles incurred whilst acting within the scope of his employment. Articles 7 and 8 make it clear that the carrier can limit his liability under the Convention. Strangely there is no express provision to the effect that the performing carrier can limit his liability. However, the provisions of Article 12 (2) and (3) clearly indicate that the performing carrier has that right.

For comments generally on the subject of aggregation of claims, see commentary on Article 9 of the 1976 Convention on page 58.

Article 13: Loss of right to limit liability

1. The carrier shall not be entitled to the benefit of the limits of liability prescribed in Articles 7 and 8 and paragraph 1 of Article 10, if it is proved that the damage resulted from an act or omission of the carrier done with the intent to cause such damage, or recklessly and with knowledge that such damage would probably result.

2. The servant or agent of the carrier or of the performing carrier shall not be entitled to the benefit of those limits if it is proved that the damage resulted from an act or omission of that servant or agent done with the intent to cause such damage, or recklessly and with knowledge that such damage would probably result.

Article 14: Basis for claims

No action for damages for the death of or personal injury to a passenger, or for the loss of or damage to luggage, shall be brought against a carrier or performing carrier otherwise than in accordance with this Convention.

Articles 13 and 14

The wording of Article 13 is similar to that of other Conventions and a general discussion of the similarities and differences between the Conventions can be found on pages 32–34 in Chapter 3, commenting on the 1976 Limitation Convention.

A number of points need to be made, specifically in relation to the Athens Convention;

(a) It is only the conduct of the carrier[17] himself which is relevant in determining whether or not he can limit his liability.[18] Therefore, if damage has been caused by the intentional or reckless act of a servant or agent of the carrier (unless that servant is the *alter ego* of the carrier), but without similar conduct on the part of the carrier himself, the carrier is entitled to limit. If a servant or agent[19] of the carrier or performing carrier, seeks to limit his liability under the Convention, he will similarly lose such right if personally guilty of intentional or reckless conduct.

(b) Article 13 appears to provide that the carrier shall lose the right to limit only if "damage" results from his conduct. It does not expressly provide that the right to limit will also be lost if the claim is for "loss" or injury to the person. However, Article 13 makes it clear that the rights to limit which will be lost are those contained in Articles 7, 8 and 10(1). These articles expressly refer to the liability of the carrier for the death of or personal injury to a passenger[20] and for "loss of or damage to luggage and/or vehicles".[21] Therefore it is unlikely that this provision will be construed as referring merely to physical damage.[22]

17. N.B. there is no express reference to the performing carrier.
18. *The "Lion"* [1990] 2 Lloyd's Rep. 144. A similar construction applies to the Hague–Visby Rules. *The "European Enterprise"* [1989] 2 Lloyd's Rep. 185.
19. The right is available whether he is an independent contractor, *contra* Article IV *bis* Rule 2 of the Hague–Visby Rules.
20. Article 7(1).
21. Article 8.
22. The position may be different under the Hague–Visby Rules, see pages 128–129.

(c) Like Article 4 of the 1976 Convention and Article 8, Rule 1, of the Hamburg Rules, Article 13 provides the right to limit is lost only if the carrier intends to cause "such" damage or acts recklessly with knowledge that "such" damage will result. Therefore, it seems clear that the right to limit is lost only if the damage complained of was the kind of damage known to be the probable result of the conduct.[23]

(d) Article 13 refers to the "carrier" and the "servants or agents" of the carrier or of the performing carrier but there is no reference to the performing carrier. Does this mean that the performing carrier has an unbreakable right to limit liability? This cannot have been the intention.

Article 14 provides that no claim for damages for death or personal injury to a passenger or for loss or damage to luggage may be brought against the carrier or performing carrier otherwise than in accordance with the Athens Convention. The effect of this Article is to ensure that no passenger can opt to pursue his claim under any other Convention which may apply (such as the 1976 Convention) or otherwise.[24]

Article 15: Notice of loss or damage to luggage

1. The passenger shall give written notice to the carrier or his agent:
   (a) in the case of apparent damage to luggage:
      (i) for cabin luggage, before or at the time of disembarkation of the passenger;
      (ii) for all other luggage, before or at the time of its re-delivery;
   (b) in the case of damage to luggage which is not apparent, or loss of luggage, within fifteen days from the date of disembarkation or re-delivery or from the time when such re-delivery should have taken place.
2. If the passenger fails to comply with this Article, he shall be presumed, unless the contrary is proved, to have received the luggage undamaged.
3. The notice in writing need not be given if the condition of the luggage has at the time of its receipt been the subject of joint survey or inspection.

23. See pages 37–38 and 129–130.
24. See commentary on pages 53–56, and also see commentary on Article 19, below.

Article 16: Time-bar for actions

1. Any action for damages arising out of the death of or personal injury to a passenger or for the loss of or damage to luggage shall be time-barred after a period of two years.

2. The limitation period shall be calculated as follows:

    (a) in the case of personal injury, from the date of disembarkation of the passenger;

    (b) in the case of death occurring during carriage, from the date when the passenger should have disembarked, and in the case of personal injury occurring during carriage and resulting in the death of the passenger after disembarkation, from the date of death, provided that this period shall not exceed three years from the date of disembarkation;

    (c) in the case of loss of or damage to luggage, from the date of disembarkation or from the date when disembarkation should have taken place, whichever is later.

3. The law of the court seized of the case shall govern the grounds of suspension and interruption of limitation periods, but in no case shall an action under this Convention be brought after the expiration of a period of three years from the date of disembarkation of the passenger or from the date when disembarkation should have taken place, whichever is later.

4. Notwithstanding paragraphs 1, 2 and 3 of this Article, the period of limitation may be extended by a declaration of the carrier or by agreement of the parties after the cause of action has arisen. The declaration or agreement shall be in writing.

Articles 15 and 16

It should be noted that in respect of damage to luggage, Article 15 provides that unless written notice of damage is given to the carrier or his agent within specified periods of time, then it is presumed, unless the contrary is proved, that the passenger received the luggage undamaged.

Article 16 provides that any action for damages for personal injury or for loss or damage to luggage must be brought within a period of two years. In the case of personal injury, the period starts to run from the date of disembarkation of the passenger. In the case of death occurring during the carriage, the period runs from the date the passenger should have disembarked. But, where death occurs subsequently as a result of injuries occurring during the carriage, then the period shall not exceed three years from the date of disembarkation.

In the case of loss or damage to luggage, the period runs

from the date of disembarkation or when disembarkation should have taken place.

Article 17: Competent jurisdiction

1. An action arising under this Convention shall, at the option of the claimant, be brought before one of the courts listed below, provided that the court is located in a State Party to this Convention:

    (a) the court of the place of permanent residence or principal place of business of the defendant, or

    (b) the court of the place of departure or that of the destination according to the contract of carriage, or

    (c) a court of the State of the domicile or permanent residence of the claimant, if the defendant has a place of business and is subject to jurisdiction in that State, or

    (d) a court of the State where the contract of carriage was made, if the defendant has a place of business and is subject to jurisdiction in that State.

2. After the occurrence of the incident which has caused the damage, the parties may agree that the claim for damages shall be submitted to any jurisdiction or to arbitration.

Article 17

Article 17 gives the claimant four alternative places in which to bring his claim "provided that the court is located in a State Party to this Convention"[25]:

    (a) the court of the place of permanent residence or principal place of business of the defendant; or

    (b) the court of the place of departure or destination according to the contract of carriage; or

    (c) a court of the domicile or permanent residence of the claimant provided that the defendant has a place of business and is subject to jurisdiction in that state; or

    (d) a court of the State where the contract of carriage is made, also provided that the defendant has a place of business and is subject to jurisdiction in that state.

Article 18: Invalidity of contractual provisions

Any contractual provision concluded before the occurrence of the incident which has caused the death of or personal injury to a passenger or the

---

25. This condition is omitted under the law of the United Kingdom S.I. 1987 No. 670.

loss of or damage to his luggage, purporting to relieve the carrier of his liability towards the passenger or to prescribe a lower limit of liability than that fixed in this Convention except as provided in paragraph 4 of Article 8, and any such provision purporting to shift the burden of proof which rests on the carrier, or having the effect of restricting the option specified in paragraph 1 of Article 17, shall be null and void, but the nullity of that provision shall not render void the contract of carriage which shall remain subject to the provisions of this Convention.

Article 18

Article 18 renders null and void any provision which attempts either to exclude the liability of the carrier, to prescribe for a lower limit than that provided in the Convention, to shift the burden of proof or to limit the options of jurisdiction as set out in Article 17.

Article 19: Other conventions on limitation of liability

This Convention shall not modify the rights or duties of the carrier, the performing carrier, and their servants or agents provided for in international conventions relating to the limitation of liability of owners of seagoing ships.

Article 19

Article 19 preserves the right of the servants or agents of the carrier or the performing carrier to limit their liability under other "international conventions relating to the limitation of liability" such as the 1976 Convention. However, to avail themselves of this right, the servant or agent must be the "owner, charterer, manager or operator of the ship or someone for whose acts such person is responsible within the meaning of Article 1 of the 1976 Convention".

In the context of the 1976 Convention, claims "for the death of or personal injury to a passenger" are subject to the right of limitation under Article 7 of that Convention. (It should be noted that if the person killed or injured is not a "passenger" as defined in Article 1(4) of the Athens Convention and Article 7(2) of the 1976 Convention, then no claim arises under the Athens Convention and the carrier's right to limit arises, if at all, under Article 6(1) rather than under Article 7 of the 1976 Convention.)

Where claims for loss of life or personal injury are presented by "passengers" as defined by Article 1(4) of the Athens Convention and Article 7(2) of the 1976 Convention, it is suggested that because of the terms of Article 14 of the Athens Convention, claims on behalf of such passengers must be presented in accordance with the Athens Convention. If, however, the total liability of the carrier to all claimants under the provisions of the Athens Convention exceeds the global limitation fund calculated in accordance with the 1976 Convention, then all claims will further abate *pro rata*.

Article 20: Nuclear damage

No liability shall arise under this Convention for damage caused by a nuclear incident:

    (a) if the operator of a nuclear installation is liable for such damage under either the Paris Convention of 29 July 1960 on Third Party Liability in the Field of Nuclear Energy as amended by its Additional Protocol of 28 January 1964, or the Vienna Convention of 21 May 1963 on Civil Liability for Nuclear Damage, or

    (b) if the operator of a nuclear installation is liable for such damage by virtue of a national law governing the liability for such damage, provided that such law is in all respects as favourable to persons who may suffer damage as either the Paris or the Vienna Conventions.

Article 21: Commercial carriage by public authorities

This Convention shall apply to commercial carriage undertaken by States or Public Authorities under contracts of carriage within the meaning of Article 1.

CHAPTER 5

LIMITATION: CARRIAGE OF GOODS

HISTORY

The law relating to the carriage of goods by sea has developed over many centuries predominantly by way of precedent established by individual cases. However, the benefit of international uniformity by codification has been appreciated for some considerable time. Therefore in 1921 the shipping community met at the Hague and a body of rules known as the "Hague Rules" was formulated. The Rules were quickly adopted into the municipal legislation of a large number of countries[1] and have been widely used ever since. The Hague Rules are in effect a collection of rules which define the rights and liabilities of the two parties concerned in an agreement to carry goods by sea, namely, the carrier and the cargo interest, including the right of the carrier to limit his liability to cargo claims.

By the 1960s it was felt that the Hague Rules were becoming anachronistic and were not totally suited to certain new trends which had developed since their formulation. For example, it was considered that the Hague Rules did not give sufficient assistance where problems arose in the container trade or indeed in the bulk cargo trade.

In the circumstances, the shipping community gathered this time at Visby in Sweden and produced the Hague–Visby Rules in 1968. Once again, these Rules have been adopted relatively quickly into the municipal legislation of a number of states.[2]

1. The Hague Rules were incorporated into the domestic legislation of the United Kingdom by the Carriage of Goods by Sea Act 1924, now repealed.
2. The Hague–Visby Rules have been incorporated into the domestic legislation of the United Kingdom by the Carriage of Goods by Sea Act 1971.

However, there existed at the time a strong ground swell of opinion to the effect that a more radical revision was necessary. Some countries considered that the balance of risk between ship and cargo in the Hague Rules and Hague–Visby Rules was weighted far too much in the favour of the carrier and that the balance should be shifted in favour of the cargo interest.

This ground swell of opinion resulted in a further meeting of the shipping community being arranged in Hamburg in 1978. This meeting produced the United Nations Convention on the Carriage of Goods By Sea 1978 ("the Hamburg Rules"). The Convention will come into force one year after 20 countries have ratified them or acceded to them.[3]

Under the Hague and Hague–Visby Rules the carrier is subject to defined obligations,[4] and has defined rights,[5] including the right of limitation of liability.[6] However, under the Hamburg Rules, there are no expressly defined rights and liabilities as such. The carrier is liable for loss of or damage to the goods and for delay unless he proves that he and his servants took all measures that could reasonably be required to avoid the occurrence and its consequences.[7] However, if he is liable, the carrier is entitled to limit his liability.[8]

RELATIONSHIP BETWEEN THE HAGUE, HAGUE–VISBY AND HAMBURG RULES AND THE 1976 LIMITATION CONVENTION

There are two separate but interlinked methods of limitation which may be available to the carrier of goods by sea;

(i) The "package" limitation in Article IV, Rule 5, of the Hague Rules and the Hague–Visby and Article 6 of the

---

3. Zambia has become the 20th country to ratify the Rules and they will come into force on 1 November 1992. In the meantime the Hamburg Rules have already been adopted into the municipal legislation of Chile and applies to carriage to or from Chile.
4. See Article III.
5. See Article IV.
6. See Article IV, Rule 5.
7. See Article 5(1).
8. See Articles 6–8.

Hamburg Rules. (This right of limitation is restricted to claims for loss or damage incurred in connection with the goods which are being carried and the limit is calculated with reference to particulars of the cargo.)

(ii) The so called "tonnage" limitation available to the carrier under any statute "relating to the limitation of liability of owners of seagoing ships".[9] Notwithstanding the fact that different countries use different bases for calculating the limit, this form of limitation is applied to claims arising not only in connection with the carriage of goods but also to the many other forms of claim which may arise out of a maritime occurrence, for example, hull and property damage and personal injury. There is no separate limitation fund for cargo claimants. Their claims rank *pari passu* with other claims arising out of the same occurrence (other than claims for loss of life or personal injury which are subject to a separate fund).[10]

Provided (a) that the carrier of goods is not guilty of conduct which debars his right to limit under the relevant Rules and/or the "tonnage" limitation statute and (b) that the claim in respect of which he wishes to limit is one which is subject to limitation under the relevant "tonnage" limitation statute,[11] there is nothing to prevent such carrier from relying on rights given by the Rules to limit his liability to the particular claim and then to the relevant "tonnage" statute to limit his liability to a sum which is lower than the "package" limitation available to him under the Hague or Hague–Visby or Hamburg Rules. Such right is expressly reserved to the carrier by Article

9. The use of the phrase "tonnage limitation" is a useful means of distinguishing this form of limitation from the "package" method of limitation. However, it should be appreciated that whilst in those countries which give effect to the 1957 Brussels Convention or the 1976 London Convention this form of limitation is calculated with reference to the tonnage of the vessel in question, in other countries such as the United States, this form of limitation is calculated by reference to the value of the ship and any freight to be paid on completion of the voyage.

10. See pages 48–49 relating to the 1976 Convention.

11. In most cases such claims will fall within Article 2(1)(a) of the 1976 Convention.

VIII of the Hague and Hague–Visby Rules[12] and Article 25 (1) of the Hamburg Rules.

Example

Cargo is carried on ship A under a contract which is subject to the Hague–Visby Rules. In a collision between ship A and ship B caused by the unseaworthiness of A, the following claims could be made against A:

1. Loss of or damage to cargo on ship A   £1,000
2. Loss of or damage to cargo on ship B   £ 900
3. Physical damage to ship B
   (after set-off of physical damage to ship A)   £1,000

Since the collision was caused by the unseaworthiness of A the owners of cargo carried on her would probably have a good cause of action against her owner as carrier for breach of Article III, Rule 1. Provided that the owner of A was not guilty of the conduct which debars his right to limit under the Hague–Visby Rules[13] he would be able to rely on the "package" limitation provisions of those Rules to restrict his liability to say, £100.[14]

However, since the owner of ship A could also expect to face other claims arising out of the same incident he could also (provided again that he is not guilty of conduct debarring his right to limit) rely on the right to limit liability under the relevant "tonnage" limitation rules. Assuming that ship A's "tonnage" limitation fund is £1,000 then even though her owner has already limited his liability to her own cargo to £100 (as against a claim for £1,000), ship A's owner will still wish to rely on the relevant "tonnage" limitation, since the total of claims 1,2 and 3 is still in excess of £1,000. The claims against the fund will therefore be:

12. For these purposes the right of a British shipowner in section 18 of the 1979 MSA to limit his liability totally in certain circumstances is treated as being a right reserved under Art. VIII of the Hague–Visby Rules—see section 6(4) of COGSA 1971 and page 25. This right is not available to a British shipowner under the Athens Convention see para. 12, Part II of Schedule 3 to the 1979 MSA.

13. See pages 127–130.

14. The actual figures would depend on the number of packages or units or the weight of the cargo see page 116.

1. Claim of cargo carried on ship A	£ 100
2. Claim of cargo carried on ship B	£ 900
3. Claim for physical damage to ship B	£1,000
Total claims against the fund	£2,000

Since each of these claims will rank *pari passu* against a fund of £1,000 it follows that the owner of the cargo carried on ship A (claim 1) can only recover 1/20 × £1,000 i.e. £50.

Therefore, by using his full rights of limitation under both the "package" and the "tonnage" limitation rules the owner of ship A has been able to limit his liability to the owners of the cargo carried on his vessel to £50 (as against a total original claim of £1,000).

Package limitation

(i) Hague Rules

In the United Kingdom and many other countries legislation giving effect to the Hague Rules has been repealed and replaced by legislation giving effect to the Hague–Visby Rules.[15] However, there are still some countries which give effect to the Hague Rules and it is common still to see the Hague Rules incorporated into charterparties by express contractual agreement in the form of a "Paramount Clause".

Article IV, Rule 5, of the Hague Rules provides that:

Neither the carrier nor the ship shall in any event[16] be or become liable for any loss or damage to or in connection with goods[17] in an amount exceeding £100[18] per package or unit[19] or the equivalent of that sum in other currency,[20] unless the nature and value of such goods have been declared by the shipper before shipment and inserted in the bill of lading.[21]

This declaration if embodied in the bill of lading shall be prima facie evidence, but shall not be binding or conclusive on the carrier.

By agreement between the carrier, Master or agent of the carrier and the

---

15. In England the Carriage of Goods by Sea Act 1924, which gave effect to the Hague Rules has been repealed and the Carriage of Goods by Sea Act 1971 now gives effect to the Hague–Visby Rules.

16. See pages 125–127.

17. See pages 134–135.

18. See page 114.

19. See pages 112–113.

20. See page 114.

21. See page 124.

shipper another maximum amount than that mentioned in this paragraph may be fixed, provided that such maximum shall not be less than the figure above named.

Neither the carrier nor the ship shall be responsible in any event for loss or damage to or in connection with goods if the nature or value thereof has been knowingly misstated by the shipper in the bill of lading.[22]

(A) "PER PACKAGE OR UNIT"

In the case of bulk cargo, it is clearly straining language to say that a bulk cargo is a "package". For example, in the English case of *Studebaker Distributors Ltd.* v. *Charlton Steam Shipping Company Ltd.*[23] Goddard J., stated that:

" 'Package' must indicate something packed. It is obvious that this clause cannot refer to all cargoes that may be shipped under the bill of lading; for instance, on a shipment of grain it could apply to grain shipped in sacks, but could not, in my opinion, possibly apply to a shipment in bulk. If the shipowners desire that it should refer to any individual piece of cargo, it would not be difficult to use, appropriate words, as for instance, 'package or unit', to use the language of the Hague Rules."

Accordingly, the debate has centred more on whether or not such a cargo or part of it can be described as a "unit". The problem is less acute in the United States where the Carriage of Goods by Sea Act 1936, section 4 (5), provides that the carrier can limit his liability to: " . . . $500 per package . . . or in case of goods not shipped in packages, per customary freight unit."

The question which has arisen in other countries which do not have such wording is whether the word "unit" means simply the physical unit received for shipment or the "freight unit" despite the absence of the word "freight". The English court, as indicated by the dictum of Goddard J. in the *Studebaker* case[24] quoted above, is likely to hold that a carrier of a bulk cargo cannot rely on any "package" limitation as the cargo is not a physical "package" or "unit" and there is no alternative "weight" limit as there is under the Hague–Visby Rules.[25]

22. See pages 124–125.
23. (1937) 59 Ll. L. Rep. 23 at page 27.
24. (1937) 59 Ll. L. Rep. 23.
25. See pages 114 and 116.

In the case of containerised or palletised cargo there would seem to be no reason in principle why the container or the pallet itself should not be considered to be a "package" or "unit". In the old case of *Whaite* v. *Lancs & Yorks Railway*[26] a railway waggon with wooden sides was held to be a "package" for the purpose of the Carriers Act 1830. Furthermore, in the case of *Standard Electrica S.A.* v. *Hamburg Sudamerikanische Dampfschiffahrts-Gesellschaft*[27] the United States court had no difficulty in finding that a pallet was a "package".

However, what happens if that container or pallet is used to contain other smaller "packages" or "units"? If the container is used to carry bulk cargo then the cases quoted above would suggest that the container itself could be the "package" or "unit" in that it does not contain smaller "packages" or "units".

However, the problem is more difficult when the container or pallet contains smaller physical units. There is not much guidance from the English court on this point and whilst there has been much debate in North American courts there would seem to be no clear answer. It is beyond the scope of this book to set out the competing arguments.[28] However, it appears that the manner in which the cargo is described in the bill of lading is "entitled to considerable weight"[29] but is not to be treated as conclusive. Therefore, a bill of lading recording the shipment of "one container said to contain 99 bales of leather" was treated as recording the shipment of 99 bales[30] whereas a bill of lading evidencing the shipment of "one container said to contain machinery" was treated as a bill of lading recording the shipment of a single "package", although in fact, it contained 350 individual cartons.[31]

---

26. (1874) L.R. 9 Ex. 67.

27. [1967] 2 Lloyd's Rep. 193.

28. For a fuller discussion see the 18th edition of *Scrutton on Charterparties* pages 441–444 and the 13th edition of Carver, *Carriage by Sea*, paras. 551–559.

29. *Standard Electrica* v. *Hamburg Sud-Amerikaniske* [1967] 2 Lloyd's Rep. 193.

30. *The "Mormaclynx"* [1971] 2 Lloyd's Rep. 276.

31. *The "Kulmerland"* [1973] 1 Lloyd's Rep. 319.

(B) "£100"

The seemingly clear reference to £100 sterling in Article IV, Rule 5, must be read in the light of Article IX which provides that: "The monetary units mentioned in these Rules are to be taken to be gold value."

The question has been asked over the years whether limitation is therefore to be £100 sterling or the value of 100 gold sovereigns (currently worth approximately £7,000 sterling) per "package or unit". However, it has now been held by the English court that the carrier is entitled to limit his liability not to £100 sterling per package or unit but to the current market value of "the gold content of 100 sovereigns of the weight and fineness specified under the Coinage Act 1870".[32]

This problem is usually avoided when the Hague–Visby Rules are incorporated into the domestic legislation of other countries since the relevant statute usually provides for a limit calculated in the currency of that country.

(ii) Hague–Visby Rules

Because of the difficulties encountered in construing the limitation provisions of the Hague Rules attempts were made to remedy such deficiencies when drafting the Hague–Visby Rules. Article IV, Rule 5, of the Hague–Visby Rules now reads as follows:

5(a) Unless the nature and value of such goods have been declared by the shipper before shipment and inserted in the bill of lading, neither the carrier nor the ship shall in any event be or become liable for any loss or damage to or in connection with the goods in an amount exceeding 666.67 units[33] of account[34] per package or unit or 2 units[35] of account per kilogramme of gross weight of the goods lost or damaged, whichever is the higher.

(b) The total amount recoverable shall be calculated by reference to the value of such goods at the place and time at which the goods are dis-

32. *The "Rosa S"* [1988] 2 Lloyd's Rep. 574.
33. See page 116.
34. For those countries who have not given effect to the Hague–Visby protocol of 1979 the relevant figures and units of account are 10,000 Poincaré francs and 30 francs respectively. A list of those countries which have adopted the 1979 protocol is set out in Appendix IX.
35. See page 116.

charged from the ship in accordance with the contract or should have been so discharged.

The value of the goods shall be fixed according to the commodity exchange price, or if there be no such price, according to the current market price, or, if there be no commodity exchange price or current market price, by reference to the normal value of goods of the same kind and quality.

(c) Where a container, pallet or similar article of transport is used to consolidate goods, the number of packages or units enumerated in the bill of lading as packed in such article of transport shall be deemed the number of packages or units for the purpose of this paragraph as far as these packages or units are concerned. Except as aforesaid such article of transport shall be considered the package or unit.[36]

(d) The unit of account mentioned in this Article is the special drawing right as defined by the International Monetary Fund.[37] The amounts mentioned in sub-paragraph (a) of this paragraph shall be converted into national currency on the basis of the value of that currency on a date to be determined by the law of the court seized of the case.[38]

(e) Neither the carrier nor the ships shall be entitled to the benefit of the limitation of liability provided for in this paragraph if it is proved that the damage resulted from an act or omission of the carrier[39] done with intent to cause damage, or recklessly and with knowledge that damage would probably result.[40]

(f) The declaration mentioned in sub-paragraph (a) of this paragraph, if embodied in the bill of lading, shall be prima facie evidence, but shall not be binding or conclusive on the carrier.

(g) By agreement between the carrier, master or agent of the carrier and the shipper other maximum amounts than those mentioned in sub-paragraph (a) of this paragraph may be fixed, provided that no maximum amount so fixed shall be less than the appropriate maximum mentioned in that sub-paragraph.

(h) Neither the carrier nor the ship shall be responsible in any event for loss or damage to, or in connection with goods if the nature or value thereof has been knowingly misstated by the shipper in the bill of lading.

The Hague–Visby Rules altered the right to limit liability set out in the Hague Rules in the following ways:

1. The sterling/gold sovereign limit is replaced by a limit expressed in terms of the Special Drawing Right (SDR)[41] the monetary value of which can be calculated each day and is

36. See pages 116–118.
37. See page 47.
38. See page 116.
39. See page 128.
40. See pages 128–130.
41. Art. IV, Rule 5(d).

reported in newspapers such as the *Financial Times* and *Lloyd's List*. The relevant date for calculation of value is the date of judgment.[42]

2. The limit per "package" or "unit" is 666.67 SDR.[43]

3. There is an alternative limitation based on weight to cater *inter alia* for bulk cargoes. This is 2 SDR per kilo of gross weight and it is the higher of the "package"/"unit" or "weight" limits which is to apply.[44] In the case of "light" cargoes it is more likely that the limitation based on the number of packages will result in a higher limit whilst the contrary is true of "heavy cargoes".

Example 1—Light cargo

1,000 packages weighing 1 kilo each

    (a) Number of packages limit = $1,000 \times 666.67$ = SDR 666.670
    (b) Weight limit = $1,000 \times 1$ kilo $\times 2$ = SDR 2,000

Example 2—Heavy cargo

3 packages weighing 1,000 kilos each

    (a) Number of packages limit = 3×666.67 = SDR 2,000.01
    (b) Weight limit = $3 \times 1,000$ kilos $\times 2$ = SDR 6,000

4. "Packages" or "units" are defined for purposes of containerised or palletised cargo. They are the number of "packages or units enumerated in the bill of lading as packed in the [container or pallet]. Except as aforesaid such [container or pallet] shall be considered the package or unit."[45]

Where the bill of lading gives the number of "packages or units" in the container or pallet without qualification no problem arises. However, in practice, the carrier of an FCL container (a container packed and sealed by the shipper before presentation to the carrier) is unlikely to agree to the inclusion of such detail without qualification since he has no means of checking the contents of the container. He may wish to utilise

42. Section 2(5) of the Merchant Shipping Act 1981.
43. Art. IV, Rule 5(a).
44. Art. IV, Rule 5(a).
45. Art. IV, Rule 5(c).

the right given to him by the proviso to Article III, Rule 3, to refuse "to state or show in the bill of lading any . . . number, quantity . . . which . . . he has had no reasonable means of checking." He may therefore wish to issue a bill which records shipment merely of "one container" in which case this will probably be the "package or unit" for the purpose of Article IV, Rule 5(c).

However, this may be unacceptable to the shipper who will require a bill of lading describing the contents of the container as one of the documents necessary for the sale of his goods. The parties will therefore often agree on a compromise by the issuance of a bill of lading recording the shipment of "one container said to contain" a number of packages or units. The question therefore arises whether the inclusion in the bill of the number of packages qualified by the words "said to contain" amounts to an "enumeration" in the bill of lading for the purposes of Article IV, Rule 5(c), since if not, the Article states that the container itself has to be "the package or unit".

The editors of the nineteenth edition of *Scrutton on Charterparties* conclude, apparently with misgivings, that such a qualified statement is a sufficient enumeration for the purposes of Article IV, Rule 5(c). However, it is also arguable that the provisions of Article IV, Rule 5(c) are intended to complement the obligations placed on the carrier by Article III, Rules 3, 4 and 5. These provisions clearly envisage an unqualified enumeration in the bill of lading of figures provided by the shippers. It has, however, been repeatedly held in this context that by addition of words such as "said to contain" or "weight unknown" the number or weight of goods inserted in the bill of lading is not even prima facie evidence of the shipment of such goods and the onus is on the cargo claimant to prove by other evidence how much cargo was shipped.[46] A bill of lading qualified in this manner is not "such a bill of lading" as will provide prima facie evidence for the purposes of Article III, Rule 4.

The Hague–Visby Rules are intended to be construed as a whole and the provisions are intended to complement each other. It would therefore be strange if a qualified enumeration which would not be binding on a carrier under Article III, Rule

---

46. *Att-Gen. of Ceylon* v. *Scindia* [1962] A.C. 60.

4, would nevertheless be binding on him for the purposes of Article IV, Rule 5(c).

Even if it is accepted that a qualified acknowledgment on the bill of the shipment of a specified number of packages in the container is not an "enumeration" for the purposes of Article IV, Rule 5(c), this does not mean that the carrier can always limit his liability merely to one "package", i.e. the container. Article IV, Rule 5(a), gives an alternative "weight" limit which is not calculated with reference to particulars recorded on the bill but with reference to the *actual weight* "of goods lost or damaged". It is the higher of the "package"/"unit" or "weight" limit which is to apply and the cargo claimant can usually produce weight certificates or other evidence to prove the weight of the goods shipped.

5. Certain misconduct on the part of the carrier can deprive him of his right to limit namely, acts or omissions done with intent to cause damage or recklessly, with knowledge that damage would probably result.[47]

6. Article IV *bis* (1) specifies that:

"The defences and limits of liability provided for in these Rules shall apply in any action against the carrier in respect of loss or damage to goods covered by a contract of carriage whether the action be founded in contract or in tort."

Under the Hague Rules it had never been universally established whether the limitation rules applied to claims in tort although, under English law, the carrier could always rely on the Hague Rules defences if the tortious claim were put forward under the contract of carriage. The purpose of this Rule was to ensure that a claimant was not placed in a better position by framing his claim in tort rather than in contract. However, the inclusion of this Rule does not mean that the carrier can always limit his liability to a tort claim. Article II of the Rules implies that the Rules apply only where there is a "contract of carriage of goods by sea by the carrier". Therefore, if a claim can and is brought against the carrier in tort other than under such a contract the Hague–Visby Rules may not apply,

47. Article IV Rule 5(e). A commentary on this provision can be found on pages 127–130 and a comparison of similar words in other Conventions including Article 4 of the 1976 Convention can be found on pages 32–39.

in which case, the carrier may not be able to rely on any "package" limitation.[48] However, as a result of the decision of the House of Lords in The "Aliakmon"[49] there would not appear to be many cases in which a claimant can now bring an action in tort outside the contract of carriage. In any event, the carrier may still be able to limit his liability under the 1976 Limitation Convention or similar legislation.[50]

7. Article IV bis, Rules 2, 3 and 4, specifies that if a claim is brought against a servant or agent (but not an independent contractor) of the carrier such servant or agent shall be entitled to avail himself of the defences and limits of liability which the carrier is entitled to invoke and the aggregate amount recoverable from the carrier, servant and agent shall not exceed the limits provided by the Rules. However, Article IV bis, Rule 4, makes it clear that if the servant or agent is guilty of intentional and reckless misconduct, whereas the carrier is not, the carrier can limit his liability but the servant or agent cannot (assuming he can be made legally liable to the claimant).

It should also be remembered that these rights benefit only a servant or agent who is not an independent contractor. The rights will probably therefore be of limited application in practice since most of the agents who are likely to be held liable, e.g. stevedores, will normally be independent contractors and not employees of the carrier. These independent contractors may nevertheless be able to limit their liability under Article 1(4) of the 1976 Convention if they are a person for whose acts the shipowner is responsible.[51]

(iii) The Hamburg Rules

The Hamburg Rules as set out in the United Nations Convention on the Carriage of Goods by Sea 1978 have now been ratified by 20 countries (Zambia being the 20th) and will come into

48. See the decision of the Court of Appeal in The "Captain Gregos" [1990] 1 Lloyd's Rep. 315.

49. [1986] 2 Lloyd's Rep. 1.

50. See the commentary on Article 2 of the 1976 Convention on pages 17–25.

51. See pages 12–13.

damage to car[...]
the decisi[...]
concern[...]

force internationally on 1 November 1992.[52] However, the Hamburg Rules have already been incorporated into the municipal legislation of Chile and apply now to claims relating to carriage of goods to or from that country.

The Hamburg Rules provide as follows:

Article 6: Limits of liability

1. (a) The liability of the carrier for loss resulting from loss of or damage to goods according to the provisions of Article 5 is limited to an amount equivalent to 835 units of account per package or other shipping unit or 2.5 units of account per kilogramme of gross weight of the goods lost or damaged whichever is the higher.
   (b) The liability of the carrier for delay in delivery according to the provisions of Article 5 is limited to an amount equivalent to two and a half times the freight payable for the goods delayed, but not exceeding the total freight payable under the contract of carriage of goods by sea.
   (c) In no case shall the aggregate liability of the carrier, under both subparagraphs (a) and (b) of this paragraph, exceed the limitation which would be established under subparagraph (a) of this paragraph for total loss of the goods with respect to which such liability was incurred.

2. For the purpose of calculating which amount is the higher in accordance with paragraph 1(a) of this Article, the following rules apply:
   (a) Where a container, pallet or similar article of transport is used to consolidate goods, the package or other shipping units enumerated in the bill of lading, if issued, or otherwise in any other document evidencing the contract of carriage by sea, as packed in such article of transport are deemed packages or shipping units. Except as aforesaid the goods in such article of transport are deemed one shipping unit.
   (b) In cases where the article of transport itself has been lost or damaged, that article of transport, if not owned or otherwise supplied by the carrier, is considered one separate shipping unit.

3. Units of account means the unit of account mentioned in Article 26.

4. By agreement between the carrier and the shipper, limits of liability exceeding those provided for in paragraph 1 may be fixed.

Article 7: Application to non-contractual claims

1. The defences and limits of liability provided for in this Convention apply in any action against the carrier in respect of loss or damage to the goods covered by the contract of carriage by sea, as well as of delay in delivery whether the action is founded in contract, in tort or otherwise.

52. The Hamburg Rules have been ratified by the countries named in Appendix IX.

2. If such an action is brought against a servant or agent of the carrier, such servant or agent, if he proves that he acted within the scope of his employment, is entitled to avail himself of the defences and limits of liability which the carrier is entitled to invoke under this Convention.

3. Except as provided in Article 8, the aggregate of the amounts recoverable from the carrier and from any persons referred to in paragraph 2 of this Article shall not exceed the limits of liability provided for in this Convention.

Article 8: Loss of right to limit liability

1. The carrier is not entitled to the benefit of the limitation of liability provided for in Article 6 if it is proved that the loss, damage or delay in delivery resulted form an act or omission of the carrier done with the intent to cause such loss, damage or delay, or recklessly and with knowledge that such loss, damage or delay would probably result.

2. Notwithstanding the provisions of paragraph 2 of Article 7, a servant or agent of the carrier is not entitled to the benefit of the limitation of liability provided for in Article 6 if it is proved that the loss, damage or delay in delivery resulted from an act or omission of such servant or agent, done with the intent to cause such loss, damage or delay, or recklessly and with knowledge that such loss, damage or delay would probably result.

The wording of the Hamburg Rules does differ (sometimes markedly) from that used in the Hague–Visby Rules. It is not within the scope of this book to enter into a detailed examination of those differences and, therefore, regard should be had to the specific provisions of the Hamburg Rules themselves when the problems arise.[53] However, the general approach to limitation adopted in the Hamburg Rules follows that adopted in the Hague–Visby Rules and the following comments adopt the numbering on pages 115–119, above, relating to the manner in which the Hague–Visby Rules amended the Hague Rules:

1. Equivalent provisions can be found in Articles 6(3) and 26.
2. The limit is 835 SDR "per package or other *shipping unit*". See Article 6(1)(a). The Hamburg Rules therefore apparently provide for the concept of a "unit" which is not merely physical and which could encompass the freight unit.

53. For a detailed discussion see the lecture of Mr. Diamond Q.C. on the Hamburg Rules given for Lloyd's of London Press on 28 September 1978. See also Christof F. Lüddeke and Andrew Johnson, *A Guide to the Hamburg Rules* (Lloyd's of London Press Ltd., 1991).

3. The limit is 2.5 SDR per kilo of the goods lost or damaged. See Article 6(1)(a).
4. Similar provisions are found in Article 6(2).
5. Similar provisions are found in Article 8.[54]
6. Similar provisions are found in Article 7(1)(i). However, Article 10 also places liability on the "actual carrier" who may not have a contractual relationship with the claimants. Therefore, "the actual carrier" may be able to rely in such circumstances on the provisions of the Rules to limit his liability to a tortious claim even though the claim against him is not brought under the contract of carriage.
7. Similar provisions are found in Article 7(2) and 7(3) and Article 8. It should be noted, however, that unlike Article IV *bis*, Rule 2, of the Hague–Visby Rules,[55] Article 7(2) gives the right of limitation to a "servant or agent" of the carrier irrespective of whether or not he is an independent contractor so long as liability arises in relation to an act done "within the scope of his employment". In determining whether the act was or was not "within the scope of his employment" the court may refer to cases on the effect of Article IV, Rule 2(q), of the Hague and Hague–Visby Rules. In *The "Chyebassa"*[56] it was held that the theft of cargo by a stevedore was an act within the duties entrusted to him whereas the theft by a stevedore of part of the ship's equipment was not.

Article 10(3) of the Hamburg Rules also gives similar right to the "actual carrier" who is defined in Article 1(2) as:

" . . . any person to whom the performance of the carriage of the goods, or of part of the carriage, has been entrusted by the Carrier, and includes any other person to whom such performance has been entrusted."

Article 10(4) specifies that where both the carrier and

54. A commentary on this provision can be found on page 130 and a comparison of similar words in other Conventions including Article 4 of the 1976 Convention can be found on pages 32–39.
55. See page 119.
56. [1966] 2 Lloyd's Rep. 193.

actual carrier are liable their liability is to be joint and several.

Unlike the Hague or Hague–Visby Rules, the Hamburg Rules provides a further express rule of limitation in the case of delay. Article 6(1)(b) provides that in such circumstances the carrier can limit his liability to an amount equivalent either to two and a half times the freight payable on the goods delayed or to the total freight payable under the contract of carriage which ever is the *lower*.

(iv) Can the carrier of goods rely on lower "package" limits?

1. Where the Hague Rules, Hague–Visby Rules or Hamburg Rules apply *as a matter of law*[57] it is not possible for the carrier to impose a package or weight limitation which is more beneficial to him than that imposed by such Rules. Article III, Rule 8, and Article IV, Rule 5, of the Hague and Hague–Visby Rules stipulate that any clause which purports to "lessen" liability otherwise than as provided in the Rules is to be "null and void and of no effect".[58] There is a provision to similar effect in Article 23(1) of the Hamburg Rules.

This principle can have effect in surprising circumstances. In *The "Hollandia/Morviken"*[59] the House of Lords considered a cargo claim against a vessel which had shipped cargo at a port in the United Kingdom after the Carriage of Goods by Sea Act 1971 had given statutory effect to the Hague–Visby Rules in the United Kingdom. The bill of lading had a Dutch law and jurisdiction clause and the carrier subsequently sought to stay English proceedings and to refer the claim to Holland where package limitation was more favourable to him since Holland was still at that time giving effect to the Hague Rules. The House of Lords held that the effect of the Dutch law and jurisdiction clause, if implemented, would be to lessen the liability of the carrier under the Hague–Visby Rules. They therefore refused to stay the English proceedings on the grounds that the law/jurisdiction clause was void under Article III, Rule 8.

57. Section 1(2) and (3) and (6) of the Carriage of Goods by Sea Act 1971 provides that the Hague–Visby Rules as set out in the Schedule to the Act shall "have the force of law" in the United Kingdom in the circumstances described in the Act and the Schedule.

58. See *The "European Enterprise"* [1989] 2 Lloyd's Rep. 185.

59. [1983] 1 Lloyd's Rep. 1.

2. Where the Hague Rules, Hague–Visby Rules or Hamburg Rules apply *as a matter of contract* (for example, by virtue of the inclusion of a clause paramount) it is a matter of construction of the whole contract whether effect would be given to a clause lessening the carrier's liability to a sum lower than that in the Rules. There is nothing in principle to prevent parties from agreeing that the Rules shall apply but that a lower figure should be substituted for the figures in the Rules themselves. However, it is likely that clear words would be required since otherwise a court or tribunal might, in view of Article III, Rule 8, of the Hague or Hague–Visby Rules or Article 23(1) of the Hamburg Rules feel constrained to apply any expressed lower limits to claims relating to incidents other than those covered by the Rules such as, for example, to incidents arising, in the case of the Hague and Hague–Visby Rules, before loading or after discharge.

(v) No "package" limit

Article IV Rule 5 of both the Hague and Hague–Visby Rules stipulate that the right of the carrier to limit his liability according to the Rules applies "unless the nature *and* value of such goods have been declared by the shipper before shipment *and* inserted in the bill of lading". If this is done then the carrier's liability is unlimited under the Rules (subject to his right to rely on "tonnage" limitation under the 1976 Limitation Convention or similar legislation). However, to achieve this end both the requirement of declaration by the shipper *and* insertion in the bill must be satisfied.[60] A bill of lading including these particulars is called an *"ad valorem"* bill and its issuance usually commands a higher freight rate.

To compensate the carrier to some extent for the loss of his right to limit his liability in such circumstances the last paragraph of Article IV, Rule 5, of the Hague Rules and Article IV, Rule 5(h), of the Hague–Visby Rules provides that if the nature *or* (NB not "and") value of the goods has been knowingly misstated "by the shipper" on the bill, "neither the carrier nor the ship shall be responsible in any event for loss or

---

60. *Pyrene Co. Ltd.* v. *Scindia Steam Navigation Co. Ltd.* [1954] 1 Lloyd's Rep. 321; 2 Q.B. 402.

damage to or in connection with the goods". This right appears to apply no matter what the cause of the damage and irrespective of whether the claim is brought by the shipper, or the receiver or any other party provided that the shipper *knew* of the misstatement.

There seems to be no similar provisions in the Hamburg Rules. Article 17(1), of the Hamburg Rules appears to envisage that if the nature of the goods is stated inaccurately on the bill of lading (whether this is known to the shipper or not) the carrier will be liable to the claimant subject to his right to limit under Article VI and can subsequently seek an indemnity from the shipper for any "loss resulting from inaccuracies in such particulars".

(vi) Loss of right to rely on package limitation

(A) HAGUE RULES

There is no specific provision in the Hague Rules which attempts to restrict the carrier's right to limit under Article IV, Rule 5. Indeed, Article IV, Rule 5, states that: "Neither the carrier nor the ship shall *in any event* become liable for any loss or damage to or in connection with goods in an amount exceeding . . . ."

The words "in any event" suggest that there is no restriction on the carrier's right to limit. This is the view adopted by the editors of the nineteenth edition of *Scrutton on Charterparties* at page 453. However, the view was not adopted in *The "Chanda"*[61] which was a case of deviation in the form of unauthorised carriage on deck. The judge held that since the provisions of the Rules were intended to apply only to under-deck carriage Article IV, Rule 5, and the words "in any event" were to be construed purely in relation to such carriage and not to loss or damage resulting from uncontemplated deck carriage.

Historically, unauthorised carriage of goods on deck has been treated as a deviation and it has been repeatedly held that a carrier guilty of such conduct is not entitled to rely on any exemption or limitation clauses in the contract of carriage but

61. [1989] 2 Lloyd's Rep. 494.

is liable as a common carrier.[62] The precise basis for the rule has been much debated over the years. On one view the principle rested on the doctrine of fundamental breach, which doctrine no longer exists after the decision of the House of Lords in *Photo Production Ltd.* v. *Securicor Transport Ltd.*[63] On another view, the principle is merely one of construction. The argument is that by promising to carry the goods under deck but actually carrying them on deck the carrier cannot rely on exemptions and limitations which were only intended to protect him if he had carried out the contract in the way which he had agreed.

It seems clear from the decisions of the Court of Appeal in *The "Antares"*[64] and of the Commercial Court in *The "Chanda"*[65] that the English court now prefers the principle based on construction. However, whereas the Court of Appeal found in *The "Antares"* that a carrier could rely on the time limit provision in Article III, Rule 6, of the Hague–Visby Rules despite the unauthorised deck carriage, it was held in *The "Chanda"* that a carrier could not rely on the limitation provisions of Article IV, Rule 5, of the Hague Rules in similar circumstances. Hirst J. held[66] that:

"neither the *Dixon* nor the *Evans* case rested on the discredited fundamental breach rule, but rather on a principle of construction, which in my judgment is to be derived from both these two cases, that clauses which are clearly intended to protect the shipowner provided he honours his contractual obligation to stow goods under deck do not apply if he is in breach of that obligation".

However, it is debatable whether Article IV, Rule 5, of the Hague Rules is "clearly intended to protect the shipowner provided he honours his contractual obligation to stow goods under deck" and does "not apply if he is in breach of that obligation". The definition of "goods" in Article I(c) of the Rules makes it clear that the Rules *are* intended to apply to the carriage of goods *on deck* unless the bill of lading is *also* stamped

---

62. See for example, *Hain S.S. Co.* v. *Tate and Lyle* (1936) 41 Com. Cas. 350.
63. [1980] 1 Lloyd's Rep. 545.
64. [1987] 1 Lloyd's Rep. 424.
65. [1989] 2 Lloyd's Rep. 494.
66. [1989] 2 Lloyd's Rep. at page 505.

to this effect.[67] Indeed, it was held by Pilcher J. in the *Svenska Traktor* case that in such circumstances the carrier could not rely on a favourable exemption clause in the bill of lading since such clause was void under Article III, Rule 8, of the Hague Rules which applied to the carriage. He went on to say[68] that: "I accordingly hold that the plaintiffs' tractors were in this case being carried by the shipowner subject to the obligations imposed upon them by Article III, Rule 2, of the Act."

Since the Hague Rules are intended to be a balance of "responsibilities and liabilities . . . and rights and immunities"[69] it would seem illogical for the carrier to be subject to the one without the other. It is also material in this regard when considering the above-quoted words of Pilcher J. that Article III, Rule 2, itself commences with the words: "Subject to the provisions of Article IV. . .".

If the correct approach is, therefore, one of construction there would seem to be grounds for saying that a carrier should be able to rely on the right to limit in Article IV, Rule 5, particularly in view of the words "in any event".

The reasoning of the court in The *"Chanda"*[70] suggests that a similar approach might not be adopted in relation to the more common case of geographical deviation where there is no unauthorised carriage of cargo on deck. However, the United States court has held that the words "in any event" do not protect a carrier in the case of unjustified deviation.[71]

Similar problems should not arise in relation to the Hague–Visby Rules in view of the express provisions of Article IV, Rule 5(e).

(B) HAGUE–VISBY RULES

Article IV, Rule 5(e), states that:

"Neither the carrier nor the ship shall be entitled to the benefit of the limitation of liability provided for in this paragraph if it is proved that the damage resulted from an act or omission of the carrier done with

---

67. *Svenska Traktor* v. *Maritime Agencies* [1953] 2 Lloyd's Rep. 124.
68. [1953] 2 Lloyd's Rep. at page 130.
69. Article II of the Hague Rules.
70. [1989] 2 Lloyd's Rep. 494.
71. *Jones* v. *Flying Clipper* (1954) 116 Fed. Supp. 386.

intent to cause damage, or recklessly and with knowledge that damage would probably result."

A general commentary in relation to the meaning of these words and of similar words in other Conventions can be found on pages 32–39. However, some points are worth re-emphasis:

1. It is only the conduct of the carrier himself which is relevant in determining whether or not he can limit his liability under this Article. Therefore, if damage has been caused by the intentional or reckless conduct of a servant or agent of the carrier (unless that servant or agent is the *alter ego* of the carrier) but without similar conduct on the part of the carrier himself, the carrier is entitled to limit his liability.[72] The situation differs, therefore, from that under Article III, Rules 1 and 2, where the "carrier" is in breach of his obligations to exercise due diligence to make the ship seaworthy and to "properly and carefully carry" etc., the goods if there is merely negligence on the part of his servants, agent or independent contractors.[73]

Similarly, if an action is brought against a servant or agent[74] of the carrier and such person wishes to limit his liability, such right is lost if that servant or agent is personally guilty of intentional or reckless conduct.[75]

2. There is a strange omission in Article IV, Rule 5(e), and Article IV *bis*, Rule 4, in that there is no mention of "loss". Throughout its other provisions the Hague–Visby Rules speak consistently of "loss or damage". Indeed, even Article IV, Rule 5(a), uses the same phrase when *establishing* the carrier's right to limit. Yet, Article IV, Rule 5(e), which is intended to *restrict* the general application of Article IV, Rule 5(a), apparently applies only to "damage" and not "loss".

A similar omission arises in Article 4 of the 1976 Convention which refers to "loss" without mention of "damage".[76] However, whereas it is possible in that context to argue that "loss"

---

72. *The "European Enterprise"* [1989] 2 Lloyd's Rep. 195. The position is the same under the Athens Convention. See *The "Lion"* [1990] 2 Lloyd's Rep. 144 and page 100.

73. See for example *The "Muncaster Castle"* [1961] 1 Lloyd's Rep. 57.

74. A servant or agent who is an independent contractor cannot limit. Article IV *bis*, Rule 2.

75. Article IV *bis*, Rule 4.

76. See pages 36–37.

means the financial loss arising from a physical loss of or damage to the goods with the result, therefore, that Article 4 is applicable to most situations, it is more difficult to do so in relation to Article IV, Rule 5(e), of the Hague–Visby Rules, since, when read in context, the word "damage" appears to contemplate merely physical damage to goods and conduct relating thereto.[77] If this is correct then, if cargo is "lost" ("not damaged") due to intentional or reckless conduct on the part of the carrier, he may be able to limit his liability under Article IV, Rule 5(a) (particularly in view of the words "in any event") since nothing in Article IV, Rule 5(e), restricts that right.[78]

3. Whereas, Article 4 of the 1976 Convention stipulates that the right to limit liability is lost only if the carrier intends to cause "such" loss or acts recklessly with knowledge that "such" loss will result, the word "such" is not present in Article IV, Rule 5(e), of the Hague–Visby Rules. In *Goldman* v. *Thai Airways*[79] the Court of Appeal considered similar words in the Warsaw Convention and came to the conclusion that the right to limit is lost if "the damage complained of is the kind of damage known to be the probable result".[80] However, Eveleigh L.J., who delivered the leading judgment, went on to say:

"It is with less confidence that I have said that the damage anticipated must be of the same kind of damage as that suffered. I have reached my conclusion because Article 25 is designed to cover cases of damage both to the person, in other words, injury, and to property."[81]

The Hague–Visby Rules do not cover injury to the person and accordingly it may be that a court construing the Hague–Visby Rules would come to the conclusion that the right to

77. Although Article 13 of the Athens Convention also speaks merely in terms of "damage", the reference in the same Article to liability under Articles 7 and 8 makes it clear that "damage" is to encompass injury to the person and damage to and loss of luggage.

78. In *The "Lion"* [1990] 2 Lloyd's Rep. 144 Hobhouse J. emphasised at page 149 the importance of "a consistent approach to the construction of similar Maritime Conventions using similar terms and expressing similar ideas". Query, however, whether such an approach is warranted where the words of the particular Convention in question appear to draw a distinction.

79. [1983] 3 All E.R. 693 (C.A.).

80. [1983] 3 All E.R. page 698.

81. [1983] 3 All E.R. page 700.

limit may be lost even if the damage anticipated is not the same as that suffered.[82]

(C) HAMBURG RULES

It is likely that, as in the case of the Hague–Visby Rules, only the conduct of the carrier himself is relevant in determining whether or not he can limit his liability under the Hamburg Rules.[83]

The Hamburg Rules do not suffer from the deficiencies referred to above in relation to the Hague–Visby Rules. Article 8(1) of the Hamburg Rules refers to "such loss, damage or delay" and, therefore, the right to limit liability can be lost in relation to all these types of claim if the carrier is personally guilty of intentional or reckless misconduct.[84]

Article 8(2) provides that the "servant or agent" of the carrier may lose the right to limit liability if (as in the case of Article IV, Rule 2, of the Hague–Visby Rules) they are personally guilty of intentional or reckless misconduct.[85]

(vii)   Persons who can limit liability

(1)   Owners and charterers

(A) HAGUE/HAGUE–VISBY/HAMBURG RULES

Article IV, Rules 5, of the Hague and Hague–Visby Rules provides that a "carrier" can limit his liability. Article I(a) of both Rules provides that: "'Carrier' includes the owner or the charterer who enters into a contract of carriage with a shipper."

Similarly Articles 6 and 10 of the Hamburg Rules provide that a "carrier" and "actual carrier" can limit their liability.

Article 1(1) defines a "carrier" as: " . . . any person by whom or in whose name a contract of carriage of goods by sea has been concluded with a shipper" and Article 1(2) defines an "actual carrier" as any person to whom the carrier has

---

82. However in *The "Lion"* [1990] 2 Lloyd's Rep. 144, Hobhouse J. emphasised at page 149 the importance of "a consistent approach to the construction of similar Maritime Conventions using similar terms and expressing similar ideas".

83. See page 128.

84. See page 129.

85. See pages 119 and 122.

entrusted part of the carriage. There is therefore no precise definition of a carrier under any of the Rules but an owner and a charterer clearly come within the definition. This is express in the case of the Hague and Hague–Visby Rules and implicit in the case of the Hamburg Rules.

However, such persons can limit their liability under the Rules only to the extent that the claim arises under a "contract of carriage". The definition of a "contract of carriage" differs under the Hague/Hague–Visby Rules on the one hand and the Hamburg Rules on the other hand.

Article I(b) of the Hague/Hague–Visby Rules describes a "contract of carriage" as: " . . . contract of carriage covered by a bill of lading or similar document of title. . . ." Article 1(6) of the Hamburg Rules defines a "contract of carriage" as: " . . . any contract whereby the carrier undertakes against payment of freight to carry goods by sea from one port to another."

A charterparty is not a "contract of carriage" for the purposes of the Hague/Hague–Visby Rules as it is not a bill of lading or a similar document of title and is equally not a "contract of carriage" for the purpose of the Hamburg Rules as Article 2(3) of the Hamburg provides that: "The provisions of this Convention are not applicable to charterparties."

Therefore an owner or charterer cannot limit his liability under any of the Rules in respect of liabilities incurred by him as a carrier under a charterparty unless the parties to such contract have expressly agreed that the Rules are to apply, for example by the inclusion of a paramount clause in the charter.

(B) 1976 CONVENTION

Owners and charterers are clearly "persons entitled to limit liability" under the Convention by virtue of the express provisions of Article 1(2).[86] Furthermore, an "actual carrier" within the meaning of Article 1(2) of the Hamburg Rules is no doubt a "person for whose act . . . the shipowner . . . is responsible" within the meaning of Article 1(4) of the 1976 Convention since Article 10(1) of the Hamburg Rules states expressly that: "The carrier is responsible, in relation to the

86. See pages 8–10.

carriage performed by the actual carrier, for the acts and omissions of the actual carrier . . . ".

(2) Other "carriers"

(A)   HAGUE/HAGUE–VISBY/HAMBURG RULES

The definition of "carrier" in the Hague,[87] Hague–Visby and Hamburg Rules[88] is clearly wide enough to include "carriers" who are not owners or charterers. Therefore, for example, a freight forwarder who issues his own bill of lading to a shipper and collects freight from him could be such a "carrier" and entitled to limit his liability under the Rules.

(B)   1976 CONVENTION

However, a freight forwarder may not be a "person entitled to limit liability" under the 1976 Convention in that he may not be an "owner, charterer, manager or operator of a" ship and not a person for whose acts such parties are liable.[89]

(3) Servants and agents of a carrier

(A)   HAGUE RULES

There is nothing in the Hague Rules to indicate that any party other than the "carrier" himself can limit his liability under the Rules. However, the common use of 'Himalaya clauses" in bills of lading may reduce the instances in which a servant or agent can be held liable to a claimant.[90] The purpose of such a clause is to oblige a claimant to claim against the carrier himself and not against his independent contractors. Such servant or agent, if personally liable to a claimant, may nevertheless be able to limit his liability under Article 1(4) of the 1976 Convention as a "person for whose act, neglect or default the shipowner or salvor is responsible".[91]

87. Article I(a).
88. Article 1(i).
89. See pages 12–13.
90. See for example *The "Eurymedon"* [1975] 2 Lloyd's Rep. 534 and *Port Jackson* v. *Salmond* [1980] 3 All E.R. 257.
91. See pages 12–13.

(B) HAGUE–VISBY RULES

Article IV *bis*, Rule 2, provides that a servant or agent of the carrier can limit his liability in the same way and to the same extent as the carrier *provided*, however, that servant or agent is not an independent contractor. It therefore follows that only a limited class of persons (predominantly the carrier's crew and other employees) can take advantage of these rights. Stevedores, ship's agents and managers are usually incorporated as independent contractors and would not therefore be able to rely on this right to limit if they were held liable in respect of a cargo claim. However, this problem is circumvented in a number of instances by the insertion into the bill of lading of a "Himalaya clause", which obliges the claimant to bring a claim only against the carrier.[92]

In determining whether or not the servant or agent can limit his liability under the Rules it is his own conduct which is relevant, not the conduct of his principal.[93]

The "servant or agent" who is an employee will also in most cases be entitled to limit his liability under Article 1(4) of the 1976 Convention as a "person for whose act, neglect or default the shipowner or salvor is responsible".[94]

Similarly, independent contractors such as stevedores (who cannot limit under the Hague–Visby Rules) can also probably rely on Article 1(4) of the 1976 Convention provided that the shipowner is liable for their actions as a matter law. However, it may be more difficult to prove that an independent contractor, as opposed to an employee, is in fact someone, "for whose act . . . the shipowner is responsible".

(C) HAMBURG RULES

Articles 7(2) and 10(2) of the Hamburg Rules have similar provisions to those of Article IV *bis*, Rule 2, of the Hague–Visby Rules except that the right to limit is afforded by the Hamburg Rules to servants or agents irrespective of whether they are independent contractors, so long as the liability which they

---

92. See page 8.
93. *The "Captain Gregos"* [1990] 1 Lloyd's Rep. at 316.
94. See pages 12–13.

wish to limit has been incurred whilst acting within the scope of their employment.

Servants or agents who are not independent contractors are likely to be entitled to limit their liability under Article 1(4) of the 1976 Convention as "persons for whose act . . . the shipowner is responsible". It may well be that a servant or agent who is an independent contractor has a similar right but, depending on the precise relationship in a particular case, it may be more difficult for the independent contractor to prove that he is a "person for whose act . . . the shipowner is responsible".

(viii)   *Claims which are subject to limitation*

(A)   HAGUE AND HAGUE–VISBY RULES

Article IV, Rule 5, of the Hague Rules, and Article IV, Rule 5(a), of the Hague–Visby Rules provide that: ". . . neither the carrier nor the ship in any event be or become liable for any loss or damage to or in connection with the goods . . .".

These words clearly give the carrier the right to limit his liability in respect of claims against him for physical loss of or damage to cargo carried on board the ship. However, the words "in connection with the goods" have been held to extend the rights of the carrier to limit his liability to other claims for "loss or damage" provided they arise "in connection with the goods".[95] For example, *G. H. Renton & Co. Ltd.* v. *Palmyra Trading Corporation (The "Caspiana")*[96] similar words in Article III, Rule 8, were held to apply where loss arose as a result of the discharge of goods at the wrong port.

Similarly, in *The "Satya Kailash"*[97] the Court of Appeal held that where the Rules are incorporated into a charter the carrier was entitled to invoke the immunities in section 4 of the U.S. Carriage of Goods by Sea Act (which includes a provision similar to Article IV, Rule 5, of the Hague Rules) in respect of the wide range of activities to be performed by the carrier under

95. *Adamastos Shipping Co. Ltd.* v. *Anglo Saxon Petroleum Co. Ltd.* [1958] 1 Lloyd's Rep. 73.
96. [1956] 2 Lloyd's Rep. 379.
97. [1984] 1 Lloyd's Rep. 588.

the charter. The carrier in that case could rely on the immunities in section 4 of the Act in respect of a claim against him for damage caused by a lightening vessel to the mother ship which was owned by the charterer.

(B) HAMBURG RULES

Article 6(1) and (2) of the Hamburg Rules are more limited in scope than Article IV, Rule 5, of the Hague and Article IV, Rule 5(a) of the Hague–Visby Rules in that the right to limit is restricted to: " . . . The liability of the carrier for loss resulting from loss of or damage to goods . . . " (Article 6(1)(a)) and "The liability of the carrier for delay in delivery . . . " (Article 6(1)(b)).

Article 6(1)(a) therefore clearly envisages claims merely for physical loss of or damage to goods and Article 6(1)(b) extends the right to limit to claims for delayed delivery. Liability for other forms of claim (such as that in *Renton* v. *Palmyra*[98] and *The "Satya Kailash"*[99] may not therefore be the subject of limitation under the Hamburg Rules.

(C) 1976 CONVENTION

Whether claims which qualify for limitation under the various Rules also qualify for limitation under the 1976 Convention depends on whether the particular claim is a "claim in respect of . . . loss of or damage to property . . . occurring on board or in direct connection with the operation of the ships . . . and consequential loss resulting therefrom" within the meaning of Article 2(1)(a)[100] or a claim "resulting from delay in the carriage by sea of cargo . . . " within the meaning of Article 2(1)(b) of the Convention.[101]

The words clearly encompass claims for loss of or damage to cargo. However, on a strict construction of the quoted words in Article 2(1)(a), the right to limit for consequential loss can only exist if there is also a claim for physical loss of or damage to the cargo. On this view a carrier who might be able to limit

98. [1956] 2 Lloyd's Rep. 379.
99. [1984] 1 Lloyd's Rep. 588.
100. See pages 19–20.
101. See pages 20–21.

his liability for a claim for loss of market or for discharging cargo at the wrong port under the Hague or Hague–Visby Rules might not be able to limit his liability under the 1976 Convention if there was no claim for physical loss of damage to the cargo.

APPENDICES

  I. Section 503 of the Merchant Shipping Act 1894 as amended by (a) Merchant Shipping (Liability of Shipowners and Others) Act 1958; (b) section 12 of the Merchant Shipping Act 1984
 II. Sections 14, 17, 18, 19, 35 and 48 of the Merchant Shipping Act 1979
III. Merchant Shipping Act 1979, Schedule 3, Parts I, II and III
 IV. Merchant Shipping Act 1979, Schedule 4, Parts I and II
  V. Merchant Shipping Act 1979, Schedule 5
 VI. Statutory Instruments
     1. Merchant Shipping Act 1979 (Commencement No.10) Order 1986
     2. Merchant Shipping (Liability of Shipowners and Others) (Calculation of Tonnage) Order 1986
     3. Merchant Shipping Act 1979 (Commencement No.11) Order 1987
     4. Merchant Shipping Act 1979 (Commencement No.13) Order 1989
     5. Carriage of Passengers and their Luggage by Sea (United Kingdom Carriers) (Amendment) Order 1989
VII. Carriage of Goods by Sea Act 1971 (The Hague–Visby Rules)
VIII. United Nations Convention on the Carriage of Goods By Sea 1978 (The Hamburg Rules)
 IX. Limitation of Liability for Maritime Claims: Summary of Limits

APPENDIX I

SECTION 503 OF THE MERCHANT SHIPPING ACT 1894 (AS AMENDED)

KEY

(1) Matter in ordinary type is what remains of original 1894 wording; (2) Matter in italics are amendments introduced by Merchant Shipping (Liability of Shipowners and Others) Act 1958; (3) Matter in bold type is a paraphrase of amendments introduced by Merchant Shipping (Liability of Shipowners and Others) Act 1958; (4) Underlined matter denotes wording introduced by section 12 of the Merchant Shipping Act 1984 to replace the original section 503(2).

Limitation of owner's liability in certain cases of loss of life, injury or damage

503.—(1) The owners of a ship, British or foreign, shall not, where all or any of the following occurrences take place without their actual fault or privity; (that is to say),

(*a*) Where any loss of life or personal injury is caused to any person being carried in the ship;

(*b*) Where any damage or loss is caused to any goods, merchandise, or other things whatsoever on board the ship;

(*c*) *where any loss of life or personal injury is caused to any person not carried in the ship through the act or omission of any person (whether on board the ship or not) in the navigation or management of the ship or in the loading, carriage or discharge of its cargo or in the embarkation, carriage or disembarkation of its passengers, or through any other act or omission of any person on board the ship;*

(*d*) *where any loss or damage is caused to any property (other than any property mentioned in paragraph (b) of this subsection) or any rights are infringed through the act or omission of any person (whether on board the ship or not) in the*

139

navigation or management of the ship, or in the loading, carriage or discharge of its cargo or in the embarkation, carriage or disembarkation of its passengers, or through any other act or omission of any person on board the ship;

be liable to damages beyond the following amounts; (that is to say),

(i) In respect of loss of life or personal injury, either alone or together with *such loss, damage or infringement as is mentioned in paragraphs (b) and (d) of this subsection*, an aggregate amount not exceeding *an amount equivalent to three thousand one hundred gold francs*, for each ton of their ship's tonnage; and

(ii) In respect of *such loss, damage or infringement as is mentioned in paragraphs (b) and (d) of this subsection*, whether there be in addition loss of life or personal injury or not, an aggregate amount not exceeding *an amount equivalent to one thousand gold francs*, for each ton of their ship's tonnage;

and the number by which the amount equivalent to three thousand one hundred gold francs mentioned in this section is to be multiplied shall be three hundred in any case where the tonnage concerned is less than three hundred tons.

For the purposes of this section a gold franc shall be taken to be a unit consisting of sixty-five and a half milligrams of gold of millesimal fineness nine hundred.

And the Minister may from time to time by order specify the amounts which for the purposes of this section are to be taken as equivalent to 3,100 and 1,000 gold francs respectively.

For the purposes of subsection (1) of this section where any obligation or liability arises—

(a) *in connection with the raising, removal or destruction of any ship which is sunk, stranded or abandoned or of anything on board such a ship, or*

(b) *in respect of any damage (however caused) to harbour works, basins or navigable waterways,*

the occurrence giving rise to the obligation or liability shall be treated as one of the occurrences mentioned in paragraphs (b) and (d) of subsection (1) of this section and the obligation or liability as a liability to damages.

The provisions of sub-paragraph (a) above, relating to an obligation or liability arising in connection with the raising, removal or destruction of any ship which is sunk, stranded or abandoned or of anything on board such ship shall not come into force until such day as the Minister may by order made by statutory instrument appoint.

The application of this section to any liability shall not be excluded by reason only that the occurrence giving rise to the liability was not due to the negligence of any person.

(2) For the purposes of this section the tonnage of a ship shall be ascertained as follows:

(a) where the register tonnage of the ship has been or can be ascertained in accordance with the tonnage regulations of this Act, the ship's tonnage shall be the register tonnage of the ship as so ascertained but without making any deduction required by those regulations of any tonnage allowance for propelling machinery space;

(b) where the tonnage of the ship cannot be ascertained in accordance with paragraph (a) above, a surveyor of ships shall, if so directed by the court, certify what, on the evidence specified in the direction, would in his opinion be the tonnage of the ship as ascertained in accordance with that paragraph if the ship could be duly measured for the purpose; and the tonnage stated in his certificate shall be taken to be the tonnage of the ship.

(3) The limits set by this section to the liabilities mentioned therein shall apply to the aggregate of such liabilities which are incurred on any distinct occasion, and shall so apply in respect of each distinct occasion without regard to any liability incurred on another occasion.

The persons whose liability in connection with a ship is excluded or limited by Part VIII of the Merchant Shipping Act, 1894, shall include any charterer and any person interested in or in possession of the ship, and, in particular, any manager or operator of the ship.

In relation to a claim arising from the act or omission of any person in his capacity as master or member of the crew or (otherwise than in that capacity) in the course of his employment as a servant of the owners or of any such person as is mentioned in subsection (1) of this section,—

(a) the persons whose liability is excluded or limited as aforesaid shall also include the master, member of the crew or servant, and, in a case where the master or member of the crew is the servant of a person whose liability would not be excluded or limited apart from this paragraph, the person whose servant he is; and

(b) the liability of the master, member of the crew or servant himself shall be excluded or limited as aforesaid notwithstanding his actual fault or privity in that capacity, except in the cases mentioned in paragraph (ii) of section five hundred and two of the said Act of 1894.

APPENDIX II

SECTIONS 14, 17, 18, 19, 35 AND 48 OF THE MERCHANT SHIPPING ACT 1979

Carriage of passengers and luggage by sea

Scheduled convention to have force of law

14.—(1) The provisions of the Convention relating to the Carriage of Passengers and their Luggage by Sea as set out in Part I of Schedule 3 to this Act (hereafter in this section and in Parts II and III of that Schedule referred to as "the Convention") shall have the force of law in the United Kingdom.

(2) The provisions of Part II of that Schedule shall have effect in connection with the Convention and the preceding subsection shall have effect subject to the provisions of that Part.

(3) On and after the date when this subsection and Part III of Schedule 3 to this Act come into force Parts I and II of that Schedule shall have effect with the modifications specified in the said Part III.

(4) If it appears to Her Majesty in Council that there is a conflict between the provisions of this section or of Part I or II of Schedule 3 to this Act and any provisions relating to the carriage of passengers or luggage for reward by land, sea or air in—

    (*a*) any convention which has been signed or ratified by or on behalf of the government of the United Kingdom before the passing of this Act (excluding the Convention); or

    (*b*) any enactment of the Parliament of the United Kingdom giving effect to such a convention,

She may by Order in Council make such modifications of this section or that Schedule or any such enactment as She considers appropriate for resolving the conflict.

(5) If it appears to Her Majesty in Council that the government of the United Kingdom has agreed to any revision of the Convention She may by Order in Council make such modifications of Parts I and II of Schedule 3 to this Act as She considers appropriate in consequence of the revision.

(6) Nothing in subsection (1), (2) or (3) of this section or in any modification made by virtue of subsection (4) or (5) of this section shall affect any rights or liabilities arising out of an occurrence which took place before the day on which the said subsection (1), (2) or (3), or as the case may be the modification, comes into force.

(7) This section shall bind the Crown, and any Order in Council made by virtue of this section may provide that the Order or specified provisions of it shall bind the Crown.

Liability of shipowners and salvors

Limitation of liability

17.—(1) The provisions of the Convention on Limitation of Liability for Maritime Claims 1976 as set out in Part I of Schedule 4 to this Act (hereafter in this section and in Part II of that Schedule referred to as "the Convention") shall have the force of law in the United Kingdom.

(2) The provisions of Part II of that Schedule shall have effect in connection with the Convention, and the preceeding subsection shall have effect subject to the provisions of that Part.

Exclusion of liability

18.—(1) Subject to subsection (3) of this section, the owner of a British ship shall not be liable for any loss or damage in the following cases, namely—

(a) where any property on board the ship is lost or damaged by reason of fire on board the ship; or

(b) where any gold, silver, watches, jewels or precious stones on board the ship are lost or damaged by reason of theft, robbery or other dishonest conduct and their nature and value were not at the time of shipment declared by their owner or shipper to the owner or master of the ship in the bill of lading or otherwise in writing.

(2) Subject to subsection (3) of this section, where the loss or damage arises from anything done or omitted by any person in his capacity as master or member of the crew or (otherwise than in that capacity) in the course of his employment as a servant of the owner of the ship, the preceding subsection shall also exclude the liability of—

(a) the master, member of the crew or servant; and

(b) in a case where the master or member of the crew is the servant of a person whose liability would not be excluded by that subsection apart from this paragraph, the person whose servant he is.

(3) This section does not exclude the liability of any person for any loss or damage resulting from any such personal act or omission of his as is mentioned in article 4 of the Convention in Part I of Schedule 4 to this Act.

(4) In this section "owner", in relation to a ship, includes any part owner and any charterer, manager or operator of the ship.

Provisions supplementary to ss. 17 and 18

19.—(1) The enactments mentioned in Schedule 5 to this Act shall have effect with the amendments there specified (which are consequential on sections 17 and 18 of this Act).

(2) Her Majesty may by Order in Council provide that the said sections 17 and 18, the preceding subsection and Schedules 4 and 5 to this Act shall extend, with such modifications, if any, as are specified in the Order, to any of the following countries, namely—

    (a) the Isle of Man;

    (b) any of the Channel Islands;

    (c) any colony;

    (d) any country outside Her Majesty's dominions in which Her Majesty has jurisdiction in right of the government of the United Kingdom.

(3) Any statutory instrument made by virtue of the preceding subsection shall be subject to annulment in pursuance of a resolution of either House of Parliament.

(4) Nothing in the said sections 17 and 18 or the said Schedule 4 shall apply in relation to any liability arising out of an occurrence which took place before the coming into force of those sections, and subsection (1) of this section and Schedule 5 to this Act shall not affect the operation of any enactment in relation to such an occurrence.

Amendment of s. 503 of Merchant Shipping Act 1894 etc.

35.—(1) Nothing in section 503 of the Merchant Shipping Act 1894 (which relates to the limitation of liability in certain cases of loss of life, injury or damage) shall apply to any liability in respect of loss of life or personal injury caused to, or loss of or damage to any property of, a person who is on board or employed in connection with the ship in question if—

    (a) he is so on board or employed under a contract of service governed by the law of any part of the United Kingdom; and

(b) the liability arises from an occurrence which took place after the coming into force of this subsection and before the coming into force of the following subsection;

and in this subsection "ship" has the same meaning as in the said section 503.

(2) The provisions having the force of law under section 17 of this Act shall not apply to any liability in respect of loss of life or personal injury caused to, or loss of or damage to any property of, a person who is on board the ship in question or employed in connection with that ship or with the salvage operations in question if—

(a) he is so on board or employed under a contract of service governed by the law of any part of the United Kingdom; and

(b) the liability arises from an occurrence which took place after the coming into force of this subsection;

and in this subsection "ship" and "salvage operations" have the same meaning as in those provisions.

Application to hovercraft

48. The enactments and instruments with respect to which provision may be made by Order in Council in pursuance of section 1(1)(*h*) of the Hovercraft Act 1968 shall include this Act and any instrument made under it.

MERCHANT SHIPPING ACT 1979 SCHEDULE 3, PARTS I, II AND III

SCHEDULE 3. CONVENTION RELATING TO THE CARRIAGE OF PASSENGERS AND THEIR LUGGAGE BY SEA

PART I. TEXT OF CONVENTION

Article 1. Definitions

In this Convention the following expressions have the meaning hereby assigned to them:

1. (a) "carrier" means a person by or on behalf of whom a contract of carriage has been concluded, whether the carriage is actually performed by him or by a performing carrier;

   (b) "performing carrier" means a person other than the carrier, being the owner, charterer or operator of a ship, who actually performs the whole or a part of the carriage;

2. "contract of carriage" means a contract made by or on behalf of a carrier for the carriage by sea of a passenger or of a passenger and his luggage, as the case may be;

3. "ship" means only a seagoing vessel, excluding an aircushion vehicle;

4. "passenger" means any person carried in a ship,

   (a) under a contract of carriage, or

   (b) who, with the consent of the carrier, is accompanying a vehicle or live animals which are covered by a contract for the carriage of goods not governed by this Convention;

5. "luggage" means any article or vehicle carried by the carrier under a contract of carriage, excluding:

   (a) articles and vehicles carried under a charterparty, bill of lading or other contract primarily concerned with the carriage of goods, and

   (b) live animals;

6. "cabin luggage" means luggage which the passenger has in his cabin or is otherwise in his possession, custody or control. Except for the application of paragraph 8 of this Article and Article 8, cabin luggage includes luggage which the passenger has in or on his vehicle;

7. "loss of or damage to luggage" includes pecuniary loss resulting from the luggage not having been re-delivered to the passenger within a reasonable time after the arrival of the ship on which the luggage has been or should have been carried, but does not include delays resulting from labour disputes;

8. "carriage" covers the following periods:

(a) with regard to the passenger and his cabin luggage, the period during which the passenger and/or his cabin luggage are on board the ship or in the course of embarkation or disembarkation, and the period during which the passenger and his cabin luggage are transported by water from land to the ship or vice-versa, if the cost of such transport is included in the fare or if the vessel used for the purpose of auxiliary transport has been put at the disposal of the passenger by the carrier. However, with regard to the passenger, carriage does not include the period which he is in a marine terminal or station or on a quay or in or on any other port installation;

(b) with regard to cabin luggage, also the period during which the passenger is in a marine terminal or station or on a quay or in or on any other port installation if that luggage has been taken over by the carrier or his servant or agent and has not been re-delivered to the passenger;

(c) with regard to other luggage which is not cabin luggage, the period from the time of its taking over by the carrier or his servant or agent onshore or on board until the time of its re-delivery by the carrier or his servant or agent;

9. "international carriage" means any carriage in which, according to the contract of carriage, the place of departure and the place of destination are situated in two different States, or in a single State if, according to the contract of carriage or the scheduled itinerary, there is an intermediate port of call in another State;

Article 2. Application

1. This Convention shall apply to any international carriage if:

(a) the ship is flying the flag of or is registered in a State Party to this Convention, or

(b) the contract of carriage has been made in a State Party to this Convention, or

(c) the place of departure or destination, according to the contract of carriage, is in a State Party to this Convention.

2. Notwithstanding paragraph 1 of this Article, this Convention shall not apply when the carriage is subject, under any other international convention concerning the carriage of passengers or luggage by another mode of transport, to a civil liability regime under the provisions of such convention, in so far as those provisions have mandatory application to carriage by sea.

Article 3. Liability of the carrier

1. The carrier shall be liable for the damage suffered as a result of the death of or personal injury to a passenger and the loss of or damage to luggage if the incident which caused the damage so suffered occurred in the course of the carriage and was due to the fault or neglect of the carrier or of his servants or agents acting within the scope of their employment.

2. The burden of proving that the incident which caused the loss or damage occurred in the course of the carriage, and the extent of the loss or damage, shall lie with the claimant.

3. Fault or neglect of the carrier or of his servants or agents acting within the scope of their employment shall be presumed, unless the contrary is proved, if the death of or personal injury to the passenger or the loss of or damage to cabin luggage arose from or in connection with the shipwreck, collision, stranding, explosion or fire, or defect in the ship. In respect of loss of or damage to other luggage, such fault or neglect shall be presumed, unless the contrary is proved, irrespective of the nature of the incident which caused the loss or damage. In all other cases the burden of proving fault or neglect shall lie with the claimant.

Article 4. Performing carrier

1. If the performance of the carriage or part thereof has been entrusted to a performing carrier, the carrier shall nevertheless remain liable for the entire carriage according to the provisions of this Convention. In addition, the performing carrier shall be subject and entitled to the provisions of this Convention for the part of the carriage performed by him.

2. The carrier shall, in relation to the carriage performed by the performing carrier, be liable for the acts and omissions of the

performing carrier and of his servants and agents acting within the scope of their employment.

3. Any special agreement under which the carrier assumes obligations not imposed by this Convention or any waiver of rights conferred by this Convention shall affect the performing carrier only if agreed by him expressly and in writing.

4. Where and to the extent that both the carrier and the performing carrier are liable, their liability shall be joint and several.

5. Nothing in this Article shall prejudice any right of recourse as between the carrier and the performing carrier.

Article 5. Valuables

The carrier shall not be liable for the loss of or damage to monies, negotiable securities, gold, silverware, jewellery, ornaments, works of art, or other valuables, except where such valuables have been deposited with the carrier for the agreed purpose of safe-keeping in which case the carrier shall be liable up to the limit provided for in paragraph 3 of Article 8 unless a higher limit is agreed upon in accordance with paragraph 1 of Article 10.

Article 6. Contributory fault

If the carrier proves that the death of or personal injury to a passenger or the loss of or damage to his luggage was caused or contributed to by the fault or neglect of the passenger, the court seized of the case may exonerate the carrier wholly or partly from his liability in accordance with the provisions of the law of that court.

Article 7. Limit of liability for personal injury

1. The liability of the carrier for the death of or personal injury to a passenger shall in no case exceed 700,000 francs per carriage. Where in accordance with the law of the court seized of the case damages are awarded in the form of periodical income payments, the equivalent capital value of those payments shall not exceed the said limit.

2. Notwithstanding paragraph 1 of this Article, the national law of any State Party to this Convention may fix, as far as carriers who are nationals of such State are concerned, a higher *per capita* limit of liability.

Article 8. Limit of liability for loss of or damage to luggage

1. The liability of the carrier for the loss of or damage to cabin luggage shall in no case exceed 12,500 francs per passenger, per carriage.

2. The liability of the carrier for the loss of or damage to vehicles including all luggage carried in or on the vehicle shall in no case exceed 50,000 francs per vehicle, per carriage.

3. The liability of the carrier for the loss of or damage to luggage other than that mentioned in paragraphs 1 and 2 of this Article shall in no case exceed 18,000 francs per passenger, per carriage.

4. The carrier and the passenger may agree that the liability of the carrier shall be subject to a deductible not exceeding 1,750 francs in the case of damage to a vehicle and not exceeding 200 francs per passenger in the case of loss of or damage to other luggage, such sum to be deducted from the loss or damage.

Article 9. Monetary unit and conversion

1. The franc mentioned in this Convention shall be deemed to refer to a unit consisting of 65.5 milligrams of gold of millesimal fineness 900.

2. The amounts referred to in Articles 7 and 8 shall be converted into the national currency of the State of the court seized of the case on the basis of the official value of that currency, by reference to the unit defined in paragraph 1 of this Article, on the date of the judgment or the date agreed upon by the parties.

Article 10. Supplementary provisions on limits of liability

1. The carrier and the passenger may agree, expressly and in writing, to higher limits of liability than those prescribed in Articles 7 and 8.

2. Interest on damages and legal costs shall not be included in the limits of liability prescribed in Articles 7 and 8.

Article 11. Defences and limits for carriers' servants

If an action is brought against a servant or agent of the carrier or of the performing carrier arising out of damage covered by this Convention, such servant or agent, if he proves that he acted within the scope of his employment, shall be entitled to avail himself of the defences and limits of liability which the carrier or the performing carrier is entitled to invoke under this Convention.

Article 12. Aggregation of claims

1. Where the limits of liability prescribed in Articles 7 and 8 take effect, they shall apply to the aggregate of the amounts recoverable in

all claims arising out of the death of or personal injury to any one passenger or the loss of or damage to his luggage.

2. In relation to the carriage performed by a performing carrier, the aggregate of the amounts recoverable from the carrier and the performing carrier and from their servants and agents acting within the scope of their employment shall not exceed the highest amount which could be awarded against either the carrier or the performing carrier under this Convention, but none of the persons mentioned shall be liable for a sum in excess of the limit applicable to him.

3. In any case where a servant or agent of the carrier or of the performing carrier is entitled under Article 11 of this Convention to avail himself of the limits of liability prescribed in Articles 7 and 8, the aggregate of the amounts recoverable from the carrier, or the performing carrier as the case may be, and from that servant or agent, shall not exceed those limits.

Article 13. Loss of right to limit liability

1. The carrier shall not be entitled to the benefit of the limits of liability prescribed in Articles 7 and 8 and paragraph 1 of Article 10, if it is proved that the damage resulted from an act or omission of the carrier done with the intent to cause such damage, or recklessly and with knowledge that such damage would probably result.

2. The servant or agent of the carrier or of the performing carrier shall not be entitled to the benefit of those limits if it is proved that the damage resulted from an act or omission of that servant or agent done with the intent to cause such damage, or recklessly and with knowledge that such damage would probably result.

Article 14. Basis for claims

No action for damages for the death of or personal injury to a passenger, or for the loss of or damage to luggage, shall be brought against a carrier or performing carrier otherwise than in accordance with this Convention.

Article 15. Notice of loss or damage to luggage

1. The passenger shall give written notice to the carrier or his agent:

   (a) in the case of apparent damage to luggage:

      (i) for cabin luggage, before or at the time of disembarkation of the passenger;

      (ii) for all other luggage, before or at the time of its re-delivery;

  (b) in the case of damage to luggage which is not apparent, or loss of luggage, within fifteen days from the date of disembarkation or re-delivery or from the time when such re-delivery should have taken place.

2. If the passenger fails to comply with this Article, he shall be presumed, unless the contrary is proved, to have received the luggage undamaged.

3. The notice in writing need not be given if the condition of the luggage has at the time of its receipt been the subject of joint survey or inspection.

Article 16. Time-bar for actions

1. Any action for damages arising out of the death of or personal injury to a passenger or for the loss of or damage to luggage shall be time-barred after a period of two years.

2. The limitation period shall be calculated as follows:

  (a) in the case of personal injury, from the date of disembarkation of the passenger;

  (b) in the case of death occurring during carriage, from the date when the passenger should have disembarked, and in the case of personal injury occurring during carriage and resulting in the death of the passenger after disembarkation, from the date of death, provided that this period shall not exceed three years from the date of disembarkation;

  (c) in the case of loss of or damage to luggage, from the date of disembarkation or from the date when disembarkation should have taken place, whichever is later.

3. The law of the court seized of the case shall govern the grounds of suspension and interruption of limitation periods, but in no case shall an action under this Convention be brought after the expiration of a period of three years from the date of disembarkation of the passenger or from the date when disembarkation should have taken place, whichever is later.

4. Notwithstanding paragraphs 1, 2 and 3 of this Article, the period of limitation may be extended by a declaration of the carrier or by agreement of the parties after the cause of action has arisen. The declaration or agreement shall be in writing.

Article 17. Competent jurisdiction

1. An action arising under this Convention shall, at the option of the claimant, be brought before one of the courts listed below, provided that the court is located in a State Party to this Convention:

    (a) the court of the place of permanent residence or principal place of business of the defendant, or

    (b) the court of the place of departure or that of the destination according to the contract of carriage, or

    (c) a court of the State of the domicile or permanent residence of the claimant, if the defendant has a place of business and is subject to jurisdiction in that State, or

    (d) a court of the State where the contract of carriage was made, if the defendant has a place of business and is subject to jurisdiction in that State.

2. After the occurrence of the incident which has caused the damage, the parties may agree that the claim for damages shall be submitted to any jurisdiction or to arbitration.

Article 18. Invalidity of contractual provisions

Any contractual provision concluded before the occurrence of the incident which has caused the death of or personal injury to a passenger or the loss of or damage to his luggage, purporting to relieve the carrier of his liability towards the passenger or to prescribe a lower limit of liability than that fixed in this Convention except as provided in paragraph 4 of Article 8, and any such provision purporting to shift the burden of proof which rests on the carrier, or having the effect of restricting the option specified in paragraph 1 of Article 17, shall be null and void, but the nullity of that provision shall not render void the contract of carriage which shall remain subject to the provisions of this Convention.

Article 19. Other conventions on limitation of liability

This Convention shall not modify the rights or duties of the carrier, the performing carrier, and their servants or agents provided for in international conventions relating to the limitation of liability of owners of seagoing ships.

Article 20. Nuclear damage

No liability shall arise under this Convention for damage caused by a nuclear incident:

(a) if the operator of a nuclear installation is liable for such damage under either the Paris Convention of 29 July 1960 on Third Party Liability in the Field of Nuclear Energy as amended by its Additional Protocol of 28 January 1964, or the Vienna Convention of 21 May 1963 on Civil Liability for Nuclear Damage, or

(b) if the operator of a nuclear installation is liable for such damage by virtue of a national law governing the liability for such damage, provided that such law is in all respects as favourable to persons who may suffer damage as either the Paris or the Vienna Conventions.

Article 21. Commercial carriage by public authorities

This Convention shall apply to commercial carriage undertaken by States or Public Authorities under contracts of carriage within the meaning of Article 1.

PART II. PROVISIONS HAVING EFFECT IN CONNECTION WITH CONVENTION

Interpretation

1. In this Part of this Schedule any reference to a numbered article is a reference to the article of the Convention which is so numbered and any expression to which a meaning is assigned by article 1 of the Convention has that meaning.

Provisions adapting or supplementing specified articles of the Convention

2. For the purposes of paragraph 2 of article 2, provisions of such an international convention as is mentioned in that paragraph which apart from this paragraph do not have mandatory application to carriage by sea shall be treated as having mandatory application to carriage by sea if it is stated in the contract of carriage for the carriage in question that those provisions are to apply in connection with the carriage.

3. The reference to the law of the court in article 6 shall be construed as a reference to the Law Reform (Contributory Negligence) Act 1945 except that in relation to Northern Ireland it shall be construed as a reference to section 2 of the Law Reform (Miscellaneous Provisions Act (Northern Ireland) 1948.

4. The Secretary of State may by order provide that, in relation to a carrier whose principal place of business is in the United Kingdom, paragraph 1 of article 7 shall have effect with the substitution for the limit for the time being specified in that paragraph of a different limit specified in the order (which shall not be lower than the limit specified in that paragraph at the passing of this Act or, if paragraph 1 of Part III of this Schedule has come into force, specified in paragraph 1 of article 7 as amended by paragraph 1 of that Part).

5. The values which in pursuance of article 9 shall be considered as the official values in the United Kingdom of the amounts in francs for the time being specified in articles 7 and 8 shall be such amounts in sterling as the Secretary of State may from time to time by order specify.

6. It is hereby declared that by virtue of article 12 the limitations on liability there mentioned in respect of a passenger or his luggage apply to the aggregate liabilities of the persons in question in all proceedings for enforcing the liabilities or any of them which may be brought whether in the United Kingdom or elsewhere.

7. Article 16 shall apply to an arbitration as it applies to an action; and section 27(3) and (4) of the Limitation Act 1939 and section 72(2) and (3) of the Statute of Limitation (Northern Ireland) 1958 (which determine when an arbitration is deemed to commence) shall apply for the purposes of article 16 as they apply for the purposes of those Acts.

8. The court before which proceedings are brought in pursuance of article 17 to enforce a liability which is limited by virtue of article 12 may at any stage of the proceedings make such orders as appear to the court to be just and equitable in view of the provisions of article 12 and of any other proceedings which have been or are likely to be begun in the United Kingdom or elsewhere to enforce the liability in whole or in part; and without prejudice to the generality of the preceding provisions of this paragraph such a court shall, where the liability is or may be partly enforceable in other proceedings in the United Kingdom or elsewhere, have jurisdiction to award an amount less than the court would have awarded if the limitation applied solely to the proceedings before the court or to make any party of its award conditional on the results of any other proceedings.

Other provisions adapting or supplementing the Convention

9. Any reference in the Convention to a contract of carriage excludes a contract of carriage which is not for reward.

10. If Her Majesty by Order in Council declares that any State

specified in the Order is a party to the Convention in respect of a particular country the Order shall, subject to the provisions of any subsequent Order made by virtue of this paragraph, be conclusive evidence that the State is a party to the Convention in respect of that country.

11. The Secretary of State may by order make provision—

(a) for requiring a person who is the carrier in relation to a passenger to give to the passenger, in a manner specified in the order, notice of such of the provisions of Part I of this Schedule as are so specified;

(b) for a person who fails to comply with a requirement imposed on him by the order to be guilty of an offence and liable on summary conviction to a fine of an amount not exceeding £500.

Application of ss. 502 and 503 of Merchant Shipping Act 1894 and sections 17 and 18 of this Act

12. Nothing in section 502 of the Merchant Shipping Act 1894 or section 18 of this Act (which among other things limit a shipowner's liability for the loss or damage of goods in certain cases) shall relieve a person of any liability imposed on him by the Convention.

13. It is hereby declared that nothing in the Convention affects the operation of section 503 of the Merchant Shipping Act 1894 or section 17 of this Act (which limit a shipowner's liability in certain cases of loss of life, injury or damage).

PART III. MODIFICATIONS OF PARTS I AND II IN CONSEQUENCE OF PROTOCOL OF 19TH NOVEMBER 1976

1. In Part I of this Schedule, in article 7 of the Convention, for the words "700,000 francs" or any other words which, by virtue of paragraph 4 of Part II of this Schedule, are specified in that article in the place of those words there shall be substituted the words "46,666 units of account".

2. In the said Part I, in article 8 of the Convention, for the word "francs" wherever it occurs there shall be substituted the words "units of account" and for the figures "12,500", "50,000", "18,000", "1,750" and "200" there shall be substituted respectively the figures "833", "3,333", "1,200", "117" and "13".

3. In the said Part I for article 9 there shall be substituted the following—

Article 9. Unit of account and conversion

The Unit of Account mentioned in this Convention is the Special Drawing Right as defined by the International Monetary Fund. The amounts mentioned in Articles 7 and 8 shall be converted into the national currency of the state of the Court seized of the case on the basis of the value of that currency on the date of the judgment or the date agreed upon by the Parties.

4. In Part II of this Schedule for paragraph 5 there shall be substituted the following—

5.—(1) For purpose of converting from special drawing rights into sterling the amounts mentioned in articles 7 and 8 of the Convention in respect of which a judgment is given, one special drawing right shall be treated as equal to such a sum in sterling as the International Monetary Fund have fixed as being the equivalent of one special drawing right for—

(a) the day on which the judgment is given; or
(b) if no sum has been so fixed for that day, the last day before that day for which a sum has been so fixed.

(2) A certificate given by or on behalf of the Treasury stating—

(a) that a particular sum in sterling has been fixed as mentioned in the preceding sub-paragraph for a particular day; or
(b) that no sum has been so fixed for that day and a particular sum in sterling has been so fixed for a day which is the last day for which a sum has been so fixed before the particular day,

shall be conclusive evidence of those matters for the purposes of articles 7 to 9 of the Convention; and a document purporting to be such a certificate shall, in any proceedings, be received in evidence and, unless the contrary is proved, be deemed to be such a certificate.

APPENDIX IV

MERCHANT SHIPPING ACT 1979 SCHEDULE 4, PARTS I AND II

SCHEDULE 4. CONVENTION ON LIMITATION OF LIABILITY FOR MARITIME CLAIMS 1976

PART I. TEXT OF CONVENTION

Chapter I. The Right of Limitation

Article 1. Persons entitled to limit liability

1. Shipowners and salvors, as hereinafter defined, may limit their liability in accordance with the rules of this Convention for claims set out in Article 2.

2. The term "shipowner" shall mean the owner, charterer, manager or operator of a seagoing ship.

3. Salvor shall mean any person rendering services in direct connexion with salvage operations. Salvage operations shall also include operations referred to in Article 2, paragraph 1 (d), (e) and (f).

4. If any claims set out in Article 2 are made against any person for whose act, neglect or default the shipowner or salvor is responsible, such person shall be entitled to avail himself of the limitation of liability provided for in this Convention.

5. In this Convention the liability of a shipowner shall include liability in an action brought against the vessel herself.

6. An insurer of liability for claims subject to limitation in accordance with the rules of this Convention shall be entitled to the benefits of this Convention to the same extent as the assured himself.

7. The act of invoking limitation of liability shall not constitute an admission of liability.

Article 2. Claims subject to limitation

1. Subject to Articles 3 and 4 the following claims, whatever the basis of liability may be, shall be subject to limitation of liability:

    (a) claims in respect of loss of life or personal injury or loss of or damage to property (including damage to harbour works, basins and waterways and aids to navigation), occurring on board or in direct connexion with the operation of the ship or with salvage operations, and consequential loss resulting therefrom;

    (b) claims in respect of loss resulting from delay in the carriage by sea of cargo, passengers or their luggage;

    (c) claims in respect of other loss resulting from infringement of rights other than contractual rights, occurring in direct connexion with the operation of the ship or salvage operations;

    (d) claims in respect of the raising, removal, destruction or the rendering harmless of a ship which is sunk, wrecked, stranded or abandoned, including anything that is or has been on board such ship;

    (e) claims in respect of the removal, destruction or the rendering harmless of the cargo of the ship;

    (f) claims of a person other than the person liable in respect of measures taken in order to avert or minimize loss for which the person liable may limit his liability in accordance with this Convention, and further loss caused by such measures.

2. Claims set out in paragraph 1 shall be subject to limitation of liability even if brought by way of recourse or for indemnity under a contract or otherwise. However, claims set out under paragraph 1(d), (e) and (f) shall not be subject to limitation of liability to the extent that they relate to remuneration under a contract with the person liable.

Article 3. Claims excepted from limitation

The rules of this Convention shall not apply to:

    (a) claims for salvage or contribution in general average;

    (b) claims for oil pollution damage within the meaning of the International Convention on Civil Liability for Oil Pollution Damage dated 29th November 1969 or of any amendment or Protocol thereto which is in force;

    (c) claims subject to any international convention or national legislation governing or prohibiting limitation of liability for nuclear damage;

    (d) claims against the shipowner of a nuclear ship for nuclear damage;

    (e) claims by servants of the shipowner or salvor whose duties are connected with the ship or the salvage operations, including claims of their heirs, dependants or other persons entitled to make such claims, if under the law governing the contract of service between the shipowner or salvor and such servants the shipowner or salvor is not entitled to limit his liability in respect of such claims, or if he is by such law only permitted to limit his liability to an amount greater than that provided for in Article 6.

Article 4. Conduct barring limitation

A person liable shall not be entitled to limit his liability if it is proved that the loss resulted from his personal act or omission, committed with the intent to cause such loss, or recklessly and with knowledge that such loss would probably result.

Article 5. Counterclaims

Where a person entitled to limitation of liability under the rules of this Convention has a claim against the claimant arising out of the same occurrence, their respective claims shall be set off against each other and the provisions of this Convention shall only apply to the balance, if any.

Chapter II. Limits of Liability

Article 6. The general limits

1. The limits of liability for claims other than those mentioned in Article 7, arising on any distinct occasion, shall be calculated as follows:

    (a) in respect of claims for loss of life or personal injury,

        (i) 333,000 Units of Account for a ship with a tonnage not exceeding 500 tons,

        (ii) for a ship with a tonnage in excess thereof, the following amount in addition to that mentioned in (i):

for each ton from 501 to 3,000 tons, 500 Units of Account;

for each ton from 3,001 to 30,000 tons, 333 Units of Account;

for each ton from 30,001 to 70,000 tons, 250 Units of Account, and

for each ton in excess of 70,000 tons, 167 Units of Account,

(b) in respect of any other claims,

    (i) 167,000 Units of Account for a ship with a tonnage not exceeding 500 tons,

    (ii) for a ship with a tonnage in excess thereof the following amount in addition to that mentioned in (i):

for each ton from 501 to 30,000 tons, 167 Units of Account;

for each ton from 30,001 to 70,000 tons, 125 Units of Account; and

for each ton in excess of 70,000 tons, 83 Units of Account.

2. Where the amount calculated in accordance with paragraph 1(a) is insufficient to pay the claims mentioned therein in full, the amount calculated in accordance with paragraph 1(b) shall be available for payment of the unpaid balance of claims under paragraph 1(a) and such unpaid balance shall rank rateably with claims mentioned under paragraph 1(b).

3. The limits of liability for any salvor not operating from any ship or for any salvor operating solely on the ship to, or in respect of which he is rendering salvage services, shall be calculated according to a tonnage of 1,500 tons.

Article 7. The limit for passenger claims

1. In respect of claims arising on any distinct occasion for loss of life or personal injury to passengers of a ship, the limit of liability of the shipowner thereof shall be an amount of 46,666 Units of Account multiplied by the number of passengers which the ship is authorised to carry according to the ship's certificate, but not exceeding 25 million Units of Account.

2. For the purpose of this Article "claims for loss of life or personal injury to passengers of a ship" shall mean any such claims brought by or on behalf of any person carried in that ship:

(a) under a contract of passenger carriage, or

(b) vehicle or live animals which are covered by a contract for the carriage of goods.

Article 8. Unit of Account

1. The Unit of Account referred to in Articles 6 and 7 is the Special Drawing Right as defined by the International Monetary Fund. The amounts mentioned in Articles 6 and 7 shall be converted into the national currency of the State in which limitation is sought, according

to the value of that currency at the date the limitation fund shall have been constituted, payment is made, or security is given which under the law of that State is equivalent to such payment.

Article 9. Aggregation of claims

1. The limits of liability determined in accordance with Article 6 shall apply to the aggregate of all claims which arise on any distinct occasion:

    (a) against the person or persons mentioned in paragraph 2 of Article 1 and any person for whose act, neglect or default he or they are responsible; or

    (b) against the shipowner of a ship rendering salvage services from that ship and the salvor or salvors operating from such ship and any person for whose act, neglect or default he or they are responsible; or

    (c) against the salvor or salvors who are not operating from a ship or who are operating solely on the ship to, or in respect of which, the salvage services are rendered and any person for whose act, neglect or default he or they are responsible.

2. The limits of liability determined in accordance with Article 7 shall apply to the aggregate of all claims subject thereto which may arise on any distinct occasion against the person or persons mentioned in paragraph 2 of Article 1 in respect of the ship referred to in Article 7 and any person for whose act, neglect or default he or they are responsible.

Article 10. Limitation of liability without constitution of a limitation fund

1. Limitation of liability may be invoked notwithstanding that a limitation fund as mentioned in Article 11 has not been constituted.

2. If limitation of liability is invoked without the constitution of a limitation fund, the provisions of Article 12 shall apply correspondingly.

3. Questions of procedure arising under the rules of this Article shall be decided in accordance with the national law of the State Party in which action is brought.

Chapter III. The Limitation Fund

Article 11. Constitution of the fund

1. Any person alleged to be liable may constitute a fund with the Court or other competent authority in any State Party in which legal

proceedings are instituted in respect of claims subject to limitation. The fund shall be constituted in the sum of such of the amounts set out in Articles 6 and 7 as are applicable to claims for which that person may be liable, together with interest thereon from the date of the occurrence giving rise to the liability until the date of the constitution of the fund. Any fund thus constituted shall be available only for the payment of claims in respect of which limitation of liability can be invoked.

2. A fund may be constituted, either by depositing the sum, or by producing a guarantee acceptable under the legislation of the State Party where the fund is constituted and considered to be adequate by the Court or other competent authority.

3. A fund constituted by one of the persons mentioned in paragraph 1(a), (b) or (c) or paragraph 2 of Article 9 or his insurer shall be deemed constituted by all persons mentioned in paragraph 1(a), (b) or (c) or paragraph 2, respectively.

Article 12. Distribution of the fund

1. Subject to the provisions of paragraphs 1 and 2 of Article 6 and of Article 7, the fund shall be distributed among the claimants in proportion to their established claims against the fund.

2. If, before the fund is distributed, the person liable, or his insurer, has settled a claim against the fund such person shall, up to the amount he has paid, acquire by subrogation the rights which the person so compensated would have enjoyed under this Convention.

3. The right of subrogation provided for in paragraph 2 may also be exercised by persons other than those therein mentioned in respect of any amount of compensation which they may have paid, but only to the extent that such subrogation is permitted under the applicable national law.

4. Where the person liable or any other person establishes that he may be compelled to pay, at a later date, in whole or in part any such amount of compensation with regard to which such person would have enjoyed a right of subrogation pursuant to paragraphs 2 and 3 had the compensation been paid before the fund was distributed, the Court or other competent authority of the State where the fund has been constituted may order that a sufficient sum shall be provisionally set aside to enable such later date to enforce his claim against the fund.

Article 13. Bar to other actions

1. Where a limitation fund has been constituted in accordance with Article 11, any person having made a claim against the fund shall be

barred from exercising any right in respect of such a claim against any other assets of a person by or on behalf of whom the fund has been constituted.

2. After a limitation fund has been constituted in accordance with Article 11, any ship or other property, belonging to a person on behalf of whom the fund has been constituted, which has been arrested or attached within the jurisdiction of a State Party for a claim which may be raised against the fund, or any security given, may be released by order of the Court or other competent authority of such State. However, such release shall always be ordered if the limitation fund has been constituted:

(a) at the port where the occurrence took place, or, if it took place out of port, at the first port of call thereafter; or
(b) at the port of disembarkation in respect of claims for loss of life or personal injury; or
(c) at the port of discharge in respect of damage to cargo; or
(d) in the State where the arrest is made.

3. The rules of paragraphs 1 and 2 shall apply only if the claimant may bring a claim against the limitation fund before the Court administering that fund and the fund is actually available and freely transferable in respect of that claim.

Article 14. Governing law

Subject to the provisions of this Chapter the rules relating to the constitution and distribution of a limitation fund, and all rules of procedure in connection therewith, shall be governed by the law of the State Party in which the fund is constituted.

Chapter IV. Scope of Application

Article 15

This Convention shall apply whenever any person referred to in Article 1 seeks to limit his liability before the Court of a State Party or seeks to procure the release of a ship or other property or the discharge of any security given within the jurisdiction of any such State.

PART II. PROVISIONS HAVING EFFECT IN CONNECTION WITH CONVENTION

Interpretation

1. In this Part of this Schedule any reference to a numbered article is a reference to the article of the Convention which is so numbered.

Right to limit liability

2. The right to limit liability under the Convention shall apply in relation to any ship whether seagoing or not, and the definition of "shipowner" in paragraph 2 of article 1 shall be construed accordingly.

Claims subject to limitation

3.—(1) Paragraph 1(d) of article 2 shall not apply unless provision has been made by an order of the Secretary of State for the setting up and management of a fund to be used for the making to harbour or conservancy authorities of payments needed to compensate them for the reduction, in consequence of the said paragraph 1(d), of amounts recoverable by them in claims of the kind there mentioned, and to be maintained by contributions from such authorities raised and collected by them in respect of vessels in like manner as other sums so raised by them.

(2) Any order under sub-paragraph (1) above may contain such incidental and supplemental provisions as appear to the Secretary of State to be necessary or expedient.

(3) If immediately before the coming into force of section 17 of this Act an order is in force under section 2(6) of the Merchant Shipping (Liability of Shipowners and Others) Act 1958 (which contains provisions corresponding to those of this paragraph) that order shall have effect as if made under this paragraph.

Claims excluded from limitation

4.—(1) The claims excluded from the Convention by paragraph (b) of article 3 are claims in respect of any liability incurred under section 1 of the Merchant Shipping (Oil Pollution) Act 1971.

(2) The claims excluded from the Convention by paragraph (c) of article 3 are claims made by virtue of any of sections 7 to 11 of the Nuclear Installations Act 1965.

The general limits

5.—(1) In the application of article 6 to a ship with a tonnage less than 300 tons that article shall have effect as if—

    (a) paragraph (a)(i) referred to 166,667 Units of Account; and

    (b) paragraph (b)(i) referred to 83,333 Units of Account.

(2) For the purposes of article 6 and this paragraph a ship's tonnage

shall be its gross tonnage calculated in such manner as may be prescribed by an order made by the Secretary of State.

(3) Any order under this paragraph shall, so far as appears to the Secretary of State to be practicable, give effect to the regulations in Annex I of the International Convention on Tonnage Measurement of Ships 1969.

Limit for passenger claims

6.—(1) In the case of a passenger steamer within the meaning of Part III of the Merchant Shipping Act 1894 the ship's certificate mentioned in paragraph 1 of article 7 shall be the passenger steamer's certificate issued under section 274 of that Act.

(2) In paragraph 2 of article 7 the reference to claims brought on behalf of a person includes a reference to any claim in respect of the death of a person under the Fatal Accidents Act 1976, the Fatal Accidents (Northern Ireland) Order 1977 or the Damages (Scotland) Act 1976.

Units of Account

7.—(1) For the purpose of converting the amounts mentioned in articles 6 and 7 from special drawing rights into sterling one special drawing right shall be treated as equal to such a sum in sterling as the International Monetary Fund have fixed as being the equivalent of one special drawing right for—
  (a) the relevant date under paragraph 1 of Article 8; or
  (b) if no sum has been so fixed for that date, the last preceding date for which a sum has been so fixed.

(2) A certificate given by or on behalf of the Treasury stating—
  (a) that a particular sum in sterling has been fixed as mentioned in the preceding sub-paragraph for a particular date; or
  (b) that no sum has been so fixed for that date and that a particular sum in sterling has been so fixed for a date which is the last preceding date for which a sum has been so fixed,
shall be conclusive evidence of those matters for the purposes of those articles; and a document purporting to be such a certificate shall, in any proceedings, be received in evidence and, unless the contrary is proved, be deemed to be such a certificate.

Constitution of fund

8.—(1) The Secretary of State may from time to time, with the concurrence of the Treasury, by order prescribe the rate of interest to be applied for the purposes of paragraph 1 of article 11.

(2) Where a fund is constituted with the court in accordance with article 11 for the payment of claims arising out of any occurrence, the court may stay any proceedings relating to any claim arising out of that occurrence which are pending against the person by whom the fund has been constituted.

Distribution of fund

9. No lien or other right in respect of any ship or property shall affect the proportions in which under article 12 the fund is distributed among several claimants.

Bar to other actions

10. Where the release of a ship or other property is ordered under paragraph 2 of article 13 the person on whose application it is ordered to be released shall be deemed to have submitted to (or, in Scotland, prorogated) the jurisdiction of the court to adjudicate on the claim for which the ship or property was arrested or attached.

Meaning of "court"

11. References in the Convention and the preceding provisions of this Part of this Schedule to the court are—
    (a) in relation to England and Wales, references to the High Court;
    (b) in relation to Scotland, references to the Court of Session;
    (c) in relation to Northern Ireland, references to the High Court of Justice in Northern Ireland.

Meaning of "ship"

12. References in the Convention and in the preceding provisions of this Part of this Schedule to a ship include references to any structure (whether completed or in course of completion) launched and intended for use in navigation as a ship or part of a ship.

Meaning of "State Party"

13. An Order in Council made for the purposes of this paragraph and declaring that any State specified in the Order is a party to the Convention shall, subject to the provisions of any subsequent Order made for those purposes, be conclusive evidence that the State is a party to the Convention.

APPENDIX V

MERCHANT SHIPPING ACT 1979
SCHEDULE 5

SCHEDULE 5. LIABILITY OF SHIPOWNERS AND SALVORS: CONSEQUENTIAL AMENDMENTS

The Merchant Shipping (Liability of Shipowners and Others) Act 1900

1.—(1) In section 2(1) of the Merchant Shipping (Liability of Shipowners and Others) Act 1900 for the reference to the actual fault or privity of the owners or authority there shall be substituted a reference to any such personal act or omission of the owners or authority as is mentioned in article 4 of the Convention in Part I of Schedule 4 to this Act.

(2) The limit of liability under that section shall be ascertained by applying to the ship mentioned in subsection (1) the method of calculation specified in paragraph 1(b) of article 6 of the Convention read with paragraph 5(1) and (2) of Part II of that Schedule.

(3) Articles 11 and 12 of the Convention in Part I of that Schedule and paragraphs 8 and 9 of Part II of that Schedule shall apply for the purposes of that section.

The Pilotage Authorities (Limitation of Liability) Act 1936

2.—(1) In section 1(1) of the Pilotage Authorities (Limitation of Liability) Act 1936 for the reference to the actual fault or privity of the pilotage authority there shall be substituted a reference to any such personal act or omission of the authority as is mentioned in article 4 of the Convention in Part I of Schedule 4 of this Act.

(2) In section 4 of that Act for the words from " by or under" to "subsequent Acts" there shall be substituted the words "under section 17 or 18 of the Merchant Shipping Act 1979".

The Crown Proceedings Act 1947

3. For section 5 of the Crown Proceedings Act 1947, including that Act as it applies in Northern Ireland, there shall be substituted—
    "5.—(1) The provisions of sections 17 and 18 of the Merchant Shipping Act 1979 and of Schedule 4 to that Act (liability of ship-owners and salvors) shall apply in relation to His Majesty's ships as they apply in relation to other ships.
    (2) In this section 'ships' has the same meaning as in those provisions."

The Hovercraft Act 1968

4. In section 1(1)(i) of the Hovercraft Act 1968 for the words "Part VIII of the Merchant Shipping Act 1894", "that Part" and "the said Part VIII" there shall be substituted respectively the words "sections 17 and 18 of the Merchant Shipping Act 1979", "those sections" and "the said sections of the Merchant Shipping Act 1979".

The Carriage of Goods by Sea Act 1971

5. In section 6(4) of the Carriage of Goods by Sea Act 1971 for the words from "section 502" to "1958" there shall be substituted the words "section 18 of the Merchant Shipping Act 1979 (which".

The Merchant Shipping (Oil Pollution) Act 1971

6.—(1) In sections 5(4)(b) and 7(b) of the Merchant Shipping (Oil Pollution) Act 1971 for the words "the Merchant Shipping (Liability of Shipowners and Others) Act 1958" there shall be substituted the words "the Merchant Shipping Act 1979".
    (2) For section 15(2) of that Act there shall be substituted—
        "(2) For the purposes of section 17 of the Merchant Shipping Act 1979 (limitation of liability) any liability incurred under this section shall be deemed to be a liability in respect of such damage to property as is mentioned in paragraph 1(a) of article 2 of the Convention in Part I of Schedule 4 to that Act."

APPENDIX VI

STATUTORY INSTRUMENTS

**The Merchant Shipping Act 1979 (Commencement No. 10) Order
1986**

(1986 No. 1052)

Made ....   *23rd June 1986*

The Secretary of State for Transport, in exercise of powers conferred
on him by section 52(2) of the Merchant Shipping Act 1979 (hereinafter referred to as "the Act") and of all other powers enabling him in
that behalf hereby makes the following Order:—

1. This Order may be cited as the Merchant Shipping Act 1979
(Commencement No. 10) Order 1986.
2. The provisions of the Act specified in the first column of the
Schedule to this Order (which relates to the matters specified in the
second column of that Schedule) shall come into force on 1st
December 1986.

                                                John Moore,
23rd June 1986.   SECRETARY OF STATE FOR TRANSPORT.

SCHEDULE

PROVISION COMING INTO FORCE ON 1ST DECEMBER 1986

Section 17	Limitation of Liability
Section 18	Exclusion of Liability
Section 19(1) and (4)	Supplementary

171

Section 50(4) so far as it relates to the provisions of Schedule 7 set out below in this Schedule	Repeals
Schedule 4	Convention on Limitation of Liability for Maritime Claims 1976
Schedule 5	Salvors: Consequential amendments
Schedule 7, Part I	Repeal of enactments relating to liability of Shipowners and salvors

EXPLANATORY NOTE

(This Note is not part of the Order)

This Order brings into operation those provisions of the Merchant Shipping Act 1979 necessary to give effect to the Convention on Limitation of Liability for Maritime Claims 1976 (set out in Schedule 4 to the Act), which comes into force on 1st December 1986, and replaces in the United Kingdom the Brussels Convention relating to the Limitation of Liability of Owners of Sea-going Ships, 1957.

NOTE TO EARLIER COMMENCEMENT ORDERS

(This Note is not part of the Order)

The following provisions of the Merchant Shipping Act 1979 have been brought into force by commencement orders made before the date of this Order:—

Provision	*Date of commencement*	*S.I. No.*
ss. 1 to 6. Sch. 1	1.8.79	1979/807
ss. 7, 8(1), (2), (4) and that part of (6) which relates to s. 14 of the Pilotage Act 1913, 9 to 11	4.7.80 and 1.9.80	1980/923
ss. 12, 13(1) in relation to Sch. 2, paras. 1 to 4, 5(2), 6, 7, 10(2), 11, 12, 14, to 19, 20(1), the former part of 20(2), 21 to 27	1.8.79, 1.10.79 and 1.1.80	1979/807

Provision	Date of commencement	S.I. No.
s. 13(1) in relation to Sch. 2, paras. 5(1), 8, 9, 10(1), 13(3) and the latter part of 20(2)	1.1.80 4.7.80 and 1.9.80	1979/807 1980/923
s. 13(2) to (5)	1.8.79	1979/807
s. 15(1) and the latter part of (2)	17.12.79	1979/1578
s. 16	1.8.79	1979/807
s. 19(2), (3)	17.12.79	1979/1578
ss. 20 to 22, 26 to 30, 32(1), 33, 34, 35(1) except in relation to fishing vessels, 36(1)	1.8.79, 1.10.79 and 1.1.80	1979/807
s. 23(7)	31.12.85	1985/1827
s. 31	3.5.83	1983/440
s. 32(2), (3)	1.7.83	1982/1616
s. 36(2)	1.4.80	1980/354
ss. 36(3), 37(1) to (3), (5), (7), (8)	1.8.79	1979/807
s. 37(4)	1.1.83	1982/1616
s. 38(5)	17.12.79	1979/1578
s. 38(1), (2), (3) and (6)	8.4.81	1981/405
ss. 39 to 45, 46 (partially), Sch. 6	1.8.79 and 1.1.80	1979/807
s. 46 (remainder)	4.7.80	1980/923
s. 47(1), (2) (partially), (3)	1.8.79, 1.10.79 and 1.1.80	1979/807
s. 47(2)	17.12.79 and 14.9.83	1979/1578 and 1983/1312
ss. 48, 49, 50(1), (2)	1.8.79	1979/807
s. 50(3)	4.7.80	1980/923
s. 50(4) and Sch. 7 (partially)	1.8.79, 1.10.79 and 1.1.80 1.4.80 4.7.80 and 1.9.80 8.4.81 3.5.83 31.12.85	1979/807 1980/354 1980/923 1981/405 1983/440 1985/1827
s. 51(1), (3), 52	1.8.79	1979/807
s. 51(2) (partially)	1.1.83	1982/1616

Provision	Date of commencement	S.I. No.
Sch. 3, Part I has been brought into force for some purposes, with modification, by the Carriage of Passengers and their Luggage by Sea (Interim Provisions) Order 1980 (S.I. 1980/1092) made under the powers in section 16(1), (2) and (5).	1.1.81	1980/1092.

Notes 1. Sections 1 to 13, Schedule 2, paragraph 2 of Schedule 5 and the entries relating to the Pilotage Act 1913 (c. 31 (2 & 3 Geo. 5)) in Part II of Schedule 7 have been repealed by and re-enacted in the Pilotage Act 1983 (c. 21) (a consolidation Act).
2. Section 35(1) ceases to have effect with the coming into operation of the repeals effected by this Order.

The Merchant Shipping (Liability of Shipowners and Others) (Calculation of Tonnage) Order 1986

(1986 No. 1040)

Made	*23rd June 1986*
Laid before Parliament	*3rd July 1986*
Coming into Operation	*1st December 1986*

The Secretary of State for Transport in exercise of the powers conferred on him by paragraph 5 of Part II of Schedule 4 to the Merchant Shipping Act 1979 and of all other powers enabling him in that behalf, hereby makes the following Order:—

1. This Order may be cited as the Merchant Shipping (Liability of Ship-owners and Others) (Calculation of Tonnage) Order 1986 and shall come into force on 1st December 1986.

2.—(1) For the purposes of article 6 of the Convention on Limitation of Liability for Maritime Claims 1976 and of paragraph 5 of Part II of Schedule 4 to the Merchant Shipping act 1979, the gross tonnage of a ship shall be calculated in accordance with regulations 4 to 6 of the Merchant Shipping (Tonnage) Regulations 1982.

(2) In the case of a ship of which, at the time when limitation is claimed, the tonnage has not been and cannot be ascertained in accordance with paragraph (1) above, the best evidence available of

the measurements of the ship shall be used in calculating the tonnage of the ship according to those regulations.

John Moore,
23rd June 1986. Secretary of State for Transport.

EXPLANATORY NOTE

(This Note is not part of the Order)

The Order provides that, for the purposes of the Convention on Limitation of Liability for Maritime Claims 1976, set out in and implemented by the Merchant Shipping Act 1979, a ship's gross tonnage (being the tonnage by relation to which the ship's liability may be limited) is to be calculated in accordance with regulations 4 to 6 of the Merchant Shipping (Tonnage) Regulations 1982. These implement the rules for measuring gross tonnage set out in Annex 1 of the International Convention on Tonnage Measurement of Ships, 1969 (Cmnd 4332). The best available evidence of the measurements of a ship will be used when the tonnage of a ship claiming limitation has not previously been ascertained and cannot be ascertained.

The Merchant Shipping Act 1979 (Commencement No. 11) Order 1987

(S.I. 1987 No. 635)

Made .... *2nd April 1987*

Whereas subsections (1) and (2) of section 14 of the Merchant Shipping Act 1979 provide for the Athens Convention relating to the Carriage of Passengers and their Luggage by Sea (set out in Schedule 3 to that Act) to have the force of law in the United Kingdom but those subsections do not come into force until an order for that purpose is made under section 5(2) of the Act:

And whereas by virtue of section 16(1) of that Act the Carriage of Passengers and their Luggage by Sea (Interim Provisions) Order 1980 provides for the said Athens Convention to apply to certain contracts for international carriage (being contracts made on or after 1st January 1981 but, by virtue of Article 3 of that Order, only until such time as subsections (1) and (2) of the said section 14 come into force:

And whereas a draft of this Order has been laid before Parliament in accordance with section 16(5) of the Merchant Shipping Act 1979 (hereinafter referred to as "the Act") and has been approved by a resolution of each House of Parliament:

Now therefore the Secretary of State for Transport, in exercise of powers conferred on him by sections 16(4) and 52(2) of the Act and of all other powers enabling him in that behalf hereby makes the following Order:—

1. This Order may be cited as the Merchant Shipping Act 1979 (Commencement No. 11) Order 1987.

2. The provisions of the Act specified in the first column of the Schedule to this Order (which relate to the matters specified in the second column of that Schedule) shall come into force on 30th April 1987.

3. Notwithstanding Article 3(1) of the Carriage of Passengers and their Luggage by Sea (Interim Provisions) Order 1980, nothing in this Order affects the operation of that Order with respect to matters arising after the commencement of this Order in connection with any contract referred to in Article 2(a) or (b) of the said Order of 1980 and made before 30th April 1987.

Michael Spicer
Signed by authority of the Secretary of State   Parliamentary Under
                                               Secretary of State,
2nd April 1987   Department of Transport

SCHEDULE. PROVISIONS COMING INTO FORCE ON 30th APRIL 1987

Provisions of the Act	*Subject matter of the provisions*
Section 14(1), (2), (4), (5), (6) (except in its application to subsection (3)) and (7).	Convention relating to the Carriage of Passengers and their Luggage by Sea to have force of law.
Section 15(2) so far as not already in force.	Provisions concerning Orders in Council under section 14(4) or (5).
Schedule 3. Parts I and II.	Text of the Convention and provisions having effect in connection with it.

EXPLANATORY NOTE

(This note is not part of the Order)

The Order brings into force on 30th April most of section 14 of the Merchant Shipping Act 1979, which gives the force of law in the United Kingdom to the Athens Convention relating to the Carriage of Passengers and their Luggage by Sea (set out in Schedule 3 to the Act). The Convention comes into force internationally on 28th April 1987.

The Order does not bring into force section 14(3) of the 1979 Act (nor consequently section 14(6) as it applies to section 14(3), because that provision implements the Protocol to the Convention (which substitutes Special Drawing Rights for gold francs as the unit of account) and this Protocol is not yet in force.

The Order also brings into force section 15(2) so far as it is not already in force, and Schedule 3, Parts I and II.

The Order also contains a transitional provision preserving the effect of the Carriage of Passengers and their Luggage by Sea (Interim Provisions) Order 1980 for contracts for international carriage made before 30th April 1987.

NOTE AS TO EARLIER COMMENCEMENT ORDERS

(This note is not part of the Order)

The following provisions of the Merchant Shipping Act 1979 have been brought into force by commencement orders made before the date of this Order:—

Provision	Date of commencement	S.I. No.
ss. 1 to 6. Sch. 1	1.8.79	1979/807
ss. 7, 8(1), (2), (4) and that part of (6) which relates to s. 14 of the Pilotage Act 1913, 9 to 11	4.7.80 and 1.9.80	1980/923
ss. 12, 13(1) in relation to Sch. 2, paras. 1 to 4, 5(2), 6, 7, 10(2), 11, 12, 14 to 19, 20(1), the former part of 20(2), 21 to 27	1.8.79, 1.10.79 and 1.1.80	1979/807

Provision	Date of commencement	S.I. No.
s. 13(1) in relation to Sch. 2, paras. 5(1), 8, 9, 10(1), 13(3) and the latter part of 20(2)	1.1.80 4.7.80 and 1.9.80	1979/807 1980/923
s. 13(2) to (5)	1.8.79	1979/807
s. 15(1) and the latter part of (2)	17.12.79	1979/1578
s. 16	1.8.79	1979/807
ss. 17, 18 and 19(1) and (4)	1.12.86	1986/1052
s. 19(2), (3)	17.12.79	1979/1578
ss. 20 to 22, 26 to 30, 32(1), 33, 34, 35(1) except in relation to fishing vessels and 36(1)	1.8.79, 1.10.79 and 1.1.80	1979/807
s. 23(7)	31.12.85	1985/1827
s. 31	3.5.83	1983/440
s. 32(2), (3)	1.7.83	1982/1616
s. 36(2)	1.4.80	1980/354
ss. 36(3), 37(1) to (3), (5), (7) and (8)	1.8.79	1979/807
s. 37(4)	1.1.83	1982/1616
s. 38(5)	17.12.79	1979/1578
s. 38(1), (2), (3) and (6)	8.4.81	1981/405
ss. 39 to 45, 46 (partially), Sch. 6	1.8.79 and 1.1.80	1979/807
s. 46 (remainder)	4.7.80	1980/923
s. 47(1), (2) (partially), (3)	1.8.79, 1.10.79 and 1.1.80	1979/807
s. 47(2)	17.12.79 and 14.9.83	1979/1578 and 1983/1312
ss. 48, 49, 50(1), (2)	1.8.79	1979/807
s. 50(3)	4.7.80	1980/923
s. 50(4) and Sch. 7 (partially)	1.8.79, 1.10.79 and 1.1.80 1.4.80 4.7.80 and 1.9.80 8.4.81 3.5.83 31.12.85 1.12.86	1979/807 1980/354 1980/923 1981/405 1983/440 1985/1827 1986/1052

Provision	Date of commencement	S.I. No.
s. 51(1), (3) and 52	1.8.79	1979/807
s. 51(2) (partially)	1.1.83	1982/1616
Sch. 3, Part I has been brought into force for some purposes, with modification, by the Carriage of Passengers and their Luggage by Sea (Interim Provisions) Order 1980 (S.I. 1980/1092) made under the powers in section 16(1), (2) and (5).	1.1.81	1980/1092
Schedules 4 and 5	1.12.86	1986/1052.

Notes 1. Sections 1 to 13, Schedule 2, paragraph 2 of Schedule 5 and the entries relating to the Pilotage Act 1913 (c. 31 (2 & 3 Geo. 5)) in Part II of Schedule 7 have been repealed by and re-enacted in the Pilotage Act 1983 (c. 21) (a consolidation Act).

2. Section 35(1) has ceased to have effect.

The Merchant Shipping Act 1979 (Commencement No. 13) Order 1989

(S.I. 1989 No. 1881)

Made .... *9th October 1989*

The Secretary of State for Transport, in exercise of powers conferred on him by section 52(2) of the Merchant Shipping Act 1979 and of all other powers enabling him in that behalf hereby makes the following Order:—

1. This Order may be cited as the Merchant Shipping Act 1979 (Commencement No. 13) Order 1989.

2.—(1) Section 35(2) of the Merchant Shipping Act 1979, so far as it is not already in force, shall come into force on 10th November 1989.

(2) Section 14, so far as it is not already in force, and Part III of Schedule 3 to the Merchant Shipping Act 1979 shall come into force on 10th November 1989.

Patrick McLoughlin
Signed by authority of the Secretary of State Parliamentary Under
Secretary of State,
9th October 1989 Department of Transport

APPENDIX VI
EXPLANATORY NOTE

(This note is not part of the Order)

The Order brings into force on 10th November 1989 section 35(2) of the Merchant Shipping Act 1979 so far as it is not in force—i.e. for fishing vessels. Section 35(2) prevents any person limiting his liability under section 17 of the Act for loss of life or personal injury or other damage caused to a person on a ship who is employed in connection with the ship or with salvage operations. By virtue of section 17 shipowners and salvors can limit their liability in accordance with the Convention on Limitation of Liability for Maritime Claims 1976 (set out in Schedule 4 to the 1979 Act).

The Order also brings into force on 10th November 1989 section 14 so far as it is not already in force and Part III of Schedule 3 to the 1979 Act, primarily as a consequence of the coming into force of the 1976 Protocol to the Athens Convention relating to the Carriage of Passengers and their Luggage 1974. The Protocol substitutes references to Special Drawing Rights for references to gold francs.

NOTE AS TO EARLIER COMMENCEMENT ORDERS

(This note is not part of the Order)

The following provisions of the Merchant Shipping Act 1979 have been or are being brought into force by commencement orders made before the date of this Order:—

Provision	Date of commencement	S.I. No.
s. 14(1), (2), (4), (5), (6) except in its application to subsections (3) and (7)	30.4.87	1987/635
s. 15(1)	17.12.79	1979/1578
s. 15(2)	17.12.79 and 30.4.87	1979/1578 and 1987/ 635
s. 16	1.8.79	1979/807
ss. 17, 18 and 19(1) and (4)	1.12.86	1986/1052
s. 19(2), (3)	17.12.79	1979/1578

Provision	Date of commencement	S.I. No.
ss. 20 to 22, 26 to 30, 32(1), 33, 34, 35(1) except in relation to fishing vessels and 36(1)	1.8.79, 1.10.79 and 1.1.80	1979/807
s. 23(7)	31.12.85	1985/1827
s. 31	3.5.83	1983/440
s. 32(2) and (3)	1.7.83	1982/1616
s. 35(2) except in relation to fishing vessels	30.4.87	1987/719
s. 36(2)	1.4.80	1980/354
ss. 36(3), 37(1) to (3), (5), (7) and (8)	1.8.79	1979/807
s. 37(4)	1.1.83	1982/1616
s. 38(5)	17.12.79	1979/1578
s. 38(1), (2), (3) and (6)	8.4.81	1981/405
ss. 39 to 45, 46 (partially), Sch. 6	1.8.79 and 1.1.80	1979/807
s. 46 (remainder)	4.7.80	1980/923
s. 47(1), (2) (partially) and (3)	1.8.79, 1.10.79 and 1.1.80	1979/807
s. 47(2)	17.12.79 and 14.9.83	1979/1578 and 1983/1312
ss. 48, 49, 50(1) and (2)	1.8.79	1979/807
s. 50(3)	4.7.80	1980/923
s. 50(4) and Sch. 7 (partially)	1.8.79, 1.10.79 and 1.1.80 1.4.80 4.7.80 and 1.9.80 8.4.81 3.5.83 31.12.85 1.12.86	1979/807 1980/354 1980/923 1981/405 1983/440 1985/1827 1986/1052
ss. 51(1), (3) and 52	1.8.79	1979/807
s. 51(2) (partially)	1.1.83	1982/1616
Schedule 3, Parts I and II	30.4.87	1987/635
Schedules 4 and 5	1.12.86	1986/1052.

Notes 1. Sections 1 to 13, Schedule 2, paragraph 2 of Schedule 5 and the entries relating to the Pilotage Act 1913 (c. 31 (2 & 3 Geo. 5)) in Part II of Schedule 7 which were in force have been repealed.
2. Section 35(1) has ceased to have effect.

The Carriage of Passengers and their Luggage by Sea (United Kingdom Carriers) (Amendment) Order 1989

(S.I. 1989 No. 1880)

Made	*9th October 1989*
Coming into force	*10th November 1989*

The Secretary of State for Transport, in exercise of the powers conferred upon him by sections 14 and 16 of, and by paragraph 4 of Part II of Schedule 3 to, the Merchant Shipping Act 1979 and of all other powers enabling him in that behalf hereby makes the following Order:—

1. This Order may be cited as the Carriage of Passengers and their Luggage by Sea (United Kingdom Carriers) (Amendment) Order 1989 and shall come into force on 10th November 1989.
2. The Carriage of Passengers and their Luggage by Sea (United Kingdom Carriers) Order 1987 shall be amended as follows:—
   (a) in article 2, for "700,000 francs" there shall be substituted "46,666 units of account"; and for "1,525,000 francs" there shall be substituted "100,000 units of account";
   (b) article 3 shall be omitted.

Patrick McLoughlin
Signed by authority of the Secretary of State   Parliamentary Under
Secretary of State,
9th October 1989   Department of Transport

EXPLANATORY NOTE

(This note is not part of the Order)

This Order amends the Carriage of Passengers and their Luggage by Sea (United Kingdom Carriers) Order 1987 as a consequence of the coming into force of the 1976 Protocol to the Athens Convention relating to the Carriage of Passengers and their Luggage 1974 (which replaces the reference to gold francs in the Athens Convention by references to Special Drawing Rights). That Order provides a higher limit for United Kingdom carriers. This Order substitutes references to gold francs by appropriate references to "units of account", (the definition and conversion into sterling of which are provided in paragraphs 3 and 4 of Part III of Schedule 3 to the Merchant Shipping Act 1979, which comes into force on the same day as this Order).

APPENDIX VII

CARRIAGE OF GOODS BY SEA ACT 1971 (THE HAGUE–VISBY RULES)

AN ACT TO AMEND THE LAW WITH RESPECT TO THE CARRIAGE OF GOODS BY SEA

Application of Hague Rules as amended

1.—(1) In this Act, "the Rules" means the International Convention for the unification of certain rules of law relating to bills of lading signed at Brussels on 25th August 1924, as amended by the Protocol signed at Brussels on 23rd February, 1968, and by Protocol signed at Brussels on December 21, 1972.

(2) The provisions of the Rules, as set out in the Schedule to this Act, shall have the force of law.

(3) Without prejudice to subsection (2) above, the said provisions shall have effect (and have the force law) in relation to and in connection with the carriage of goods by sea in ships where the port of shipment is a port in the United Kingdom, whether or not the carriage is between ports in two different States within the meaning of Article X of the Rules.

(4) Subject to subsection (6) below, nothing in this section shall be taken as applying anything in the Rules to any contract for the carriage of goods by sea, unless the contract expressly or by implication provides for the issue of a bill of lading or any similar document of title.

(5) [*Repealed by section 5(3) of and Schedule to the Merchant Shipping Act, 1981.*]

(6) Without prejudice to Article X(c) of the Rules, the Rules shall have the force of law in relation to—

    (a) any bill of lading if the contract contained in or evidenced by it expressly provides that the Rules shall govern the contract, and

(b) any receipt which is a non-negotiable document marked as such if the contract contained in or evidenced by it is a contract for the carriage of goods by sea which expressly provides that the Rules are to govern the contract as if the receipt were a bill of lading,

but subject, where paragraph (b) applies, to any necessary modification and in particular with the omission in Article III of the Rules of the second sentence of paragraph 4 and of paragraph 7,

(7) If and so far as the contract contained in or evidenced by a bill of lading or receipt within paragraph (a) or (b) of subsection (6) above applies to deck cargo or live animals, the Rules as given the force of law by that subsection shall have effect as if Article I(c) did not exclude deck cargo and live animals.

In this subsection "deck cargo" means cargo which by the contract of carriage is stated as being carried on deck and is so carried.

Contracting States, etc.

2.—(1) If Her Majesty by Order in Council certifies to the following effect, that is to say, that for the purpose of the Rules—

(a) a State specified in the Order is a contracting State, or is a contracting State in respect of any place or territory so specified; or

(b) any place or territory specified in the Order forms part of a State so specified (whether a contracting State or not),

the Order shall, except so far as it has been superseded by a subsequent Order, be conclusive evidence of the matters so certified.

(2) An Order in Council under this section may be varied or revoked by a subsequent Order in Council.

Absolute warranty of seaworthiness not to be implied in contracts to which Rules apply

3. There shall not be implied in any contract for the carriage of goods by sea to which the Rules apply by virtue of this Act any absolute undertaking by the carrier of the goods to provide a seaworthy ship.

Application of Act to British possession, etc.

4.—(1) Her Majesty may by Order in Council direct that this Act shall extend, subject to such exceptions, adaptations and modifications as may be specified in the Order, to all or any of the following territories that is—

(a) any colony (not being a colony for whose external relations a country other than the United Kingdom is responsible),

(b) any country outside Her Majesty's dominions in which Her Majesty has jurisdiction in right of Her Majesty's Government of the United Kingdom.

(2) An Order in Council under this section may contain such transitional and other consequential and incidental provisions as appear to Her Majesty to be expedient, including provisions amending or repealing any legislation about the carriage of goods by sea forming part of the law of any of the territories mentioned in paragraphs (a) and (b) above.

(3) An Order in Council under this section may be varied or revoked by a subsequent Order in Council.

Extension of application of Rules to carriage from ports in British possessions, etc.

5.—(1) Her Majesty may by Order in Council provide that section 1(3) of this Act shall have effect as if the reference therein to the United Kingdom included a reference to all or any of the following territories, that is—

(a) the Isle of Man;

(b) any of the Channel Islands specified in the Order;

(c) any colony specified in the Order (not being a colony for whose external relations a country other than the United Kingdom is responsible);

(d) any associated state (as defined by section 1(3) of the West Indies Act 1967, specified in the Order;

(e) any country specified in the Order, being a country outside Her Majesty's dominions in which her Majesty has jurisdiction in right of Her Majesty's Government of the United Kingdom.

(2) An Order in Council under this section may be varied or revoked by a subsequent Order in Council.

Supplemental

6.—(1) This Act may be cited as the Carriage of Goods by Sea Act 1971.

(2) It is hereby declared that this Act extends to Northern Ireland.

(3) The following enactments shall be repealed, that is—

(a) the Carriage of Goods by Sea Act 1924,

(b) section 12(4) of the Nuclear Installations Act 1965,

and without prejudice to section 38(1) of the Interpretation Act 1889, the reference to the said Act of 1924 in section 1(1)(i)(ii) of the Hovercraft Act 1968 shall include a reference to this Act.

(4) It is hereby declared that for the purpose of Article VIII of the Rules section 502 of the Merchant Shipping Act 1894 (which, as amended by the Merchant Shipping (Liability of Shipowners and Others) Act 1958, entirely exempts shipowners and others in certain circumstances from liability for loss of, or damage to, goods) is a provision relating to limitation of liability.

(5) [*Provisions for coming into force*].

SCHEDULE. THE HAGUE RULES AS AMENDED BY THE BRUSSELS PROTOCOL 1968[1]

Article I

In these Rules the following words are employed, with the meanings set out below:—

(a) "Carrier" includes the owner or the charterer who enters into a contract of carriage with a shipper.

(b) "Contract of carriage" applies only to contracts of carriage covered by a bill of lading or any similar document of title, in so far as such document relates to the carriage of goods by sea, including any bill of lading or any similar document as aforesaid issued under or pursuant to a charter-party from the moment at which such bill of lading or similar document of title regulates the relations between a carrier and a holder of the same.

(c) "Goods" includes goods, wares, merchandise, and articles of every kind whatsoever except live animals and cargo which by the contract of carriage is stated as being carried on deck and is so carried.

(d) "Ship" means any vessel used for the carriage of goods by sea.

(e) "Carriage of goods" covers the period from the time when the goods are loaded on to the time they are discharged from the ship.

Article II

Subject to the provisions of Article VI, under every contract of carriage of goods by sea the carrier, in relation to the loading, handling,

1. Those provisions of the Hague–Visby Rules which differ from the Hague Rules are underlined.

stowage, carriage, custody, care and discharge of such goods, shall be subject to the responsibilities and liabilities, and entitled to the rights and immunities hereinafter set forth.

Article III

1. The carrier shall be bound before and at the beginning of the voyage to exercise due diligence to—
   (a) Make the ship seaworthy.
   (b) Properly man, equip and supply the ship.
   (c) Make the holds, refrigerating and cool chambers, and all other parts of the ship in which goods are carried, fit and safe for their reception, carriage and preservation.

2. Subject to the provisions of Article IV, the carrier shall properly and carefully load, handle, stow, carry, keep, care for, and discharge the goods carried.

3. After receiving the goods into his charge the carrier or the master or agent of the carrier shall, on demand of the shipper, issue to the shipper a bill of lading showing among other things—
   (a) The leading marks necessary for identification of the goods as the same are furnished in writing by the shipper before the loading of such goods starts, provided such marks are stamped or otherwise shown clearly upon the goods if uncovered, or on the cases or coverings in which such goods are contained, in such a manner as should ordinarily remain legible until the end of the voyage.
   (b) Either the number of packages or pieces, or the quantity, or weight, as the case may be, as furnished in writing by the shipper.
   (c) The apparent order and condition of the goods.

Provided that no carrier, master or agent of the carrier shall be bound to state or show in the bill of lading any marks, number, quantity, or weight which he has reasonable ground for suspecting not accurately to represent the goods actually received, or which he has had no reasonable means of checking.

4. Such a bill of lading shall be prima facie evidence of the receipt by the carrier of the goods as therein described in accordance with paragraph 3(a), (b) and (c). However, proof to the contrary shall not be admissible when the bill of lading has been transferred to a third party acting in good faith.[2]

---

2. This sentence does not appear in Article III, Rule 4, of the Hague Rules and its effect is to do away (in those cases where the Hague–Visby Rules apply) with the old principle of English law laid down in *Grant* v. *Norway* (1851) 10 C.B. 665 that no

5. The shipper shall be deemed to have guaranteed to the carrier the accuracy at the time of shipment of the marks, number, quantity and weight, as furnished by him, and the shipper shall indemnify the carrier against all loss, damages and expenses arising or resulting from inaccuracies in such particulars. The right of the carrier to such indemnity shall in no way limit his responsibility and liability under the contract of carriage to any person other than the shipper.

6. Unless notice of loss or damage and the general nature of such loss or damage be given in writing to the carrier or his agent at the port of discharge before or at the time of the removal of the goods into the custody of the person entitled to delivery thereof under the contract of carriage, or, if the loss or damage be not apparent, within three days, such removal shall be prima facie evidence of the delivery by the carrier of goods as described in the bill of lading.

The notice in writing need not be given if the state of the goods has, at the time of their receipt, been the subject of joint survey or inspection.

Subject to paragraph 6bis[3] the carrier and the ship shall in any event be discharged from all liability whatsoever[3] in respect of the goods, unless suit is brought within one year of their delivery or of the date whey they should have been delivered. This period may, however, be extended if the parties so agree after the cause of action has arisen.[3]

In the case of any actual or apprehended loss or damage the carrier and the receiver shall give all reasonable facilities to each other for inspecting and tallying the goods.

6bis. An action for indemnity against a third person may be brought even after the expiration of the year provided for in the preceding paragraph if brought within the time allowed by the law of the Court seized of the case. However, the time allowed shall be not less than three months, commencing from the day when the person bringing such action for indemnity has settled the claim or has been served with process in the action against himself.[4]

7. After the goods are loaded the bill of lading to be issued by the carrier, master, or agent of the carrier, to the shipper shall, if the shipper so demands, be a "shipped" bill of lading, provided that if the shipper shall have previously taken up any document of title to such goods, he shall surrender the same as against the issue of the

estoppel arose in relation to quantum (as opposed to apparent good order and condition) when the bill of lading was negotiated.

3. These words do not appear in the Hague Rules.

4. These words do not appear in the Hague Rules and were introduced to do away with the uncertainty which had arisen under those Rules as to whether the one year time limit applied to indemnity claims.

"shipped" bill of lading, but at the option of the carrier such document of title may be noted at the port of shipment by the carrier, master, or agent with the name or names of the ship or ships upon which the goods have been shipped and the date or dates of shipment, and when so noted if it shows the particulars mentioned in paragraph 3 of Article III, shall for the purpose of this article be deemed to constitute a "shipped" bill of lading.

8. Any clause, covenant, or agreement in a contract of carriage relieving the carrier or the ship from liability for loss or damage to, or in connection with, goods arising from negligence, fault, or failure in the duties and obligations provided in this article or lessening such liability otherwise than as provided in these Rules, shall be null and void and of no effect. A benefit of insurance _in favour of the carrier_[5] or similar clause shall be deemed to be a clause relieving the carrier from liability.

Article IV

1. Neither the carrier nor the ship shall be liable for loss or damage arising or resulting from unseaworthiness unless caused by want of due diligence on the part of the carrier to make the ship seaworthy, and to secure that the ship is properly manned, equipped and supplied, and to make the holds, refrigerating and cool chambers and all other parts of the ship in which goods are carried fit and safe for their reception, carriage and preservation in accordance with the provisions of paragraph 1 of Article III. Whenever loss or damage has resulted from unseaworthiness the burden of proving the exercise of due diligence shall be on the carrier or other person claiming exemption under this Article.

2. Neither the carrier nor the ship shall be responsible for loss or damage arising or resulting from—

(a) Act, neglect, or default of the master, mariner, pilot, or the servants of the carrier in the navigation or in the management of the ship.

(b) Fire, unless caused by the actual fault or privity of the carrier.

(c) Perils, dangers and accidents of the sea or other navigable waters.

(d) Act of God.

(e) Act of war.

(f) Act of public enemies.

5. These words do not appear in the Hague Rules.

(g) Arrest or restraint of princes, rulers or people, or seizure under legal process.

(h) Quarantine restrictions.

(i) Act or omission of the shipper or owner of the goods, his agent or representative.

(j) Strikes or lockouts or stoppage or restraint of labour from whatever cause, whether partial or general.

(k) Riots and civil commotions.

(l) Saving or attempting to save life or property at sea.

(m) Wastage in bulk or weight or any other loss or damage arising from inherent defect, quality or vice of the goods.

(n) Insufficiency of packing.

(o) Insufficiency of inadequacy of marks.

(p) Latent defects not discoverable by due diligence.

(q) Any other cause arising without the actual fault or privity of the carrier, or without the fault or neglect of the agents or servants of the carrier, but the burden of proof shall be on the person claiming the benefit of his exception to show that neither the actual fault or privity of the carrier nor the fault or neglect of the agents or servants of the carrier contributed to the loss or damage.

3. The shipper shall not be responsible for loss or damage sustained by the carrier or the ship arising or resulting from any cause without the act, fault or neglect of the shipper, his agents or his servants.

4. Any deviation in saving or attempting to save life or property at sea or any reasonable deviation shall not be deemed to be an infringement on breach of these Rules or of the contract of carriage, and the carrier shall not be liable for any loss or damage resulting therefrom.

5.[6] (a) Unless the nature and value of such goods have been declared by the shipper before shipment and inserted in the bill of lading, neither the carrier nor the ship shall in any event be or become liable for any loss or damage to or in connection with the goods in any amount exceeding the equivalent of 666.67 units of account[7] per package or unit or 2 units of account[7] per kilo of gross weight of the goods lost or damaged, whichever is the higher.

(b) The total amount recoverable shall be calculated by reference to the value of such goods at the place and time at which the goods

6. The wording of Article IV, Rule 5, of the Hague Rules is substantially different. The Hague Rules wording is quoted in full on pages 111–112.

7. These figures and units were introduced by s. 2(3) of the Merchant Shipping Act 1981 to give effect to the Hague–Visby Protocol. The unit of account is the SDR and the figures and units replaced by the 1981 Act were 10,000 Poincaré francs per package or unit or 30 Poincaré francs per kilo.

are discharged from the ship in accordance with the contract or should have been so discharged.

The value of the goods shall be fixed according to the commodity exchange price, or, if there be no such price, according to the current market price, or, if there be no commodity exchange price or current market price, by reference to the normal value of goods of the same kind and quality.

(c) Where a container, pallet or similar article of transport is used to consolidate goods, the number of packages or units enumerated in the bill of lading as packed in such article of transport shall be deemed the number of packages or units for the purpose of this paragraph as far as these packages or units are concerned. Except as aforesaid such article of transport shall be considered the package or unit.

(d) The unit of account mentioned in this Article is the special drawing right as defined by the International Monetary Fund. The amounts mentioned in subparagraph (a) of this paragraph shall be converted into national currency on the basis of the value of the court seized of the case.[8]

(e) Neither the carrier nor the ship shall be entitled to the benefit of the limitation of liability provided for in this paragraph if it is proved that the damage resulted from an act or omission of the carrier done with intent to cause damage, or recklessly and with knowledge that damage would probably result.

(f) The declaration mentioned in subparagraph (a) of this paragraph, if embodied in the bill of lading shall be prima facie evidence, but shall not be binding or conclusive on the carrier.

(g) By agreement between the carrier, master or agent of the carrier and the shipper other maximum amounts than those mentioned in subparagraph (a) of this paragraph may be fixed, provided that no maximum amount so fixed shall be less than the appropriate maximum mentioned in that subparagraph.

(h) Neither the carrier nor the ship shall be responsible in any event for loss or damage to, or in connection with goods if the nature or value thereof has been knowingly mis-stated by the shipper in the bill of lading.

6. Goods of an inflammable, explosive or dangerous nature to the shipment whereof the carrier, master or agent of the carrier has not consented with knowledge of their nature and character, may at any time before discharge be landed at any place, or destroyed or rend-

8. This provision was introduced by s. 2(3) of the Merchant Shipping Act 1981 to give effect to the Hague–Visby Protocol which replaced the Poincaré franc with the SDR as the relevant unit. The wording of (d) prior to this amendment was:

ered innocuous by the carrier without compensation and the shipper of such goods shall be liable for all damages and expenses directly or indirectly arising out of or resulting from such shipment. If any such goods shipped with such knowledge and consent shall become a danger to the ship or cargo, they may in like manner be landed at any place, or destroyed or rendered innocuous by the carrier without liability on the part of the carrier except to general average, if any.

Article IV bis[9]

1. The defences and limits of liability provided for in these Rules shall apply in any action against the carrier in respect of loss or damage to goods covered by a contract of carriage whether the action be founded in contract or in tort.
   2. If such an action is brought against a servant or agent of the carrier (such servant or agent not being an independent contractor), such servant or agent shall be entitled to avail himself of the defences and limits of liability which the carrier is entitled to invoke under these Rules.
   3. The aggregate of the amounts recoverable from the carrier, and such servants and agents, shall in no case exceed the limit provided for in these Rules.
   4. Nevertheless, a servant or agent of the carrier shall not be entitled to avail himself of the provisions of this article, if it is provided that the damage resulted from an act or omission of the servant or agent done with intent to cause damage or recklessly and with knowledge that damage would probably result.

Article V

A carrier shall be at liberty to surrender in whole or in part all or any of his rights and immunities or to increase any of his responsibilities and obligations[10] under these Rules, provided such surrender or increase shall be embodied in the bill of lading issued to the shipper. The provisions of these Rules shall not be applicable to charter parties, but if bills of lading are issued in the case of a ship under a charterparty they shall comply with the terms of these Rules. Nothing in these Rules shall be held to prevent the insertion in a bill of lading of any lawful provision regarding general average.

"A franc means a unit consisting of 65.5 milligrams of gold of millesimal fineness 900. The date of conversion of the sum awarded into national currencies shall be governed by the law of the Court seized of the case."
   9. This provision does not appear in the Hague Rules.
   10. The Hague Rules has the words: ". . . and liabilities".

Article VI

Notwithstanding the provisions of the preceding Articles, a carrier, master or agent of the carrier and a shipper shall in regard to any particular goods be at liberty to enter into any agreement in any terms as to the responsibility and liability of the carrier for such goods, and as to the rights and immunities of the carrier in respect of such goods, or his obligation as to seaworthiness, so far as this stipulation is not contrary to public policy, or the care or diligence of his servants or agents in regard to the loading, handling, stowage, carriage, custody, care and discharge of the goods carried by sea, provided that in this case no bill of lading has been or shall be issued and that the terms agreed shall be embodied in a receipt which shall be a non-negotiable document and shall be marked as such.

Any agreement so entered into shall have full legal effect.

Provided that this Article shall not apply to ordinary commercial shipments made in the ordinary course of trade, but only to other shipments where the character or condition of the property to be carried or the circumstances, terms and conditions under which the carriage is to be performed are such as reasonably to justify a special agreement.

Article VIII

The provisions of these Rules shall not affect the rights and obligations of the carrier under any statute for the time being in force relating to the limitation of the liability of owners of sea-going vessels.

Article IX

These Rules shall not affect the provisions of any international Convention or national law governing liability for nuclear damage.[11]

Article X[12]

The provisions of these Rules shall apply to every bill of lading relating to the carriage of goods between ports in two different States if:—

---

11. These words do not appear in the Hague Rules. Article IX of the Hague Rules deals with a completely different point, namely, gold value, and reads as follows: "The monetary units mentioned in these Rules are to be taken to be gold value." In view of the amended provisions of Article IV, Rule 5, in the Hague–Visby Rules, gold value is not relevant.

12. This provision does not appear in the Hague Rules and was introduced to extend the circumstances in which the Hague–Visby Rules would apply. Countries giving effect to the Hague Rules had usually provided that those Rules would apply only to exports from that country.

(a) the bill of lading is issued in a contracting State, or

(b) the carriage is from a port in a contracting State, or

(c) the contract contained in or evidenced by the bill of lading provides that these Rules or legislation of any State giving effect to them are to govern the contract,

whatever may be the nationality of the ship, the carrier, the shipper, the consignee, or any other interested person.

UNITED NATIONS CONVENTION ON THE CARRIAGE OF GOODS BY SEA 1978 (THE HAMBURG RULES)

Preamble

THE STATES PARTIES TO THIS CONVENTION,
HAVING RECOGNIZED the desirability of determining by agreement certain rules relating to the carriage of goods by sea,
HAVE DECIDED to conclude a Convention for this purpose and have thereto agreed as follows:

PART I. GENERAL PROVISIONS

Article 1. Definitions

In this Convention:

1. "Carrier" means any person by whom or in whose name a contract of carriage of goods by sea has been concluded with a shipper.

2. "Actual carrier" means any person to whom the performance of the carriage of the goods, or of part of the carriage, has been entrusted by the carrier, and includes any other person to whom such performance has been entrusted.

3. "Shipper" means any person by whom or in whose name or on whose behalf a contract of carriage of goods by sea has been concluded with a carrier, or any person by whom or in whose name or on whose behalf the goods are actually delivered to the carrier in relation to the contract of carriage by sea.

4. "Consignee" means the person entitled to take delivery of the goods.

5. "Goods" includes live animals; where the goods are consolidated in a container, pallet or similar article of transport or where they are packed, "goods" includes such article of transport or packaging if supplied by the shipper.

6. "Contract of carriage by sea" means any contract whereby the

carrier undertakes against payment of freight to carry goods by sea from one port to another; however, a contract which involves carriage by sea and also carriage by some other means is deemed to be a contract of carriage by sea for the purposes of this Convention only in so far as it relates to the carriage by sea.

7. "Bill of lading" means a document which evidences a contract of carriage by sea and the taking over or loading of the goods by the carrier, and by which the carrier undertakes to deliver the goods against surrender of the document. A provision in the document that the goods are to be delivered to the order of a named person, or to order, or to bearer, constitutes such an undertaking.

8. "Writing" includes, *inter alia*, telegram and telex.

Article 2. Scope of application

1. The provisions of this Convention are applicable to all contracts of carriage by sea between two different States, if:
   (a) the port of loading as provided for in the contract of carriage by sea is located in a Contracting State, or
   (b) the port of discharge as provided for in the contract of carriage by sea is located in a Contracting State, or
   (c) one of the optional ports of discharge provided for in the contract of carriage by sea is the actual port of discharge and such port is located in a Contracting State, or
   (d) the bill of lading or other document evidencing the contract of carriage by sea is issued in a Contracting State, or
   (e) the bill of lading or other document evidencing the contract of carriage by sea provides that the provisions of this Convention or the legislation of any State giving effect to them are to govern the contract.

2. The provisions of this Convention are applicable without regard to the nationality of the ship, the carrier, the actual carrier, the shipper, the consignee or any other interested person.

3. The provisions of this Convention are not applicable to charter-parties. However, where a bill of lading is issued pursuant to a charter-party, the provisions of the Convention apply to such a bill of lading if it governs the relation between the carrier and the holder of the bill of lading, not being the charterer.

4. If a contract provides for future carriage goods in a series of shipments during an agreed period, the provisions of this Convention apply to each shipment. However, where a shipment is made under a charter-party, the provisions of paragraph 3 of this article apply.

Article 3. Interpretation of the Convention

In the interpretation and application of the provisions of this Convention regard shall be had to its international character and to the need to promote uniformity.

PART II. LIABILITY OF THE CARRIER

Article 4. Period of responsibility

1. The responsibility of the carrier for the goods under this Convention covers the period during which the carrier is in charge of the goods at the port of loading, during the carriage and at the port of discharge.

2. For the purpose of paragraph 1 of this article, the carrier is deemed to be in charge of the goods
    (a) from the time he has taken over the goods from:
        (i) the shipper, or a person acting on his behalf; or
        (ii) an authority or other third party to whom, pursuant to law or regulations applicable at the port of loading, the goods must be handed over for shipment;
    (b) until the time he has delivered the goods:
        (i) by handing over the goods to the consignee; or
        (ii) in cases, where the consignee does not receive the goods from the carrier, by placing them at the disposal of the consignee in accordance with the contract or with the law or with the usage of the particular trade, applicable at the port of discharge; or
        (iii) by handing over the goods to an authority or other third party to whom, pursuant to law or regulations applicable at the port of discharge, the goods must be handed over.

3. In paragraphs 1 and 2 of this article, reference to the carrier or to the consignee means, in addition to the carrier or the consignee, the servants or agents, respectively of the carrier or the consignee.

Article 5. Basis of liability

1. The carrier is liable for loss resulting from loss of or damage to the goods, as well as from delay in delivery, if the occurrence which caused the loss, damage or delay took place while the goods were in his charge as defined in article 4, unless the carrier proves that he, his servants or agents took all measures that could reasonably be required to avoid the occurrence and its consequences.

2. Delay in delivery occurs when the goods have not been delivered

at the port of discharge provided for in the contract of carriage by sea within the time expressly agreed upon or, in the absence of such agreement, within the time which it would be reasonable to require of a diligent carrier, having regard to the circumstances of the case.

3. The person entitled to make a claim for the loss of goods may treat the goods as lost if they have not been delivered as required by article 4 within 60 consecutive days following the expiry of the time for delivery according to paragraph 2 of this article.

4. (a) The carrier is liable
    (i) for loss of or damage to the goods or delay in delivery caused by fire, if the claimant proves that the fire arose from fault or neglect on the part of the carrier, his servants or agents;
    (ii) for such loss, damage or delay in delivery which is proved by the claimant to have resulted from the fault or neglect of the carrier, his servants or agents, in taking all measures that could reasonably be required to put out the fire and avoid or mitigate its consequences.
  (b) In case of fire on board the ship affecting the goods, if the claimant or the carrier so desires, a survey in accordance with shipping practices must be held into the cause and circumstances of the fire, and a copy of the surveyor's report shall be made available on demand to the carrier and the claimant.

5. With respect to live animals, the carrier is not liable for loss, damage or delay in delivery resulting from any special risks inherent in that kind of carriage. If the carrier proves that he has complied with any special instructions given to him by the shipper respecting the animals and that, in the circumstances of the case, the loss, damage or delay in delivery could be attributed to such risks, it is presumed that the loss, damage or delay in delivery was so caused, unless there is proof that all or a part of the loss, damage or delay in delivery resulted from fault or neglect on the part of the carrier, his servants or agents.

6. The carrier is not liable, except in general average, where loss, damage or delay in delivery resulted from measures to save life or from reasonable measures to save property at sea.

7. Where fault or neglect on the part of the carrier, his servants or agents combines with another cause to produce loss, damage or delay in delivery the carrier is liable only to the extent that the loss, damage or delay in delivery is attributable to such fault or neglect, provided that the carrier proves the amount of the loss, damage or delay in delivery not attributable thereto.

Article 6. Limits of liability

1. (a) The liability of the carrier for loss resulting from loss of or
   damage to goods according to the provisions of article 5 is
   limited to an amount equivalent to 835 units of account per
   package or other shipping unit or 2.5 units of account per
   kilogramme of gross weight of the goods lost or damaged,
   whichever is the higher.
   (b) The liability of the carrier for delay in delivery according to
   the provisions of article 5 is limited to an amount equivalent
   to two and a half times the freight payable for the goods
   delayed, but not exceeding the total freight payable under
   the contract of carriage of goods by sea.
   (c) In no case shall the aggregate liability of the carrier, under
   both subparagraphs (a) and (b) of this paragraph, exceed
   the limitation which would be established under subparagraph (a) of this paragraph for total loss of the goods with
   respect to which such liability was incurred.

2. For the purpose of calculating which amount is the higher in
accordance with paragraph 1(a) of this article, the following rules
apply:
   (a) Where a container, pallet or similar article of transport is
   used to consolidate goods, the package or other shipping
   units enumerated in the bill of lading, if issued, or otherwise
   in any other document evidencing the contract of carriage
   by sea, as packed in such article of transport are deemed
   packages or shipping units. Except as aforesaid the goods in
   such article of transport are deemed one shipping unit.
   (b) In cases where the article of transport itself has been lost or
   damaged, that article of transport, if not owned or otherwise supplied by the carrier, is considered one separate shipping unit.

3. Unit of account means the unit of account mentioned in article
26.

4. By agreement between the carrier and the shipper, limits of liability exceeding those provided for in paragraph 1 may be fixed.

Article 7. Application to non-contractual claims

1. The defences and limits of liability provided for in this Convention apply in any action against the carrier in respect of loss or
damage to the goods covered by the contract of carriage by sea, as
well as of delay in delivery whether the action is founded in contract,
in tort or otherwise.

2. If such an action is brought against a servant or agent of the carrier, such servant or agent, if he proves that he acted within the scope of his employment, is entitled to avail himself of the defences and limits of liability which the carrier is entitled to invoke under this Convention.

3. Except as provided in article 8, the aggregate of the amounts recoverable from the carrier and from any persons referred to in paragraph 2 of this article shall not exceed the limits of liability provided for in this Convention.

Article 8. Loss of right to limit responsibility

1. The carrier is not entitled to the benefit of the limitation of liability provided for in article 6 if it is proved that the loss, damage or delay in delivery resulted from an act or omission of the carrier done with the intent to cause such loss, damage or delay, or recklessly and with knowledge that such loss, damage or delay would probably result.

2. Notwithstanding the provisions of paragraph 2 of article 7, a servant or agent of the carrier is not entitled to the benefit of the limitation of liability provided for in article 6 if it is proved that the loss, damage or delay in delivery resulted from an act or omission of such servant or agent, done with the intent to cause such loss, damage or delay, or recklessly and with knowledge that such loss, damage or delay would probably result.

Article 9. Deck cargo

1. The carrier is entitled to carry the goods on deck only if such carriage is in accordance with an agreement with the shipper or with the usage of the particular trade or is required by statutory rules or regulations.

2. If the carrier and the shipper have agreed that the goods shall or may be carried on deck, the carrier must insert in the bill of lading or other document evidencing the contract of carriage by sea a statement to that effect. In the absence of such a statement the carrier has the burden of proving that an agreement for carriage on deck has been entered into; however, the carrier is not entitled to invoke such an agreement against a third party, including a consignee, who has acquired the bill of lading in good faith.

3. Where the goods have been carried on deck contrary to the provisions of paragraph 1 of this article or where the carrier may not under paragraph 2 of this article invoke an agreement for carriage on

deck, the carrier, notwithstanding the provisions of paragraph 1 of article 5, is liable for loss of or damage to the goods, as well as for delay in delivery, resulting solely from the carriage on deck, and the extent of his liability is to be determined in accordance with the provisions of article 6 or article 8 of this Convention, as the case may be.

4. Carriage of goods on deck contrary to express agreement for carriage under deck is deemed to be an act or omission of the carrier within the meaning of article 8.

Article 10. Liability of the carrier and actual carrier

1. Where the performance of the carriage or part thereof has been entrusted to an actual carrier, whether or not in pursuance of a liberty under the contract of carriage by sea to do so, the carrier nevertheless remains responsible for the entire carriage according to the provisions of this Convention. The carrier is responsible, in relation to the carriage performed by the actual carrier, for the acts and omissions of the actual carrier and of his servants and agents acting within the scope of their employment.

2. All the provisions of this Convention governing the responsibility of the carrier also apply to the responsibility of the actual carrier for the carriage performed by him. The provisions of paragraphs 2 and 3 of article 7 and of paragraph 2 of article 8 apply if an action is brought against a servant or agent of the actual carrier.

3. Any special agreement under which the carrier assumes obligations not imposed by this Convention or waives rights conferred by this Convention affects the actual carrier only if agreed to by him expressly and in writing. Whether or not the actual carrier has so agreed, the carrier nevertheless remains bound by the obligations or waivers resulting from such special agreement.

4. Where and to the extent that both the carrier and the actual carrier are liable, their liability is joint and several.

5. The aggregate of the amounts recoverable from the carrier, the actual carrier and their servants and agents shall not exceed the limits of liability provided for in this Convention.

6. Nothing in this article shall prejudice any right of recourse as between the carrier and the actual carrier.

Article 11. Through carriage

1. Notwithstanding the provisions of paragraph 1 of article 10, where a contract of carriage by sea provides explicitly that a specified part of the carriage covered by the said contract is to be performed by

a named person other than the carrier, the contract may also provide that the carrier is not liable for loss, damage or delay in delivery caused by an occurrence which takes place while the goods are in the charge of the actual carrier during such part of the carriage. Nevertheless, any stipulation limiting or excluding such liability is without effect if no judicial proceedings can be instituted against the actual carrier in a court competent under paragraph 1 or 2 of article 21. The burden of proving that any loss, damage or delay in delivery has been caused by such an occurrence rests upon the carrier.

2. The actual carrier is responsible in accordance with the provisions of paragraph 2 of article 10 for loss, damage or delay in delivery caused by an occurrence which takes place while the goods are in his charge.

PART III. LIABILITY OF THE SHIPPER

Article 12. General rule

The shipper is not liable for loss sustained by the carrier or the actual carrier, or for damage sustained by the ship, unless such loss or damage was caused by the fault or neglect of the shipper, his servants or agents. Nor is any servant or agent of the shipper liable for such loss or damage unless the loss or damage was caused by fault or neglect on his part.

Article 13. Special rules on dangerous goods

1. The shipper must mark or label in a suitable manner dangerous goods as dangerous.

2. Where the shipper hands over dangerous goods to the carrier or an actual carrier, as the case may be, the shipper must inform him of the dangerous character of the goods and, if necessary, of the precautions to be taken. If the shipper fails to do so and such carrier or actual carrier does not otherwise have knowledge of their dangerous character:

    (a) the shipper is liable to the carrier and any actual carrier for the loss resulting from the shipment of such goods, and

    (b) the goods may at any time be unloaded, destroyed or rendered innocuous, as the circumstances may require, without payment of compensation.

3. The provisions of paragraph 2 of this article may not be invoked by any person if during the carriage he has taken the goods in his charge with knowledge of their dangerous character.

4. If, in cases where the provisions of paragraph 2, subparagraph (b), of this article do not apply or may not be invoked, dangerous goods become an actual danger to life or property, they may be unloaded, destroyed or rendered innocuous as the circumstances may require, without payment of compensation except where there is an obligation to contribute in general average or where the carrier is liable in accordance with the provisions of article 5.

PART IV. TRANSPORT DOCUMENTS

Article 14. Issue of bill of lading

1. When the carrier or the actual carrier takes the goods in his charge, the carrier must, on demand of the shipper, issue to the shipper a bill of lading.

2. The bill of lading may be signed by a person having authority from the carrier. A bill of lading signed by the master of the ship carrying the goods is deemed to have been signed on behalf of the carrier.

3. The signature on the bill of lading may be in handwriting, printed in facsimile, perforated, stamped, in symbols, or made by any other mechanical or electronic means, if not inconsistent with the law of the country where the bill of lading is issued.

Article 15. Contents of bill of lading

1. The bill of lading must include, *inter alia*, the following particulars:

    (a) the general nature of the goods, the leading marks necessary for identification of the goods, an express statement, if applicable, as to the dangerous character of the goods, the number of packages or pieces, and the weight of the goods or their quantity otherwise expressed, all such particulars as furnished by the shipper;

    (b) the apparent condition of the goods;

    (c) the name and principal place of business of the carrier;

    (d) the name of the shipper;

    (e) the consignee if named by the shipper;

    (f) the port of loading under the contract of carriage by sea and the date on which the goods were taken over by the carrier at the port of loading;

    (g) the port of discharge under the contract of carriage by sea;

(h) the number of originals of the bill of lading, if more than one;

(i) the place of issuance of the bill of lading;

(j) the signature of the carrier or a person acting on his behalf;

(k) the freight to the extent payable by the consignee or other indication that freight is payable by him;

(l) the statement referred to in paragraph 3 of article 23;

(m) the statement, if applicable, that the goods shall or may be carried on deck;

(n) the date or the period of delivery of the goods at the port of discharge if expressly agreed upon between the parties; and

(o) any increased limit or limits of liability where agreed in accordance with paragraph 4 of article 6.

2. After the goods have been loaded on board, if the shipper so demands, the carrier must issue to the shipper a "shipped" bill of lading which, in addition to the particulars required under paragraph 1 of this article, must state that the goods are on board a named ship or ships, and the date or dates of loading. If the carrier has previously issued to the shipper a bill of lading or other document of title with respect to any of such goods, on request of the carrier, the shipper must surrender such document in exchange for a "shipped" bill of lading. The carrier may amend any previously issued document in order to meet the shipper's demand for a "shipped" bill of lading if, as amended, such document includes all the information required to be contained in a "shipped" bill of lading.

3. The absence in the bill of lading of one or more particulars referred to in this article does not affect the legal character of the document as a bill of lading provided that it nevertheless meets the requirements set out in paragraph 7 of article 1.

Article 16. Bills of lading: reservations and evidentiary effect

1. If the bill contains particulars concerning the general nature, leading marks, number of packages or pieces, weight or quantity of the goods which the carrier or other person issuing the bill of lading on his behalf knows or has reasonable grounds to suspect do not accurately represent the goods actually taken over or, where a "shipped" bill of lading is issued, loaded, or if he had no reasonable means of checking such particulars, the carrier or such other person must insert in the bill of lading a reservation specifying these inaccuracies, grounds of suspicion or the absence of reasonable means of checking.

2. If the carrier or other person issuing the bill of lading on his behalf fails to note on the bill of lading the apparent condition of the

goods, he is deemed to have noted on the bill of lading that the goods were in apparent good condition.

3. Except for particulars in respect of which and to the extent to which a reservation permitted under paragraph 1 of this article has been entered:

  (a) the bill of lading is *prima facie* evidence of the taking over or, where a "shipped" bill of lading is issued, loading, by the carrier of the goods as described in the bill of lading; and

  (b) proof to the contrary by the carrier is not admissible if the bill of lading has been transferred to a third party, including a consignee, who in good faith has acted in reliance on the description of the goods therein.

4. A bill of lading which does not, as provided in paragraph 1, sub-paragraph (k) of article 15, set forth the freight or otherwise indicate that freight is payable by the consignee or does not set forth demurrage incurred at the port of loading payable by the consignee, is *prima facie* evidence that no freight or such demurrage is payable by him. However, proof to the contrary by the carrier is not admissible when the bill of lading has been transferred to a third party, including a consignee, who in good faith has acted in reliance on the absence in the bill of lading of any such indication.

Article 17. Guarantees by the shipper

1. The shipper is deemed to have guaranteed to the carrier the accuracy of particulars relating to the general nature of the goods, their marks, number, weight and quantity as furnished by him for insertion in the bill of lading. The shipper must indemnify the carrier against the loss resulting from inaccuracies in such particulars. The shipper remains liable even if the bill of lading has been transferred by him. The right of the carrier to such indemnity in no way limits his liability under the contract of carriage by sea to any person other than the shipper.

2. Any letter of guarantee or agreement by which the shipper undertakes to indemnify the carrier against loss resulting from the issuance of the bill of lading by the carrier, or by a person acting on his behalf, without entering a reservation relating to particulars furnished by the shipper for insertion in the bill of lading, or to the apparent condition of the goods, is void and of no effect as against any third party, including a consignee, to whom the bill of lading has been transferred.

3. Such letter of guarantee or agreement is valid as against the shipper unless the carrier or the person acting on his behalf, by omitting

the reservation referred to in paragraph 2 of this article, intends to defraud a third party, including a consignee, who acts in reliance on the description of the goods in the bill of lading. In the latter case, if the reservation omitted relates to particulars furnished by the shipper for insertion in the bill of lading, the carrier has no right of indemnity from the shipper pursuant to paragraph 1 of this article.

4. In the case of intended fraud referred to in paragraph 3 of this article the carrier is liable, without the benefit of the limitation of liability provided for in this Convention, for the loss incurred by a third party, including a consignee, because he has acted in reliance on the description of the goods in the bill of lading.

Article 18. Documents other than bills of lading

Where a carrier issues a document other than a bill of lading to evidence the receipt of the goods to be carried, such a document is *prima facie* evidence of the conclusion of the contract of carriage by sea and the taking over by the carrier of the goods as therein described.

PART V. CLAIMS AND ACTIONS

Article 19. Notice of loss, damage or delay

1. Unless notice of loss or damage, specifying the general nature of such loss or damage, is given in writing by the consignee to the carrier not later than the working day after the day when the goods were handed over to the consignee, such handing over is *prima facie* evidence of the delivery by the carrier of the goods as described in the document of transport or if no such document has been issued, in good condition.

2. Where the loss or damage is not apparent, the provisions of paragraph 1 of this article apply correspondingly if notice in writing is not given within 15 consecutive days after the day when the goods were handed over to the consignee.

3. If the state of the goods at the time they were handed over to the consignee has been the subject of a joint survey or inspection by the parties, notice in writing need not be given of loss or damage ascertained during such survey or inspection.

4. In the case of any actual or apprehended loss or damage the carrier and the consignee must give all reasonable facilities to each other for inspecting and tallying the goods.

5. No compensation shall be payable for loss resulting from delay

in delivery unless a notice has been given in writing to the carrier within 60 consecutive days after the day when the goods were handed over to the consignee.

6. If the goods have been delivered by an actual carrier, any notice given under this article to him shall have the same effect as if it had been given to the carrier, and any notice given to the carrier shall have effect as if given to such actual carrier.

7. Unless notice of loss or damage, specifying the general nature of the loss or damage, is given in writing by the carrier or actual carrier to the shipper not later than 90 consecutive days after the occurrence of such loss or damage or after the delivery of the goods in accordance with paragraph 2 of article 4, whichever is later, the failure to give such notice is *prima facie* evidence that the carrier or the actual carrier has sustained no loss or damage due to the fault or neglect of this shipper, his servants or agents.

8. For the purpose of this article, notice given to a person acting on the carrier's or the actual carrier's behalf, including the master or the officer in charge of the ship, or to a person acting on the shipper's behalf is deemed to have been given to the carrier, to the actual carrier or to the shipper, respectively.

Article 20. Limitation of actions

1. Any action relating to carriage of goods under this Convention is time-barred if judicial or arbitral proceedings have not been instituted within a period of two years.

2. The limitation period commences on the day on which the carrier has delivered the goods or part thereof or, in cases where no goods have been delivered, on the last day on which the goods should have been delivered.

3. The day on which the limitation period commences is not included in the period.

4. The person against whom a claim is made may at any time during the running of the limitation period extend that period by a declaration in writing to the claimant. This period may be further extended by another declaration or declarations.

5. An action for indemnity by a person held liable may be instituted even after the expiration of the limitation period provided for in the preceding paragraphs if instituted within the time allowed by the law of the State where proceedings are instituted. However, the time allowed shall not be less than 90 days commencing from the day when the person instituting such action for indemnity has settled the claim or has been served with process in the action against himself.

Article 21. Jurisdiction

1. In judicial proceedings relating to carriage of goods under this Convention the plaintiff, at his option, may institute an action in a court which, according to the law of the State where the court is situated, is competent and within the jurisdiction of which is situated one of the following places:

(a) the principal place of business or, in the absence thereof, the habitual residence of the defendant; or

(b) the place where the contract was made provided that the defendant has there a place of business, branch or agency through which the contract was made; or

(c) the port of loading or the port of discharge; or

(d) any additional place designated for that purpose in the contract of carriage by sea.

2. (a) Notwithstanding the preceding provisions of this article, an action may be instituted in the courts of any port or place in a Contracting State at which the carrying vessel or any other vessel of the same ownership may have been arrested in accordance with applicable rules of the law of that State and of international law. However, in such a case, at the petition of the defendant, the claimant must remove the action, at his choice, to one of the jurisdictions referred to in paragraph 1 of this article for the determination of the claim, but before such removal the defendant must furnish security sufficient to ensure payment of any judgment that may subsequently be awarded to the claimant in the action.

(b) All questions relating to the sufficiency or otherwise of the security shall be determined by the court of the port or place of the arrest.

3. No judicial proceedings relating to carriage of goods under this Convention may be instituted in a place not specified in paragraph 1 or 2 of this article. The provisions of this paragraph do not constitute an obstacle to the jurisdiction of the Contracting States for provisions or protective measures.

4. (a) Where an action has been instituted in a court competent under paragraph 1 or 2 of this article or where judgment has been delivered by such a court, no new action may be started between the same parties on the same grounds unless the judgment of the court before which the first action was instituted is not enforceable in the county in which the new proceedings are instituted;

(b) for the purpose of this article the institution of measures with a view to obtaining enforcement of a judgment is not to be considered as the starting of a new action;

(c) for the purpose of this article, the removal of an action to a different court within the same country, or to a court in another country, in accordance with paragraph 2(a) of this article, is not to be considered as the starting of a new action.

5. Notwithstanding the provisions of the preceding paragraphs, an agreement made by the parties, after a claim under the contract of carriage by sea has arisen, which designates the place where the claimant may institute an action, is effective.

Article 22. Arbitration

1. Subject to the provisions of this article, parties may provide by agreement evidenced in writing that any dispute that may arise relating to carriage of goods under this Convention shall be referred to arbitration.

2. Where a charter-party contains a provision that disputes arising thereunder shall be referred to arbitration and a bill of lading issued pursuant to the charter-party does not contain a special annotation providing that such provision shall be binding upon the holder of the bill of lading, the carrier may not invoke such provision as against a holder having acquired the bill of lading in good faith.

3. The arbitration proceedings shall, at the option of the claimant, be instituted at one of the following places:

(a) a place in a State within whose territory is situated:

    (i) the principal place of business of the defendant or, in the absence thereof, the habitual residence of the defendant; or

    (ii) the place where the contract was made, provided that the defendant has there a place of business, branch or agency through which the contract was made; or

    (iii) the port of loading or the port of discharge; or

(b) any place designated for that purpose in the arbitration clause or agreement.

4. The arbitrator or arbitration tribunal shall apply the rules of this Convention.

5. The provisions of paragraphs 3 and 4 of this article are deemed to be part of every arbitration clause or agreement, and any term of such clause or agreement which is inconsistent therewith is null and void.

6. Nothing in this article affects the validity of an agreement relating

to arbitration made by the parties after the claim under the contract of carriage by sea has arisen.

PART VI. SUPPLEMENTARY PROVISIONS

Article 23. Contractual stipulations

1. Any stipulation in a contract of carriage by sea, in a bill of lading, or in any other document evidencing the contract of carriage by sea is null and void to the extent that it derogates, directly or indirectly, from the provisions of this Convention. The nullity of such a stipulation does not affect the validity of the other provisions of the contract of document of which it forms a part. A clause assigning benefit of insurance of the goods in favour of the carrier, or any similar clause, is null and void.

2. Notwithstanding the provisions of paragraph 1 of this article, a carrier may increase his responsibilities and obligations under this Convention.

3. Where a bill of lading or any other document evidencing the contract of carriage by sea is issued, it must contain a statement that the carriage is subject to the provisions of this Convention which nullify any stipulation derogating therefrom to the detriment of the shipper or the consignee.

4. Where the claimant in respect of the goods has incurred loss as a result of a stipulation which is null and void by virtue of the present article, or as a result of the omission of the statement referred to in paragraph 3 of this article, the carrier must pay compensation to the extent required in order to give the claimant compensation in accordance with the provisions of this Convention for any loss of or damage to the goods as well as for delay in delivery. The carrier must, in addition, pay compensation for costs incurred by the claimant for the purpose of exercising his right, provided that costs incurred in the action where the foregoing provision is invoked are to be determined in accordance with the law of the State where proceedings are instituted.

Article 24. General average

1. Nothing in this Convention shall prevent the application of provisions in the contract of carriage by sea or national law regarding the adjustment of general average.

2. With the exception of article 20, the provisions of this Convention relating to the liability of the carrier for loss of or damage to the goods also determine whether the consignee may refuse contribution in general average and the liability of the carrier to indemnify the consignee in respect of any such contribution made or any salvage paid.

Article 25. Other conventions

1. This Convention does not modify the rights or duties of the carrier, the actual carrier and their servants and agents, provided for in international conventions or national law relating to the limitation of liability of owners of seagoing ships.

2. The provisions of articles 21 and 22 of this Convention do not prevent the application of the mandatory provisions of any other multilateral convention already in force at the date of this Convention relating to matters dealt with in the said articles, provided that the dispute arises exclusively between parties having their principal place of business in the States members of such other convention. However, this paragraph does not affect the application of paragraph 4 of article 22 of this Convention.

3. No liability shall arise under the provisions of this Convention for damage caused by a nuclear incident if the operator of a nuclear installation is liable for such damage:

   (a) under either the Paris Convention of 29 July 1960 on Third Party Liability in the Field of Nuclear Energy as amended by the Additional Protocol of 28 January 1964 or the Vienna Convention of 21 May 1963 on Civil Liability for Nuclear Damage, or

   (b) by virtue of national law governing the liability for such damage, provided that such law is in all respects as favourable to persons who may suffer damage as either the Paris or Vienna Conventions.

4. No liability shall arise under the provisions of this Convention for any loss of or damage to or delay in delivery of luggage for which the carrier is responsible under any international convention or national law relating to the carriage of passengers and their luggage by sea.

5. Nothing contained in this Convention prevents a Contracting State from applying any other international convention which is already in force at the date of this Convention and which applies mandatorily to contracts of carriage of goods primarily by a mode of transport other than transport by sea. This provision also applies to

any subsequent revision or amendment of such international convention.

Article 26. Unit of account

1. The unit of account referred to in article 6 of this Convention is the Special Drawing Right as defined by the International Monetary Fund. The amounts mentioned in article 6 are to be converted into the national currency of a State according to the value of such currency at the date of judgment or the date agreed upon by the parties. The value of a national currency, in terms of the Special Drawing Right, of a Contracting State which is a member of the International Monetary Fund is to be calculated in accordance with the method of valuation applied by the International Monetary Fund in effect at the date in question for its operations and transactions. The value of a national currency in terms of the Special Drawing Right of a Contracting State which is not a member of the International Monetary Fund is to be calculated in a manner determined by that State.

2. Nevertheless, those States which are not members of the International Monetary Fund and whose law does not permit the application of the provisions of paragraph 1 of this article may, at the time of signature, or at the time of ratification, acceptance, approval or accession or at any time thereafter, declare that the limits of liability provided for in this Convention to be applied in their territories shall be fixed as:

12,500 monetary units per package or other shipping unit of 37.5 monetary units per kilogramme of gross weight of the goods.

3. The monetary unit referred to in paragraph 2 of this article corresponds to sixty-five and a half milligrammes of gold of millesimal fineness nine hundred. The conversion of the amounts referred to in paragraph 2 into the national currency is to be made according to the law of the State concerned.

4. The calculation mentioned in the last sentence of paragraph 1 and the conversion mentioned in paragraph 3 of this article is to be made in such a manner as to express in the national currency of the Contracting State as far as possible the same real value for the amounts in article 6 as is expressed there in units of account. Contracting States must communicate to the depositary the manner of calculation pursuant to paragraph 1 of this article, or the result of the conversion mentioned in paragraph 3 of this article, as the case may be, at the time of signature or when depositing their instruments of ratification, acceptance, approval or accession, or when availing themselves of the option provided for in paragraph 2 of this article

and whenever there is a change in the manner of such calculation or in result of such conversion.

PART VII. FINAL CLAUSES

Article 27. Depositary

The Secretary-General of the United Nations is hereby designated as the depositary of this Convention.

Article 28. Signature, ratification, acceptance, approval, accession

1. This Convention is open for signature by all States until 30 April 1979 at the Headquarters of the United Nations, New York.

2. This Convention is subject to ratification, acceptance or approval by the signatory States.

3. After 30 April 1979, this Convention will be open for accession by all States which are not signatory States.

4. Instruments of ratification, acceptance, approval and accession are to be deposited with the Secretary-General of the United Nations.

Article 29. Reservations

No reservations may be made to this Convention.

Article 30. Entry into force

1. This Convention enters into force on the first day of the month following the expiration of one year from the date of deposit of the 20th instrument of ratification, acceptance, approval or accession.

2. For each State which becomes a Contracting State to this Convention after the date of the deposit of the 20th instrument of ratification, acceptance, approval or accession, this Convention enters into force on the first day of the month following the expiration of one year after the deposit of the appropriate instrument on behalf of that State.

3. Each Contracting State shall apply the provisions of this Convention to contracts of carriage by sea concluded on or after the date of the entry into force of this Convention in respect of that State.

Article 31. Denunciation of other conventions

1. Upon becoming a Contracting State to this Convention, any State Party to the International Convention for the Unification of

Certain Rules relating to Bills of Lading signed at Brussels on 25 August 1924 (1924 Convention) must notify the Government of Belgium as the depositary of the 1924 Convention of its denunciation of the said Convention with a declaration that the denunciation is to take effect as from the date when this Convention enters into force in respect of that State.

2. Upon the entry into force of this Convention under paragraph 1 of article 30, the depositary of this Convention must notify the Government of Belgium as the depositary of the 1924 Convention of the date of such entry into force, and of the names of the Contracting States in respect of which the Convention has entered into force.

3. The provisions of paragraphs 1 and 2 of this article apply correspondingly in respect of States parties to the Protocol signed on 23 February 1968 to amend the International Convention for the Unification of Certain Rules relating to Bills of Lading signed at Brussels on 25 August 1924.

4. Notwithstanding article 2 of this Convention, for the purposes of paragraph 1 of this article, a Contracting State may, if it deems it desirable, defer the denunciation of the 1924 Convention and of the 1924 Convention as modified by the 1968 Protocol for a maximum period of five years from the entry into force of this Convention. It will then notify the Government of Belgium of its intention. During this transitory period, it must apply to the Contracting States this Convention to the exclusion of any other one.

Article 32. Revision and amendment

1. At the request of not less than one-third of the Contracting States to this Convention, the depositary shall convene a conference of the Contracting States for revising or amending it.

2. Any instrument of ratification, acceptance, approval or accession deposited after the entry into force of an amendment to this Convention, is deemed to apply to the Convention as amended.

Article 33. Revision of the limitation amount and unit of account on monetary unit

1. Notwithstanding the provisions of article 32, a conference only for the purpose of altering the amount specified in article 6 and paragraph 2 of article 26, or of substituting either or both of the units defined in paragraphs 1 and 3 of article 26 by other units is to be convened by the depositary in accordance with paragraph 2 of this

article. An alteration of the amounts shall be made only because of a significant change in their real value.

2. A revision conference is to be convened by the depositary when not less than one-fourth of the Contracting States so request.

3. Any decision by the conference must be taken by a two-thirds majority of the participating States. The amendment is communicated by the depositary to all the Contracting States for acceptance and to all the States signatories of the Convention for information.

4. Any amendment adopted enters into force on the first day of the month following one year after its acceptance by two-thirds of the contracting States. Acceptance is to be effected by the deposit of a formal instrument to that effect with the depositary.

5. After entry into force of an amendment a Contracting State which has accepted the amendment is entitled to apply the Convention as amended in its relations with Contracting States which have not within six months after the adoption of the amendment notified the depositary that they are not bound by the amendment.

6. Any instrument of ratification, acceptance, approval or accession deposited after the entry into force of an amendment to this Convention, is deemed to apply to the Convention as amended.

Article 34. Denunciation

1. A Contracting State may denounce this Convention at any time by means of notification in writing addressed to the depositary.

2. The denunciation takes effect on the first day of the month following the expiration of one year after the notification is received by the depositary. Where a longer period is specified in the notification, the denunciation takes effect upon the expiration of such longer period after the notification is received by the depositary.

DONE at Hamburg, this thirty-first day of March one thousand nine hundred and seventy-eight, in a single original, of which the Arabic, Chinese, English, French, Russian and Spanish texts are equally authentic.

IN WITNESS WHEREOF the undersigned plenipotentiaries, being duly authorized by their respective Governments, have signed the present Convention.

ANNEX II. COMMON UNDERSTANDING ADOPTED BY THE UNITED NATIONS CONFERENCE ON THE CARRIAGE OF GOODS BY SEA

It is the common understanding that the liability of the carrier under this Convention is based on the principle of presumed fault or neglect. This means that, as a rule, the burden of proof rests on the carrier but with respect to certain cases, the provisions of the Convention modify this rule.

LIMITATION OF LIABILITY FOR MARITIME CLAIMS: SUMMARY OF LIMITS

LONDON CONVENTION ON LIMITATION OF LIABILITY FOR MARITIME CLAIMS 1976

Contracting States

Australia	Finland	North Yemen	Switzerland
Bahamas	France	Netherlands	U.K.
Belgium	Germany	Norway	
Benin	Greece	Poland	
Denmark	Japan	Spain	
Egypt	Liberia	Sweden	

Amount

A (i) Loss of Life/Personal Injury only

Ships	Less than 500 tons	333,000 SDR[2]
	More than 500 tons	333,000 SDR

plus for each additional ton between

501–3,000	extra	500 SDR per ton
3,001–30,000	extra	333 SDR per ton
30,001–70,000	extra	250 SDR per ton
70,001 upwards	extra	167 SDR per ton

Salvors not operating from any ship:

[fixed tonnage—1,500 tons]   833,000 SDR

(ii) Other claims

Ships	Less than 500 tons	167,000 SDR[2]
	More than 500 tons	167,000 SDR

plus for each additional ton between

501–30,000	extra	167 SDR
30,001–70,000	extra	125 SDR
70,001 upwards	extra	83 SDR

Salvors not operating from any ship:

[fixed tonnage—1,500 tons]   334,000 SDR

(iii) Loss of Life/Personal injury and other claims

Ships	Less than 500 tons	500,000 SDR[2]
	More than 500 tons	500,000 SDR

plus for each additional ton between

501–3,000	extra	667 SDR
3,001–30,000	extra	500 SDR
30,001–70,000	extra	375 SDR
70,001 upwards	extra	250 SDR

Salvors not operating from any ship:

[fixed tonnage—1,500 tons]   1,167,000 SDR

B. Passenger claims

For each passenger which a ship is certified to carry	46,666 SDR
Subject to maximum	25,000,000 SDR

ATHENS CONVENTION RELATING TO THE CARRIAGE OF PASSENGERS AND THEIR LUGGAGE BY SEA 1974

Contracting States

Argentina	Liberia	Spain	Vanuatu
Bahamas	Luxembourg	Switzerland	U.K.
Belgium	North Yemen	Tonga	
G.D.R.	Poland	U.S.S.R.	

Amount

Death or personal injury (per passenger)[4]	46,666 SDR[5]
Loss of or damage to vehicles (per vehicle)	3,333 SDR

Loss of or damage to cabin luggage (per
   passenger) 833 SDR
Other luggage 1,200 SDR

HAGUE RULES 1924

Amount

£100 gold[6] per package or unit.

Note

The Hague Rules as enacted by the Carriage of Goods by Sea Act
1924 have been superseded in the United Kingdom by the Hague–
Visby Rules. However, in cases where the Hague–Visby Rules do not
apply by operation of law, the Hague Rules may still be applicable by
contract.

HAGUE–VISBY RULES 1968

Enacted or substantially adopted by

*Belgium	Hong Kong	Sir Lanka
Bermuda	Italy	*Sweden
*Denmark	Lebanon	Switzerland
East Germany	*Netherlands	Syria
Ecuador	*Norway	Tonga
Egypt	*Poland	*West Germany
*Finland	Singapore	*U.K. (Carriage of Goods By Sea
*France	*Spain	Act 1971)

Amount

The higher of 30 francs Poincaré (*2 SDR) per kilo or 10,000 francs
Poincaré (*666.67 SDR) per package or unit.

* The figures in brackets are the limits contained in the Hague-Visby Protocol 1979 to
which the countries asterisked are ratifying parties. The Protocol was brought into
effect in the U.K. in February 1984.

APPENDIX IX

HAMBURG RULES

Ratified or acceded to by

Barbados	Kenya	Senegal
Botswana	Lebanon	Sierra Leone
Burkhina Fasso	Lesotho	Tanzania
Chile	Malawi	Tunisia
Egypt	Morocco	Uganda
Guinea	Nigeria	Zambia
Hungary	Rumania	

and will come into force internationally on 1 November 1992.

Amount

Loss or damage

835 SDR per package or other shipping unit or 2.5 SDR per kilo of gross weight of the goods lost or damaged whichever is the higher.

Delay

Two and a half times the freight payable for the goods delayed or the total freight payable under the contract of carriage, whichever is the lower.

NOTES

1. Tonnage is calculated in accordance with the 1969 Tonnage Convention.

2. In the United Kingdom the first tranche is divided into vessels with a tonnage not exceeding 299 tons and vessels with a tonnage not exceeding 500 tons. For vessels with a tonnage not exceeding 299 tons the limit is 166,667 SDR for loss of life/personal injury claims, 83,333 SDR for other claims and 250,000 SDR when both types of claim arise.

3. The SDR exchange rate is calculated at the date of constitution of the fund or payment of the claim.

4. In the United Kingdom the Secretary of State for Transport in exercise of the powers conferred on him by sections 14 and 16 of and paragraph 4 of Part II of Schedule 3 to the Merchant Shipping Act 1979 has ordered that where *United Kingdom Carriers* are involved

the limit per passenger shall be 100,000 SDR. (S.I. 1989 No. 1880 —
Carriage of passengers and their Luggage by Sea (United Kingdom
Carriers) (Amendment) Order 1989.)

5. In Articles 7 and 8 of the Athens Convention limits are stated in
gold francs and the basis for conversion into national currencies is set
out in Article 9. However the 1976 Protocol to the Athens Convention substituted SDR for gold francs. The Protocol was brought into
force in the United Kingdom on 10 November 1989 (S.I. 1989
No. 1881 — Merchant Shipping Act 1979 (Commencement No. 13)
Order 1989.)

6. "Gold value" is defined as "the gold content of 100 sovereigns
of the weight and fineness specified under the Coinage Act 1870".
See *The "Rosa S."* [1988] 2 Lloyd's Rep. 574.

7. On 12 July 1988 Chile adopted a new Maritime Code which
gives effect to a substantial part of the Hamburg Rules. The Code
applies to all vessels carrying cargoes to or from Chile.

INDEX

Aggregation of claims, 57–59
  "distinct occasion", 58
Aircushion vehicles, 17, 79–81
Athens Convention 1974, 86–105
  aggregation of claims, 98–99,
    151–152
  amendment by 1976 Protocol, 182
  applications, 92–93, 148–149
  basis for claims, 99, 101, 152
  cabin luggage, 90–91
  carriage, 91
  carrier, 88
  carriers' servants
    defences, 98–99
    limits, 98–99
  commercial carriage by public
    authorities, 105
  competent jurisdiction, 103, 154
  contract of carriage, 88–89
  contributory fault, 94, 150
  damage to luggage, 91
  defences and limits for carriers'
    servants, 151
  definitions, 86–92, 147–148
  exclusion of liability, 144–145
  force of law in United Kingdom,
    143–144
  hovercraft, and, 146
  interest, 97
  international carriage, 92
  invalidity of contractual
    provisions, 103–104, 154
  liability of carrier, 93, 149
    burden of proof, 94
    defect in the ship, 95
    fault of passenger, 95
    "fault or neglect", 94

Athens Convention—cont.
  liability of carrier—cont.
    joint liability with performing
      carrier, 95
    "other luggage", 95
    "shipwreck, collision,
      stranding, explosion and
      fire", 95
  limit of liability for loss of or
    damage to luggage, 150–151
  limit of liability for personal
    injury, 150
  limitation of liability, 144, 145
  limits of liability
    agreement of passenger to
      higher limits, 96
  loss of luggage, 91
  loss of or damage to luggage, 96
  loss of right to limit liability, 99,
    100–101, 152
  luggage, 90–91
  monetary unit, 96, 151
    convention, 96, 151
  notice of loss or damage to
    luggage, 101, 152
  nuclear damage, 105, 154–155
  other Conventions, and, 104–105,
    154
  passenger, 90
  passenger claims, 86–105
  performing carrier, 88, 93,
    149–150
  personal injury, 96
  provisions adopting or
    supplementing, 155–157
  ship, 89–90
  summary of limits, 218–219

223

Athens Convention—*cont.*
  supplementary provisions on
      limits of liability, 151
  time-bar for actions, 102, 153
  unit of account, 158
    conversion, 158
  valuables, 94, 150

Cabin luggage
  meaning, 90–91
Calculation of tonnage, 174–175
Carriage
  claims subject to limitation,
      134–136
    Convention 1976, 135–136
    Hague Rules, 134–135
    Hague-Visby Rules, 134–135
    Hamburg Rules, 135
  Hague Rules, 107–136
  Hague-Visby Rules, 107–136
  Hamburg Rules, 119–123
    application to non-contractual
        claims, 120–121
    delay, 123
    joint and severable liability, 122
    limits of liability, 120
    loss of right to limit liability,
        121
  history, 107–108
  Limitation Convention 1976,
      107–136
  loss of right to rely on package
      limitation, 125–130
    construction of contract, and,
        126
    goods, meaning, 126–127
    Hague Rules, 125–127
    Hague-Visby rules, 127–130
    Hamburg Rules, 130
    "in any event", 127
    intentional or reckless conduct
        of servant or agent, 128
    "loss", 128–129
    "such", 129
  lower "package" limits, 123–124
    construction of contract,
        123–124
  meaning, 91
  no "package" limit, 124–125
    "ad valorem" bill, 124–125

Carriage—*cont.*
  "package" limitation, 108–109
    claim against servant or agent,
        119
    containerised or palletised
        cargo, 113
    contract of carriage, and, 118
    Hague Rules, 111–114
    Hague-Visby Rules, 114–119
    heavy cargo, 116
    light cargo, 116
    misconduct of carrier, and,
        118
    "per package or unit", 112–113
    "£100", 114
    Special Drawing Right (SDR),
        115–116
  persons who can limit liability,
      130–134
    "carrier", 132
    charterers, 130–132
    Convention of 1976, 131–132
    freight forwarder, 132
    Hague Rules, 130–131, 132
    Hague-Visby Rules, 130–131,
        133
    Hamburg Rules, 130–131,
        133–134
    owners, 130–132
    servants and agents of carrier,
        132–134
  "tonnage" limitation, 109–111
Carrier
  meaning, 88, 132
Carriage of goods by sea, 183–194
  absolute warranty of
      seaworthiness, and, 184
  application of Act of 1971 to
      British possessions,
      184–185
  application of Hague Rules as
      amended, 183–184
  contracting states, 184
  extension of application of
      Hague-Visby Rules to
      carriage from ports in British
      possessions, 185
  Hague-Visby Rules, 183–194
Claims
  aggregation of. *See* Aggregation
      of claims

Claims excepted from limitation,
    25–30
    contracts of employment, and,
        28–29
    contracts of service, and, 28–29
    nuclear damage, 27–28
    nuclear ship, and, 28
    oil pollution damage, 26–27
    salvage or contribution in general
        average, 26
Claims subject to limitation, 17–25
    costs of removal or destruction of
        wrecks, 21–22
    damages, 18–19
    delay in carriage of cargo,
        passengers or luggage, 20–21
    drydock, and, 20
    fire, loss or damage by, 25
    "infringement of rights", 21
    "management", 19
    measures taken to avert or
        minimise loss, 23–24
    "on board", 19–20
    recourse or indemnity, by way of,
        24–25
    remoteness of damage, and, 20
    salvage of cargo, 22–23
    valuables, loss of or damage to,
        25
Conduct barring limitation, 30–42
    "actual fault", 32
    "actual fault or privity of the
        owner", 31
    construction of Conventions,
        33–34
    "intent to cause such loss", 38
    "loss", 36–37
    onus of proof, 39–40
    "or recklessly and with knowledge
        that such loss would probably
        result", 38–39
    overall effect of changes made by
        1976 Convention, 40–41
    "owner", 31–32
    "personal", 35
    "personal act or omission", 32–34
    "person liable", 35–36
    "privity", 32
    section 502, MSA 1894, 41–42
    section 503, MSA 1894, 41–42
    "such loss", 37–38

Contract of carriage
    meaning, 88–89
Counterclaims, 42–44
    identity of persons to whom
        provision appllicable, 42–44
    negligent salvor, and, 43–44
Convention relating to Carriage of
    Passengers and their Luggage
    by Sea. See Athens Convention
    1974
Court
    meaning, 168

Distinct occasion
    meaning, 58

Floating platforms, 17, 79–81
Freely transferable
    meaning, 75

Gold value
    meaning, 221
Goods
    meaning, 126–127

Hague Rules
    Brussels Protocol 1968, as
        amended by, 186–194
    definitions, 186
    summary of limits, 219
Hague-Visby Rules
    Carriage of Goods by Sea Act
        1971, and, 183–194
    summary of limits, 219
Hamburg Rules, 195–216
    acceptance, 213
    accession, 213
    amendment, 214
    approval, 213
    arbitration, 209–210
    bill of lading, 203
        contents, 203–204
        evidentiary effect, 204–205
        issue, 203
        reservations, 204–205
    common understanding, 216
    contractual stipulations, 210
    definitions, 195–196
    denunciation, 215
    denunciation of other
        Conventions, 213–214
    depositary, 213

Hamburg Rules—*cont.*
documents other than bills of
lading, 206
entry into force, 213
general average, 210–211
guarantees by shipper, 205–206
interpretation, 197
jurisdiction, 208–209
liability of carrier, 197–202
application to non-contractual
claims, 199–200
basis of, 197–198
carrier and actual carrier, 201
deck cargo, 200–201
limits, 199
loss of right to limit, 200
period of responsibility, 197
through carrier, 201–202
liability of shipper, 202–203
dangerous goods, 202–203
limitation of actions, 207
notice of loss, damage or delay,
206–207
other Convetnions, and, 211–212
ratification, 213
reservations, 213
revision, 214
revision of limitation amount,
214–215
revision of unit of account, 214
scope of application, 196
signature, 213
summary of limits, 220
unit of account, 212–213
Hovercraft, 146. *See also* Air
cushion vehicles
limitation of liability, and, 11

International carriage
meaning, 92
International Conference on
Limitation of Liability for
Maritime Claims 1976, 1–2, 7 *et
seq.*
International Convention on
Limitation of Liability for
Maritime Claims, 1976
accession, 81
aggregation of claims, 163. *See
also* Aggregation of claims
amendment, 82

Int. Conv. on Limitation—*cont.*
claims excepted from limitation,
160–161. *See* Claims excepted
from limitation
claims subject to limitation,
159–160. *See also* Claims
subject to limitation
compromise, as, 1–2
conduct barring limitation, 161.
See also Conduct barring
limitation
counterclaims, 161. *See also*
Counterclaims
denunciation, 82
depository, 83
en bloc adoption by United
Kingdom, 5–6
entry into force, 81–82, 84
languages, 83–84
limit for passenger claims, 162
limitation fund, 163–165. *See also*
Limitation fund
bar to other actions, 164–165
constitution, 163–164
distribution, 164
governing law, 165
limitation of liability without
constitution of limitation
fund, 59–63
limitation without constitution of
limitation fund, 163
limits of liability, 161–163. *See
also* Limits of Liability
persons entitled to limit liability,
159. *See also* Persons entitled
to limit liability
provisions having effect, 165–168
ratification, 81
reservations, 82, 84
revision, 82
revision of limitation amount, 83
revision of monetary unit, 83
revision of unit of account, 83
right of limitation. *See* Right of
limitation
scope of application, 76–81, 165
aircushion vehicles, 79–81
drilling, 79
floating platforms, 79–81
national regulations, 79
non-sea-going ships, 77–78

Int. Conv. on Limitation—*cont.*
  scope of application—*cont.*
    principal place of business, and,
      77
    residence, and, 77
    ships of less than 300 tons, 78
  signature, 81
  summary of limits, 217–218
  unit of account, 162–163

Liability insurer
  entitlement to limit liability,
    14–16
Limitation action
  commencement of, 61
Limitation fund, 59 *et seq.*
  amount, 65
  "any person alleged to be liable",
    constitution by, 67
  availability, 66
  bar to other actions, 64, 70–75
    aim of Article 13, 70, 71, 72–73
    attachment of assets, and,
      71–72
    discretion of court, 74
    establishment of fund, and, 74
    "freely transferable", 75
    mechanics of Article 13(2),
      73–75
    presumption of entitlement to
      limitation, and, 73
    warning to would-be arrestors,
      70–71
  cash, 66
  constitution, 63, 65–67
  distribution, 63–64, 67–70
    "established" claims, and, 68
    future liability, and, 69
    interest, and, 67
    liens, and, 69–70
    subrogation, and, 69
  governing law, 64, 75–76
  guarantee, 66
  interest rate, 65–66
  limitation of liability without
    constitution of, 59–63
  obligation to constitute, 59–63
  United Kingdom position, 60–63
Limitation of liability
  commencement of action, 61
  defence, as, 60–61

Limitation of liability—*cont.*
  history in United Kingdom, 5–6
  Merchant Shipping Act 1894,
    s.503, 139–142
  summary of limits, 217–221
  ways of pleading, 60–63
  without constitution of limitation
    fund. *See* Limitation fund
Limits of liability, 44 *et seq.*
  calculation of tonnage, 50–53
    "best evidence", 52–53
    gross, 51
    International Tonnage
      Certificates, 51–52
    net, 51
    transitional provisions, 52–53
  death or personal injury claims,
    48–49
  general, 44–45
  harbour works, damage to
    national legislation, 49
  passenger claims, 45, 53–55
    Athens Convention, 53–55
    number of passengers, 54
    time limit, 54–55
    United Kingdom position,
      55–56
  Poincaré franc, 47–48
  property claims, 48–49
  salvor not operating from ship,
    49–50
  salvor operating on ship to which
    salvage services rendered,
    49–50
  sliding scale, 47
  Special Drawing Right (SDR),
    47–48
  summary of limits, 56–57
  tonnage measurement rules, 50
  unit of account, 45–46, 57
Luggage
  meaning, 90–91

Merchant Shipping Act 1979
  commencement, 171–174,
    175–181

Non-sea-going ships, 77–78

Owner/master
  entitlement to limit liability,
    13–14

Package
  meaning, 112–113, 116–117
Passenger
  meaning, 90
Passenger claims, 85–105
  Athens Convention 1974, 86–105.
    See also Athens Convention
    1974
Passenger contract
  general principles, 85
Pecuniary
  meaning, 91
Performing carrier
  meaning, 88
Persons entitled to limit liability,
    7–17
  aircushion vehicles, and, 17
  excluded persons, 16–17
  excluded vessels, 16–17
  floating platforms, and, 17
  hovercraft, 11
  liability insurer, 14–16
    stable affordable insurance
      cover, and, 15
    third parties, and, 14–15
  owner/master, 13–14
  "person interested in . . . the
    ship", 9
  persons for whom shipowner or
    salvor responsible, 12–13
    claims for damage to cargo,
      and, 12
  salvors, 10–11

Persons entitled to limit liability—
    cont.
  seagoing ships, 11
  shipowners, 8–9
  slot charterers, 9–10
£100
  meaning, 114

Responsible
  meaning, 12, 13
Right of limitation, 7 *et seq.*

Salvors
  entitlement to limit liability,
    10–11
  liability, 169–170
Seagoing ships
  limitation of liability, and, 11
Ship
  meaning, 89–90, 168
Shipowners
  entitlement to limit liability, 8–9
  liability, 169–170
  meaning, 9
Ships of less than 300 tons, 78
Slot charterers
  entitlement to limit liability, 9–10
State Party
  meaning, 168
Summary of limits, 217–221

Unit
  meaning, 116–117